"The Triple Whammy" and Other Russian Stories

By the same author:

MOSCOW BELIEVES IN TEARS: Russians and Their Movies

EL SALVADOR: Central America in the New Cold War (Co-editor)

TEACH-INS, U.S.A.: Reports, Opinions, Documents (Co-editor)

"The Triple Whammy" and Other Russian Stories

A Memoir

LOUIS MENASHE

Washington DC

New Academia Publishing, 2018

Printed in the United States of America

Library of Congress Control Number: 2017958812
ISBN 978-0-9995572-0-4 paper (alk. paper)
ISBN 978-0-9995572-1-1 hardcover (alk. paper)

An imprint of New Academia Publishing

4401-A Connecticut Ave., NW #236 - Washington DC 20008
info@newacademia.com - www.newacademia.com

For Sheila, Claudia, and David

And in Memory of John R. Anderson (1953-2012)

Two roads diverged in a yellow wood,
And sorry I could not travel both
And be one traveler....
—Robert Frost

When you come to a fork in the road, take it.
—Yogi Berra

CONTENTS

ILLUSTRATIONS

PROLOGUE: Warsaw, 1962

"Moskva?," I asked.

"V Moskvu," answered the old guy in uniform, with a nod, a smile, and his eyes really twinkled. He stood outside a train door, welcoming us.

My god, I thought, the attendant is right out of a Russian novel, and I'm about to board a Russian train. Is that Anna Karenina on the platform?

The Soviet Union, the Great Promised Land, here we come, at last! How exciting! How fulfilling! How validating! And how primitive was my Russian. I wanted to know if we were boarding the right train, and I thought to show off: I used *Moskva*, as the Russians call their capital, not "Moscow," as we call it. The old attendant confirmed the destination, but put it in correct grammatical form, and with the proper *case ending* on the noun; yes, the train was heading *"to Moscow"*. Neat, but my facility in Russian grammar with its declensions and case endings was just starting. The Spanish and French I knew had none of that.

No matter. We were on our way, four *fellow travelers,* in both senses of the term: I, an NYU graduate student, a budding *Russianist* or, if you will, given the times, *Sovietologist;* my wife Sheila, just out of graduate school in Social Work; Betty Ofsevit, another Social Work student on her way to a degree; and her husband, Stanley, ditto. The young American Left—in New York, at any rate—had an affinity for the help professions, and Social Work was a leading choice. Although the political sympathies of these four pilgrims were in sync, only Stanley could boast authentic "Red Diaper" credentials – his parents were in, or very close to, the American Communist Party—and Stanley's outlook and opinions had a harder edge than ours on most issues. Sheila and Betty came from Lower East Side lower middle-class families with pronounced labor-union sympathies. Nothing in my family background pointed to Russia or to politics, much less Left politics. The strongest identity of my Brooklyn family, also lower middle class, came from their Sephardic origins, especially since their birthplace was the venerated "Mother of Israel," the "Jerusalem of the Mediterranean"—*Selanik/ Salonique/Salonica* or, after the Greeks took back the city from the Turks and insisted on its original name, *Thessaloniki*. One day, that Sephardic identity would grip me too, coexisting with other leanings, be they Left-political, or Russianist-professional. But what put me on that train to Moscow the summer of 1962?

With Stanley, Betty, and Sheila at the Margolins' Peugeot 403 in Paris before heading East, 1962.

I

IT WAS LOTS OF THINGS

I'm always thinking of Russia
I can't keep her out of my head.
I don't give a damn for Uncle Sham,
I'm a left-wing radical Red.
— H.H. Lewis

Paul Richardson, the Publisher and Editor of *Russian Life* magazine, describes an incident during his first visit to the USSR in 1982 – he spurned an offer of black-market icons in favor of swapping his down coat for two *shapkas* (fur hats) – that triggered his "Russophilia disease," which he describes this way:

"A disproportionate interest in tsars, commissars and any author whose last name ends in ov, oy, or sky; a strange affinity for potatoes, dill and vodka; a grudging acceptance of the role of Fate and Serendipity in one's life; and an irrational tendency to argue about things from the Russian worldview, while simultaneously realizing that such arguments are often ridiculous."

Not a bad description of the Russophilic disorder. For Harlow Robinson, a distinguished scholar of Russian language and music, David Lean's *Doctor Zhivago* was a trigger. Its cinematically reconstructed Russia, he writes, "seduced me utterly and forever," setting Robinson on the Russianist path.

Several things that captivated the novelist Elif Batuman led her to "end up spending seven years…studying the form of the Russian novel…" There was her infatuation with Maxim, her Russian violin teacher. "Tatyana's Dream" from Pushkin's *Eugene Onegin* played a part, as did *Anna Karenina*, "a perfect book."

For me, as with Batuman, no one incident, no single seduction or epiphany put me on the Russian road. *It was lots of things*. And they took shape long before my first trip to the Soviet Union.

People always assumed that since I wanted to go into Russian studies I must have Russian family roots. I still get the same reaction today when I identify my calling. No; I've had to explain otherwise. Having Russia in their family backgrounds was true of many of the friends of my youth, mainly those Jewish friends whose parents and grandparents came from the *guberniyas* of the old Russian Empire, from Byelorussia or Ukraine or the Baltic regions. There was even some Russian spoken in their households, in addition to Yiddish. My people were from another part of the world, the Graeco-Turkish realms of the Eastern Mediterranean, and Ladino, or Judeo-Spanish, was the language at home. Russia, Russians, the Russian language meant little to me as a youngster, save for their association with the Soviet Union, a powerful, inescapable presence in the America of the Cold War I grew up in.

It so happened that in the Williamsburg neighborhood I called home, decades before sections of it turned ultra-hip and gentrified, there was a Slavic, non-Jewish population – Ukrainians and Poles mainly, but some Russians too, among whom there was Nick and John. We learned from the street that his name was Nick, but he was better known by all simply as *Russian*, as in "Hey, *Russian*, do you want to play some stickball?" Unlike the sport in other precincts of Brooklyn, stickball as it was played in Williamsburg's P.S. 50 schoolyard called for a tennis ball pitched to a softball bat. In one of those games with me behind the plate without a mask, *Russian* swung at a pitch, didn't connect, and the bat flew straight back out of his hands on the follow-through. *BAM*! The tip of the bat barrel met my forehead right between the eyes. My forehead swelled immediately, black and blue and the subject of concern and conversation for many days. It occurs to me now, as I write these lines, that *Russian's* errant bat also possessed some peculiar, metaphorical significance, pointing to a future that bound up my fate with Russia and Russians. *Thanks, Russian.*

John Hooz, the other Williamsburg Russian I knew, had a strong Russianizing impact on me, through no overt intent on his or my part; the cumulative Russian effect came from a series of little things between me and him. He was a close friend, from elementary school through Eastern District high school, through our college years and after, but his being Russian didn't concern me or even him in the first years of our friendship. Was he Ukrainian? Byelorussian? Great Russian? From the Baltic region? He had the fleshy face, the blue eyes, and the straight blondish-brown hair of many Lithuanian men I have met. I didn't care or even know about such national distinctions then, and I suspect that John, like many American-born sons of immigrants, was not very interested in which part of the old world his parents came from, or, if he was, it was not something he was eager to publicize. I knew that he and his sister Olga spoke Russian (Ukrainian? Byelorussian?), but never in public, just as I kept my fluent Ladino at home.

Still, there were *Russian things* coming from John that piqued my interest. At his apartment once, he flashed the cover of a book he was reading, Dostoevsky's *Crime and Punishment*. We were both avid readers at the time, roughly our early high school years, and I knew Mark Twain and Dickens, but *Dusty* was new to me. (*Dusty*: the cute sobriquet I picked up much later from Nabokov.) Not long after John's *Crime and Punishment* revelation, a young substitute teacher for the formidable Mrs. Gold of our high school honors English class happened to mention that he turned to a novel called *Brothers Karamazov* for treating certain theological questions. Hmmm.... *Dusty*, again.

Then there was John's introducing me to another great artist. Together we went to see the movie, *Carnegie Hall*, at a local theater. I was eager to catch the big-band trumpeter Harry James in the film; John, who played violin, wanted to watch the performance by Jascha Heifitz – a greater musician than James, he assured me. Well, Heifitz was Jewish, not Russian, but he was born in Vilnius, Lithuania, then part of Imperial Russia, so he counted as still one more Russian *thing* in the *Russian*-ness I associated with John. And that name, *Jascha*: so Russian. There was another film John and I attended together, Henry Hathaway's *The Desert Fox: The Story of Rommel*. At the entrance to our neighborhood RKO Republic Theater, we were met by a group of pickets protesting the film that included Dotty Osofsky, our friend Gilly's sister. She spotted us, and began shouting, "Why are they honoring this Fascist General?! Why don't they make films about the brave Polish soldiers who resisted the Nazis?!" John and I averted our eyes and walked in past Dotty and her fellow protesters. "That was meant for me," John whispered. I didn't get it. "She thinks I'm Polish," he explained.

John once informed me that the Empress Catherine the Great was sexually voracious, and known to have had intercourse with a horse. Where did that come from? I later learned that this piece of intelligence was widespread in Russian popular lore. Visiting my workplace office at Monitor Records, distributors of ethnic music from the USSR, John noticed a record jacket for *Russian Folk Songs* and read aloud its Cyrillic title – *Russkiye narodniye pesni.* That really impressed me.

John and I went our separate ways, starting with his choosing Brooklyn College and a chemistry major, while I attended City College, quite vague as to interests and future career intentions, but finally choosing, rather indifferently, History as my major. Chemistry took John to Canada after graduation and graduate studies; he was Professor of Organic Chemistry and Dean of Faculty at the University of Alberta before lung cancer cut him down at an early age. We had kept in touch over the years. There even came a moment – I was no longer directionless then—when I went to meet him at some family event, and his sister Olga greeted me with, "we've heard you speak Russian". I was proud and touched. As I am touched now, having collected these Russian flavored memory fragments. *Thanks, John.*

My opting for City College led to many unforeseen consequences. The Eastern District guys I knew were divided broadly into two groups after high school graduation – those who went out looking for jobs or, in the neighborhood argot, *woyk;* and those who went to college. I was in the second group, and college for us meant, where else? one of the City Colleges. Would it be Brooklyn or City? None of us considered Queens or Hunter. As for out of town campuses, they were simply out of the question for most families of the recent high school graduates among my friends, for mainly financial reasons. My family could have afforded some place outside of the city, but I didn't ask for it; the thought never even crossed my mind. I was a pretty clueless 16-year old, and I just went along with what my peers were doing. My brother Bobby, seven years my senior, was no role model or guide on this score either. He spent a few months at Brooklyn College, dropped out, and got a job working at Sam Goody's record shop in Manhattan, soon to become the foremost retailer of LP's, the novel long-playing disks of the day.

I was ready to go to Brooklyn College too, having the high grade average required for admission to all the City Colleges at the time, but I decided against it when I learned a "reading test" was scheduled the spring before entrance the following autumn. I assumed that this meant reading aloud from a text to a faculty group for some kind of placement evaluation. I was a very fluent reader, but I also suffered from Essential Tremor, an accursed inherited condition that manifested itself at an unusually early age in my case. It happened publicly for the first time at a standard eye-test in junior high school, the one where you held a card to cover one eye, while you read the chart on the wall opposite with the other. My card-holding hand shook very noticeably, friends teased me about it, and thereafter the fear of public, classroom reading as I held a book or paper plagued my school years. It could have been that the "reading test" was really and merely a reading *comprehension* test, but I didn't bother inquiring; just the *thought* of a public reading experience was enough to set me against Brooklyn College. There was another reason, though. Several of my immediate friends, John included, were headed for Brooklyn College, and I resolved to test my wings, embark on a solo flight – go to City, not Brooklyn College. Not really a very great act of bravery or independence, yet one with very great bearing on my future.

From the point of view of setting up the academic foundations for a career in Russian studies, or accelerating my choice of that career, Brooklyn College then was probably the better place than City. Jesse Clarkson, a nationally known historian of Russia was there; his *History of Russia* would be one of the many texts in the "know your enemy" literature coming from academia during the Cold War. I also heard from friends of a popular Professor Fan Parker who taught Russian language and headed the department. At City, no one in the faculty whose courses I took encouraged me to embrace Mother Russia. I believe Stanley Page, a Lenin specialist, was there, but I had no contact with him. Many years later our paths did cross. I was an already established historian of revolutionary Russia, and after my comments at a seminar, Page directed a question to me: "Are you the representative of Trotsky?," he asked, provocatively. "No," I replied, "are you the representative of Admiral Denikin?" (Denikin was a leader of reactionary "White" forces against the Bolsheviks during the Civil War following the Revolution.) "*Touché*," Page acknowledged, and gave me a friendly grin.

At City, still unsure of myself and unsure as to where I was heading, I didn't seek encouragement or look for that possibly energizing faculty member who could guide me toward a Russian career. In fact, an odd, ill-conceived decision led me to enter City College first at its Baruch business branch, *Downtown*. How green, how naïvely impressionable I was. I heard that among friends of my family there were some men in the "import-export" trade. I didn't think of consulting them to find out what it was all about. It was enough for me that the term "import-export" had the sound of something faintly exotic. And if it was a business career I was heading for, "import-export" seemed to promise foreign travel; it was business with an international kick. So I enrolled at Baruch for my "import-export" education. I lasted half a semester there. Not for me were boring courses in business administration, accounting, and so on, especially since by welcome contrast, an idiosyncratic Professor Sanderson taught a general history course that made a strong impression on me. He was good on military affairs, and told colorful stories, explaining the Washington Monument, for example, in explicitly phallic terms. He whetted my appetite for a more intellectual academic experience than marketing and management, and that pointed to the main City College campus, *Uptown*; the City College of New York, the Subway Harvard. There, I met Stanley Ofsevit.

Stanley had a fine voice, deep and booming—he could do excellent covers of Paul Robeson songs—and in his clothes and manners and opinions he presented a gruff tough exterior to the world that was partly affected, partly authentic. It's as if Stanley were ever ready to do battle, to show off his working-class consciousness and let everyone know which side he was on. When I told him I was reading, and was impressed by, the poems of T.S. Eliot, he shot back, "You mean *Tough Shit* Eliot?" There was a sweeter part of him, however, and he recognized me at once as innocent and lonely on campus – "This is Lou," he would introduce me to friends, "he doesn't know anyone." There was, to be sure, a proselytizing undercurrent to his kindness; he made sure I met some of his Left-wing comrades at City, a place long known for its powerful political culture on the Left. In class, I helped him with Spanish. Outside of class, he helped me with Marxism. My first assignment from Stanley was Stalin's pamphlet on *Dialectical Materialism.* He also loaned me his copy of *Ten Classics of Marxism,* a book I still have on my shelves. The *Classics* included Lenin's *State and Revolution* and Stalin's *Foundations of Leninism* – works that naturally pointed to the Russian Revolution, to Russian History, to the Soviet Union. *Thanks, Stanley.*

Not that the formal study of the Russian Revolution and the Soviet Union would now carry me through my undergraduate years at City College; far from it, I was still quite rudderless as to career intentions. I was very impressed by CCNY's imposing college Gothic architecture, its terra cotta details and walls of Manhattan schist, all confirming in my eyes of having entered a first-rate academic institution that could awaken new interests in arts and letters. I affected the manner of the seriously intellectual student; I liked to sit in the campus Quadrangle, reading a book (Camus? Sartre?), smoking a pipe. *Was that Colin Powell in his ROTC uniform I spotted walking past me?* I knew of all the distinguished CCNY alumni, Nobel Prize winners among them. Einstein had lectured at City. Professors there who had taught at Ivy League schools were fond of reporting to us that we were the superior students. I was stimulated by a range of courses in the Liberal Arts, but where would they take me? History became my major by default, but the academy-as-career had no attraction for me. After my second year, I succumbed to a mixed-up, slightly hopeless mood that prompted me to drop out of the full-time day session. But I hung on, and finished my degree at night.

By day I worked in the Sam Goody organization, later at Monitor Records, mentioned above. A roundabout path led me to Monitor, beginning with a part-time job at my brother Bobby's 9th Avenue record shop in Manhattan, an offshoot of his association with Goody, whose daughter he had married. Above the record shop was Phonotapes, an enterprise established by Goody and the legendary founder of Folkways Records, Moe Asch, to produce and market literary and historical pre-recorded audio tapes designed for educators at all levels. It was managed by a sophisticated New Yorker with a background in music and broadcasting, Gene Bruck, who offered me a full-time job after many visits to Phonotapes "upstairs". I enjoyed the whole milieu, commerce with a strong cultural flavor, but Phonotapes collapsed after a couple of years. Reel-to-reel monaural tapes had little place in the burgeoning stereophonic music scene. Next stop for me: Monitor Records, where Rose Rubin and Mischa Stillman hired me as Production Manager. So I had landed in the record business. Ah, but Monitor was a special kind of business, and my experience there helped me pass through double doors, one marked Politics, the other marked the Soviet Union.

Monitor was founded by Rubin and Stillman, each of whom brought unique features to the enterprise that nicely complemented each other. Rose was an Old Lefty who packed tremendous energy and organizing skills, including capitalist-entrepreneurial ones, into her small frame. I never learned if she was a member, but there was no doubt about her close connection to the Communist Party, U.S.A. Before Monitor, she had been active in a variety of ventures associated with the CP, especially if they involved cultivating Soviet-American friendship. Once every year, she would excuse herself from coming to the office on a weekday. She had to prepare her big Upper West Side apartment for her annual fund-raiser on behalf of what she described to me as "The Cause". I had no trouble figuring out what that Cause was. Friends – comrades—of hers who fought for the famed, communist dominated Lincoln Brigade during the Spanish Civil War visited the office regularly. I remember Moe Fishman, who limped from a serious thigh wound he suffered from a sniper's bullet in a battle near Madrid. There was Steve Nelson, a prominent labor activist, Comintern agent and Lincoln Brigade Political Commissar. Still politically raw in these matters, I didn't really know them or their full back stories when I chatted with them at Monitor. Rose once asked me to make sure I ordered stationery from a firm whose sales rep visited us; his name was Alger Hiss. I knew who he was; he looked just like newspaper photos of him. On the phone Rose often spoke to "Corliss" – that would be Corliss

Lamont, the Left-leaning scion of the affluent banking family who, like her, was friendly to the Soviet Union.

Mischa Stillman, an easy-going contrast to the dynamo Rose Rubin, had no substantial political background, as far as I knew, but he was connected to the USSR in two other ways. He was fluent in Russian (born in Saratov, before the Revolution), and he could read music. Both talents made him ideal for a job at Leeds Music in New York, which, among other specialties, published Russian and Soviet scores by arrangement with Moscow. Rose and Mischa came up with the idea of putting their respective connections and commitments to logical, potentially lucrative and certainly politically tinged ends: founding a record company that produced music from the USSR. Offering American audiences folk music from all parts of the multi-ethnic Soviet Union, plus classical scores by Soviet luminaries like David Oistrakh and Sviatoslav Richter was a fine way to advance a softer view of the USSR, via its rich musical endowments in those Cold War years of the late 1950s. Those efforts had a personal side-effect on me. They were my cultural primer of sorts in Russian/Soviet studies, and they also pushed me along that certain political path in a direction I was already on. *Thanks, Rose. Thanks, Mischa. Thanks, Monitor Records.*

Stanley, again. He and Betty were a couple at City College and Betty had a friend named Sheila, a Hunter College student she met working at a summer day camp. Stanley, Betty, and Sheila moved in a common political orbit on the Left—civil rights campaigns, the peace movement—and were also part of the same social work milieu—jobs at summer camps, community centers, hospitals. I was outside both realms, but Betty and Stanley arranged for me to meet Sheila on a blind date. "You need a date tonight?" Stanley barked at me one afternoon, half question, half command. *Sure.* Before arriving at Betty's apartment for the date, I kept reminding myself that in their circle of Commie culture, sex—"free love"—was a given, and I wondered if Betty's friend shared that credo, especially after I saw her glide toward me, with her rich ebon-dark hair, and big, gorgeous green eyes. I had done *heavy petting,* as we called it, even "down below," but hadn't *gone all the way,* as we called it. Same with her, it turned out; Commies or not, these were the '50s, remember, we were not too long out of our teens, and both of us were hardly radicals in these matters. We hit it off that night, sans sex. There was more to Sheila than her dark hair and green eyes. That date was in October. We married the following June.

I earned my undergraduate degree at City College, while Sheila was finishing up at Hunter. My salary as production manager at Monitor got us through the early years of our marriage, and the road seemed pretty clear for me as a rising young man in the record business. Monitor also provided terrific extracurricular perquisites besides augmenting our record collection – when the Bolshoi Ballet came to town, or Sviatoslav Richter made his first American appearance, Rose was sure to provide tickets for me and Sheila. Sometimes I even met some of those Soviet artists, and presented them with their recordings on the Monitor label. I remember giving one of the Moiseyev Dancers an album of ours with him on the cover, a pleasure for both of us. After I sent the composer Aram Khachaturian a disk of one of his works, he thanked me in a hand-written signed note.

A livelihood that was rewarding and fun was a great thing, but I began to feel constricted by just being in *business*, even if it was the unique Monitor business. I felt the pull of politics plus a strong Russian temptation. They were linked in my mind, and Sheila encouraged me to consider graduate school in the Russian/Soviet field. Sheila's crowd was made up of politically active social workers (like Betty and Stanley), and students in medicine, journalism, architecture. I appreciated them as intellectuals and envied their future roles as professionals. I would join them. *Thanks, Sheila.* (*Thanks to you too, Betty, and to you, Stanley, again.*)

Maybe learning about *Dusty* was the incentive for planting another Russian bug, the literary one. At my father's boardwalk ice-cream parlor in Rockaway Beach where I worked summers, I had plenty of time to read during off hours. Sometime in my middle or later teens, coinciding with my high-school years, I picked up a collection of Russian short stories. You know, one of those volumes with classical tales from the pens of Chekhov, Pushkin, Turgenev and others. They dazzled me, Turgenev's *First Love*, especially. (The big, Tolstoyan novels came later, along with *Dusty* and others.) What was it about these tales that was so beguiling? I had nothing in common with all those hussars, coachmen, house servants, serfs, merchants, barons and princesses and their country estates near the towns of N. or S., populated by Sonyas and Dunyas and Volodyas and Kolyas. Well, perhaps I identified with the young, dreamy hero of Turgenev's story, 16 years old at the time, and rapturously in love with a beautiful, slightly older neighbor, only to discover that she is carrying on a clandestine affair with....his father. Nothing quite like that in my experience, at that age (and later, too), though there were always beautiful but unattainable young women around in my teens who left me melancholic with longing.

Russian literature didn't need endings with brilliant twists, as in *First Love.* There could be lots of color, as in Lermontov's work set in the Caucasus, yet Chekhov's power came from a strong grey tonality. It was something else in those Russian stories, something likely to exert a spell over any sensitive young man or woman – a feeling for the wretched, for the underdog, sympathy for the "insulted and injured" in all social classes. A broad humanism keyed the stories and novels to very Russian characters in their very Russian places and situations against the background of Russia's sad and turbulent 19th century development. Those Russian specifics have always had a universal appeal.

The enchantment with Russian literature, cued by that short story collection, stayed with me, stays with me still. *Spasibo, Turgenev, et al.*

Over different periods of time other seductive Russian motifs popped up well before my academic studies. I have a dim memory of a film that thrilled me when I watched it on our small black and white television set —*Michael Strogoff,* based on the Jules Verne novel of the tsar's courier vs. the Tatars. Later, a still more powerful impression came from another movie, Eisenstein's *Alexander Nevsky,* which I caught at the old, now long gone Stanley theater in Manhattan, a small house specializing in foreign, often Soviet films. I was late and walked into the film at which moment I don't remember now: was it the Teutonic Knights terrorizing the population of Pskov? Or when they are preparing for the "battle on the ice"? Oh, those sinister masks, and that music on the soundtrack! Wow; I had never seen or heard anything like that. It was my first taste of Prokofiev, whose compositions I got to know and love later, but it was another composer and another score that worked greater magic on me the first time I heard it: Stravinsky and his *Petrushka.* Listen to those shimmering strings and the slightly sad, slightly gay fluttering flute that opens the ballet score; then strands of Russian folk melodies are woven into the carnival-tinged music. The Gogolesque tale of the unrequited sentient puppet *Petrushka* rivaled Turgenev's *First Love* in my mental museum of Russian pathos. I heard the recording one evening in our Williamsburg apartment and I remember how it bewitched me. Can you believe that I can still see the rendering of the forlorn *Petrushka* on the bright red sleeve of the LP that had Ernest Ansermet conducting *L'Orchestre de la Suisse Romande*? And I've continued to hear that opening shimmer in my inner ear, as I first heard it that evening in Williamsburg.

Thank you, Stravinsky, *Petrushka, Nevsky,* Eisenstein, Prokofiev, and *Strogoff.*

Lenin and Krupskaya poster over our staircase at home. Non-Russian visitors always asked, "Who are they?" I bought it in a Moscow bookstore, 1973.

II

SOVIET RUSSIA AND POLITICAL COMMITMENT

There you have them and it—*Russian-John-Dusty-Jascha-Stanley-Monitor-Sheila-Turgenev-Strogoff-Cold War-Nevsky-Petrushka-Stravinsky-Eisenstein-Stalin-Lenin-Prokofiev-Moiseyev.* That mix-tape mash-up transmuted into a compulsion to study the history of Russia and the Soviet Union. Rose Rubin was disappointed when I told her I'd be leaving my full-time Monitor post to enter graduate school. Ah, I teased her, "You're too much of a Hegelian to worry about one guy leaving." "Yes, but I'm also a realist," she countered. That was very flattering, but of course Monitor survived and did very well without me. (Founders of the label in 1956, Rose and Mischa donated over 250 Monitor recordings to Smithsonian Folkways when they retired in 1999.) Rose also understood and supported my reasoning. I wanted to advance the cause of socialism in the U.S.A. – it was her cause, too—and a serious study of the first socialist state was fundamental to that project. Additionally, it was imperative in the thermonuclear endangered world to help correct what I thought were stereotypical pictures of the USSR and the hostile attitudes that went with them, in Washington and among the public at large. I needed knowledge and credentials to strengthen my voice as a public intellectual seeking policy changes toward the Soviet Union in Cold War America. As for the university students I looked forward to teaching, well I didn't aim to "indoctrinate" them, strictly speaking, but I was hoping to convey an image of Russians, through their literature and history, later, most successfully, through their films, as peace-seeking people, not dangerous enemies.

That sassy doggerel by the Communist writer H.H. Lewis, the epigraph to the previous chapter, conveys well both the Russian inclinations and political swagger I was proud of in those days.

About graduate studies and graduate school. Sheila was set on a Masters Degree at Columbia University's School of Social Work, the leading New York institution in her field. With her experience and sterling recommendations she had no trouble getting admitted, tuition free no less, and with scholarship money to boot. No such luck for me. I wish I could have joined her at Columbia, but my checkered record at City College didn't help. And I just didn't know the ropes of applying for admission to Columbia's Russian Institute, one of the premier places in the U.S. at the time for graduate studies in the Russian-Soviet area. As someone I got to know who was a student there told me, after the fact, you should have asked for an interview with the Institute's Director, *before* you applied.

I didn't, and my application package naturally included my City College transcript. I had graduated *Cum Laude*, and made Phi Beta Kappa, but that wasn't enough to offset certain embarrassing details in the transcript. The first grade that appeared on it was a "D" for English 101. I can picture the admissions officer dropping my application into the "Reject" pile the moment he noticed it. The "D" was a gift from Professor Joseph Tynan, teaching his last classes after decades on the City College faculty. I remember someone telling me when I registered for the course, "Drop it, drop it! Tynan likes to fail people." Who me? Never. I thought dropping a course at the outset of my intellectually adventurous *City College studies* was somehow cowardly. Besides, I was a successful high school Honors English student sailing along in confidence of my ability to handle a literature or composition class with or without a Tynan. Well, I was warned, and should have listened. It was a small class, maybe a dozen students, even less when some dropped out after poor grades for early reports and papers. At our first meeting Professor Tynan treated us to a hectoring introduction that insisted how poorly we compared to students of City College yore. That was his derisive tone through the rest of the semester, but I stuck it out and hoped for a decent grade. Vain hope; all of us save for two students who received, generous for Tynan "C" grades, got either "F" or "D" marks. Much later, as a college instructor myself, I regularly experienced students coming to protest their grades, invariably getting me to reconsider and upping the mark. As that green City College undergraduate in my first year *Uptown*, I never thought of doing such a thing.

Anyway, it probably wasn't just that prominent "D" grade that blocked my admission to the Russian Institute. I hadn't studied the language; my History and Political Science grades were OK, not outstanding; no faculty member, not to mention some celebrated scholar, championed my application. I had taken a couple of courses in European History with Professor Louis L. Snyder. Professor Snyder had a reputation as an editor and author who published a lot on the subject of Nationalism. Wearing a green visor, he often sat at the back of the room going over his manuscripts and proofs while students presented the oral reports he was prone to assign the whole semester. He was kind enough, though he didn't know me from Adam, to write a letter of recommendation on my behalf after I told him I got good grades in his courses and that I wanted to specialize in Russian/Soviet studies. "You're very wise to have chosen that as a career in these times," he said. As part of my Columbia application I included copies of jacket "liner notes," that I had written for Monitor recordings of Russian music. I would be a graduate student who was already in print; shouldn't that have helped me get in? Obviously not.

I still feel a certain twinge when I read newsletters from that still prominent center for Russian studies, now renamed the Harriman Institute. I've numbered among my friends and colleagues many with graduate degrees from Columbia's Russian Institute – Jonathan and Jane Harris, Lynn Turgeon, Barbara Engel, Cliff Rosenthal, Manuela Dobos, Susan Heuman, Steve Cohen, Michael Brainerd. That Columbia portal wasn't open for me, and I had to settle for admission to the graduate History Department at New York University, to which, I should say, I owe immense gratitude for a wide range of reasons. It was fairly clear that NYU wasn't prohibitively rigorous in their admissions standards at that time, but it wasn't an intellectual/academic backwater either. There were some distinguished scholars in the History Department, and requirements for Master's and Ph.D. degrees were quite exacting. A big plus for me and Sheila was that most courses were offered evenings, allowing me to work part-time by day at Monitor. Moreover, unlike at Columbia, I could be a part-time student as well. When

I explained my new, scholarly resolve, my father kindly wrote me a check to cover tuition the first year. I think Papa always understood that I was never cut out for business. He shook his head when I scooped massive globs of ice cream into milkshakes, or topped cones with big mounds of Breyer's Butter Almond at the Rockaway Beach store, as he took note of my ignorance in how to turn a profit. Besides, he had a solid respect for schooling and learning, and was probably proud of my electing serious studies, graduate work at NYU.

That summer of 1960, our first semesters at Columbia and NYU ahead of us, Sheila and I knew we'd be facing hard work. What of it? We felt we had the energy and commitment to take on any challenges standing in our way, on that path leading to a better world.

But first, there was political action, then Cuba.

III

POLITICAL APPRENTICE

Stanley was responsible for my elementary Marxist education. He also helped get my feet wet in political *action* – picketing at a Woolworth store in the Bronx. Sheila, a born social worker and a protester from an early age, was a veteran at that sort of thing. She once confronted Mayor Robert Wagner at a street demonstration over some labor issue at a settlement house where she worked. He listened quietly, turned to an aide, and ordered him to "look into this." Sheila's side won. But public protests were new to me.

Four Black students – "the Greensboro Four" – sat in at a local North Carolina Woolworth lunch counter when they were refused service, and their act triggered a powerful wave of supporting actions across the country early in 1960. The movement spread to New York and we followed the lead of the Congress of Racial Equality's youth division which called for boycotting Woolworths and demanding a stop to discrimination at all their stores. Led by Stanley, a small group of us picketed one of the stores in the Bronx; we shouted slogans and displayed our hand-lettered signs to generally sympathetic customers. Woolworth management desegregated their chain of stores five months after the Greensboro protest. We were proud of doing our bit, and my personal pride swelled when Stanley complimented me at the end of the action, my political baptism. "You did very well," he allowed, as we enjoyed some pizza after the picketing.

There were other protests, other organizing efforts in those days before NYU and Columbia graduate schools claimed most of our time, but even during our studies we were available for action. I don't remember who recruited us – it wasn't Stanley – but Sheila and I worked one weekend on behalf of the Harlem tenants' rights advocate, Jesse Gray. We climbed the steps of many local tenements to record instances of flagrant neglect of basic apartment and hallway maintenance throughout often rodent-infested buildings. We gave our findings to Gray, who used them for documenting protests directed at negligent landlords. He impressed us as an honest, committed, and smart community organizer who would gain media attention for leading an extensive rent strike in Harlem that featured a presentation of rats at a court hearing in 1963. Later, he headed a National Tenants Organization and also served as a New York State Assemblyman, examples of working against the system from within and outside of it. That issue – as radicals, do we fight within or outside of the structures of power? – was always a major preoccupation. Another was the question of local versus national activity – community organizing at the base, or building a party that targeted the larger arena? My political orientation and learning about these issues went hand and hand with my graduate studies. I pondered such matters in terms of Alinsky vs. Lenin, *Rules for Radicals* vs. *What Is To Be Done*? Or, community organizing and trade unionism vs. national politics and political-party leadership?

Participating in Left cultural activity was in its way a form of protest politics, a mark of self- and group-identity. We didn't need a picket line or a petition to show our hostility to war and capitalism, or sympathy for peace and socialism. We could do it with music. Most of the ensemble of songs, their singers, and the ambience surrounding them was new to me. Stanley encouraged me once to attend a concert at City College to hear Pete Seeger. *Who*? I asked. I did know who Paul Robeson was, even well before Monitor issued a couple of his albums. I remember watching him sign autographs and chat with students at City after a concert appearance organized, I learned years and years later, by my good friend Sima Szaluta when she headed the City College Chapter of the "Young Progressives of America," a youth division offshoot of the Progressive Party, most famous for running presidential candidate Henry Wallace against Harry Truman in 1948. I didn't know Sima or her group then. The only "YPA" I knew in my freshman year was what anti-Left students called themselves at one of their mock demonstrations I happened to walk into – "Young Padookies of America".

The wickedly satirical nature of their antics was not lost on me, but I had little idea of the political nuances and cross-currents behind them. Neither was I at all familiar with the history of City's famous cafeteria alcoves that harbored competing factions across the political spectrum, Trotskyists battling Stalinists or Anarchists battling Marxists; what Irving Howe, an active alcove denizen, later called, in Kantian fashion, "Politics as pure mind."

Sheila was already immersed in the folk culture prized by the Left. She attended hootenannies, danced the Jesse Polka, hung out among the banjo pickers and guitar strummers filling the air with their songs at the Circle in Washington Square Park in the Village. She knew who Pete Seeger was. But I caught on quickly enough and joined right in. I too raised my voice in group sings of the union-oriented and populist repertory of the Almanac Singers – I loved their *Union Maid, Banks of Marble, Miner's Life,* especially.

As for "internationalist" fare, there was the spirited *Avanti popolo,* from the Italian Communist Party (*Bandiera rossa la trionfera / Evviva comunismo e la liberta*!), or the songbook from the Spanish Civil War brought home by veterans of the Lincoln Brigade, with its references to *Jarama* and *Gandesa,* and *Los Cuatro Generales,* the "Four Generals" who led the reactionary attack on the Republic with General Francisco Franco at their head. And we all cheered recordings of the Red Army Chorus, particularly their rendition of the pulsating, triumphal *Meadowlands.* Closer to home, you might say—close, that is, to the East European, especially Polish, Byelorussian, and Ukrainian Jewish children of immigrants who comprised so much of the New York Left – were songs like *Hey, Zhankoye*!, translated from the Yiddish, inspired by a Jewish Collective Farm in Soviet Crimea of the 1930s (*Who says Jews cannot be farmers? / Spit 'em in the face who would so harm us*...). Was there some trans-political, *emotional* connection to the USSR operating among those Lefties, old and young, whose ancestry lay in the pre-Soviet Russian Empire and its environs? Generations of their forebears suffered from anti-Semitism and were bloodied by *pogroms.* Now, to know that the Soviets were building a dam in Ukraine, or putting up housing in Minsk, or, above all, defeating the Nazis in WW II perhaps touched some kind of strong *national,* not political or ideological chord. I speculated along these lines because so many of our Left comrades were Jewish, with family roots over there, in Old Russia and Eastern Europe.

Cold War hostilities and the doomsday nuclear clouds they threatened were prominent issues for us. We marched and rallied and signed petitions for SANE (the Committee for a Sane Nuclear Policy). When the Kennedy administration announced its intention to blanket the country with pamphlets from the government on how to prepare for a nuclear attack, we organized a campaign to explain the danger this implied. Such a document, sent to every American home, was, we argued, psychologically preparing the public for war. Our plan was to urge all citizens to *"Send it Back!"* A clever tactic, we thought, but in the end, Washington decided against the pamphlet campaign.

So, I've drawn some pictures of my evolving political experience, from neophyte picketer to seasoned protester/activist. Notice that directly, or indirectly, the Russian or Soviet thing is frequently implicated in what I've described, whether it's *Meadowlands* or SANE. But none of those scenes can compare to our Cuban affair.

IV

¡VIVA LA REVOLUCIÓN! ¡VENCEREMOS!

Our trip to revolutionary Cuba late in the summer of 1960 was the most exhilarating and most rewarding political adventure yet. It was also potentially the most hazardous, not because of Cuba and the Cubans (tensions were already building between Washington and Havana), but because of our drive down the Southern United States to Key West, Florida.

The trip was the brainchild of our friend Ada Dritsas, who met Sheila at Hunter College and later was a social-work colleague of hers. Ada's father was a militant Greek-American member of the Communist Party, USA, whose specialty was organizing cafeteria and other food-service workers. He also helped recruit volunteers for the Lincoln Brigade to fight in Spain. Ada followed in daddy's footsteps. We never knew if Ada was "on assignment" from her Party unit to look into the Cuban revolution at first hand, or whether she thought it was just a nice idea for a vacation-cum-politics. We jumped at the idea. Political tourism on the Left was a feature of the 20th Century, most notably with travelers to Petrograd in 1917, and to the young USSR in the '20s and '30s. John Reed, who witnessed events in the Mexican Revolution of 1910, was also on hand for those historic Petrograd days he described in his classic account of the Bolshevik coup, *Ten Days That Shook the World*. Others followed Reed, and had mixed feelings about the "Soviet experiment" after experiencing it up close. Some were ecstatic – "I have seen the future, and it works!" exclaimed Lincoln Steffens. Others, Bertrand Russell, Malcolm Muggeridge among them, were not taken in by their Soviet hosts and were appalled by the dark side of their politics. We weren't writers or journalists, and didn't see ourselves as would-be John Reeds of the Cuban Revolution, but we did want a direct taste of history-in-the making, just "90 miles from our shores," as the intentionally ominous phrase of the time had it. Later trails of that kind would lead us and others to France, 1968; Chile, 1972; Portugal, 1974; and the Peoples Republic of China after 1949.

Our Cuba delegation consisted of Sheila and me; Ada and her boyfriend Richie; and Lew Kinsey, another social worker. On a hot summer morning we piled into our Studebaker, a sleek black "Silver Hawk," a wedding gift from my parents. No Chevy, Ford, or Chrysler for us; we wanted to show our counter-cultural credentials, sort of, and we picked the Studebaker as a car we saw as outside the mainstream. It turned out to be a lemon, but it got us to Cuba, and did duty there, and back. We drove a couple of full days and nights, Richie and I taking the wheel. There were no nighttime stops at motels: Lew was Black, and we were sensible enough to avoid challenging Jim Crow. We knew about "Colored Only" at water fountains and restrooms, but they still shocked us when we saw them for the first time.

No motels, then, but this meant sleeping at night in the car in hollows at roadsides. Not smart. What if some wandering locals somewhere in South Carolina peeked through the windshield with a flashlight, or a red-neck sheriff came by, summoned by others, and spotted this mixed Black and White band asleep in a car with New York plates? A night in jail on some charge or other? Or worse? At a different time, and in very different circumstances, in a deeper part of the South, the mixed group, James Cheney, Michael Schwerner and Andrew Goodman, in Mississippi to assist Black voter registration, were ambushed and murdered only four years after our journey. Our pulses raced at a Georgia service station one evening, as a young attendant twirled a pistol, Wild-West style, staring at us coldly while he gassed us up.

We pulled into Jacksonville, Florida at a very inauspicious moment. The local NAACP had led student sit-ins at Woolworths and violence ensued, as might be guessed by the description of one episode called "Axe Handle Saturday". Again, not too sensibly, we all walked into a tavern for some refreshments. The bartender pulled me aside, and told me, very politely, but with a tight-lipped edge,

"You ought to know better than to bring *him* in here. Don't you know what's been goin' on in Jacksonville?" Sorry, I said, as I led us out. We felt bad for Lew, bad and embarrassed for our country, and enraged too, over these examples of racism experienced up close.

Our short-term destination was the Miami home of some transplanted New York friends, the Millsteins, also from the social-worker community. We stayed overnight. Next day as we lounged on their porch, friends of Phil and Mickey's children kept staring at Lew. Later we learned that their neighbors let it be known they didn't approve of our mixed group spending time there. These incidents were fresh in our minds in Cuba, where we were willing believers in the claims that the Revolution had eliminated racism. Look, everyone noted, a Black man, *Commandante* Almeida, heads the armed forces!

Out of Miami that evening we headed toward, then down, the Keys. I drove as others slept. I woke them early of a morning to catch sight of a big, brilliant sun rising out of the sea to the East. At Key West we gave the Silver Hawk a lube job and an oil change, and drove her up the ramp onto the Key West-to-Havana ferry. *Olé*! Before we docked in the beautiful harbor of *La Habana,* I had a chance to practice my Spanish with the ship's purser, a friendly young man; no politics, just a tourist asking about some of the harbor sights drifting by. What's that monumental statue there, I asked. He told me. Who's that? He looked at me in amazement. I hadn't got used to the dropped endings and elided consonants of Cuban Spanish. *J-e-s-u- c-r-i-s-t-o,* he repeated, considerably slower. I said forgive me; he understood, and we laughed. I never saw him again. Pity; I suspect he might have offered us some cooler, more objective opinions at the outset of our stay about what was going on in Cuba than those we brought with our baggage, or got from the people we sought out.

We lodged at a hotel close by the Havana Hilton, re-dubbed the *Havana Libre,* a prominent hubbub of political tourists, journalists, and, we were sure, international intrigue. Politics aside, this was our first trip abroad for all of us—well, I was once on the Canadian side of Niagara Falls with the family—and we loved the place. We enjoyed the old colonial sections of town, and its cafes. I learned to smoke cigars and drink strong black coffee in tiny cups. We got caught in a spectacular rainstorm walking along the magnificent *Malecón* at seaside – and giggled happily. We joined our voices to those of spontaneous street singers and musicians. Lew relaxed. Ada said she felt more at home than in New York. Richie, not very interested in the politics, was fascinated by all the American cars and their owners who painstakingly improvised spare parts. Cuban men couldn't take their eyes off Sheila and Ada in their short skirts, and I ogled Cuban women in their tight outfits (worn because, they told us, our men like us that way). I spotted Saul Landau, a New Left luminary out of the University of Wisconsin and soon a prominent defender and promoter of Castro and the Cuban Revolution in the U.S., ambling one day with an arm around the waist of a curvy young Cuban woman.

But we were there for a higher purpose. We were supporting the Revolution by just *being there*. We were sympathetic *gringos*, Yankees defying the increasingly hostile U.S. postures toward the Revolution. When word of our presence got around, it was easy to meet people, and we were glad to spend time together. A popular meeting place was at Havana University, traditionally a center of political activity. Fidel himself had been a student there. On the steps of the school we got to know a young man known colorfully as "Pluto," and his wife, both of whom had been in the larger supporting movement that brought the *Barbudos* to power. They were delighted by our having a car, and with them we toured the countryside near Havana, in the province of Pinar del Río.

Pluto assured us that thanks to the Revolution peasants were reclaiming U.S.-corporate owned lands, and he pointed out much housing construction. We happened on a village festival of some kind, and were invited to join the party. We watched a suckling pig roasting on a revolving spit, and *ummm,* how delicious it was, served to us with some rice and beans. Another highlight: A visit to the celebrated frog farm run by a *Commandante,* an *Americano* by the name of William Morgan. A burly, rough-hewn guy with closely cropped blond hair who had fought with the Fidelistas in the mountains, Morgan impressed us a lot by his helping construct the new Cuba, and we told him so. Stay here, and join us, he said. (Spoiler alert: Ada did, eventually. Morgan met his fate as a "counterrevolutionary" before a firing squad in Havana several months after we met him.)

Our circle of enthusiasts came to include Vitaly Borovsky, none other than the local correspondent for *Pravda,* official organ of the Soviet Communist Party. We exchanged mutual admirations of the Revolution, but in his cups one evening, Vitaly confessed he didn't care much for Cubans, on a personal level. Too showy, he thought. We never did follow up on his invitation to write an article for *Pravda.* I imagined the headline: *Young Americans Hail the Revolution in Cuba, and Oppose Washington War Mongers.*

Amidst all the comradeship and warmth and high political spirits we all shared, one dissonant note stood out, for me, at least. A proprietor of some retail outlet I shopped in openly expressed distaste for the Revolution, and said the new Cuba was not for him; people like him will decide to leave, or be forced to leave, he said. I listened, surprised and a bit deflated by this sentiment which I failed to explore with him. Just a disgruntled *petit bourgeois,* a minority voice, I rationalized at the time. Many years later, I came to understand one of the major failings of Left tourism: seeking out and talking only to the Left. It amounts to a thoughtless self-deception (or wish fulfillment) that hides the full political picture. In Cuba, this *gusano,* as people like him came to be vilified by the Castro regime, was telling me something I didn't want to hear. We were heady with the energy and romance of this tropical revolution, crafted, we thought, by a unique band of humanist warriors with little connection to the ideologies associated with Moscow or Beijing. That was the message we wanted to take home with us. After almost two weeks in Cuba, we were anxious to deliver that message. Besides, Sheila and I had to get back to begin graduate school, and I also had to return to my job at Monitor.

Mother Nature threw us a curve, however. Its name was hurricane Donna. Torrential rains and winds that reached 140 mph hit the Keys and knocked out ferry docking facilities at Key West the second week in September. It looked like we were marooned on the island of Cuba with our Studebaker. I telegraphed Rose Rubin at Monitor: *"Your man in Havana stranded here by hurricane. Will try to fly back soon."* Full of militant virtue, Sheila and I told our Cuban friends that as an act of revolutionary solidarity, we would be happy to donate the Silver Hawk to the Revolution. Pluto, expressing the "personalism" we noticed that often marked a connection between ordinary people and Havana's leaders, said "I'll try to speak to Fidel about getting you home!"

No, Fidel wasn't involved. Saul Landau came to the rescue of the Silver Hawk. He was lingering in Havana for a while (with that girlfriend, why not?), and he offered to drive the car back to New York just as soon as docking facilities in Key West were repaired. That's what he did, under the wire, for Washington was about to impose a travel ban and an embargo that, with some ameliorations, lasted five decades until Barack Obama altered course. Cubana Airlines flew us out of Havana to Miami. Any anxiety we suffered on the first flight for all of us were eased by the frozen daiquiris generously distributed by the crew. Also distributed were fresh copies of the regime newspaper, *Granma*. A cheer went up when we read the big headline telling us Fidel was going to address the United Nations! In Miami, I called Brother Bob, who wired me the cash we needed to fly back to New York.

Weeks later, back in New York, I picked up the keys to the Silver Hawk from a Landau comrade, another Wisconsin Left luminary, Jim Weinstein. I got to know Jim much later as editor and publisher of New Left organs, and in other capacities, but no words were exchanged at his Upper West Side apartment. We saw Richie only once after Cuba, at a fruit juice stand where he was working. He had grown a long beard and looked very pre-hippy. He and Ada had separated, and we never saw him again. Lew Kinsey and I saw each other occasionally after he told me his cousin, who owned a service station on Atlantic Avenue in Brooklyn, could take care of the Silver Hawk. After a while, we lost touch. As for Ada.... ah, Ada. Her affair with Cuba was no summer romance. She went on to identify her political commitments with the Revolution. She was even arrested once in New Jersey on some gun-running charge related to the Cubans. Ada made her way back to Cuba after our visit, worked as an English-language instructor, married a Cuban, but returned to the U.S. to deliver their child so he'd be a U.S. citizen. She returned to Cuba and stayed several years, then eventually settled in different parts of the U.S. We had on-and-off contacts with her over the years, but, to our regret, we lost sight of her long ago. According to our mutual friend, Marilyn McGregor, with whom she once shared a Brooklyn apartment, Ada offered many candid reports about her Cuban experiences—the sexism of Cuban men, the rampant corruption in the Cuban Communist Party, and she had some amusing, unflattering stories about American Lefties visiting Cuba.

Housing construction in PInar del Río province, Cuba, thanks to the Revolution, according to our Havana comrade who went by the name, "Pluto". 1960. Photo by the author.

V

GRADUATE WORK AND OTHER TEMPTATIONS

Back in New York, Sheila and I were intoxicated with the Cuban Revolution, and the compulsion to defend what we saw as its achievements against the hostility developing in Washington, in the media, and at large. We met the hostility the moment we got into a cab at Idlewild (as JFK was then called), and mentioned we had been to Cuba. When the driver chattered on about "Castro, the dictator," we let him know we were on Fidel's side.

Our views then were more or less what C. Wright Mills spelled out in his popular *Listen, Yankee!*, his attempt to explain the legitimate reasons for the revolutionary eruption led by Fidel Castro, and why we should support, not condemn it. It's also what we had heard from the Cubans themselves. It went something like this: *The U.S. relationship to Cuba was historically both politically and economically exploitive. Even the term for the conflict that embedded us in Cuban affairs was insensitive and insulting – we called it the Spanish-American War, while for the Cubans it was the culmination of a long battle for independence from Spain. If anything, it should have been called the Cuban-Spanish-American War. We also maimed Cuban sovereignty by attaching the Platt Amendment to the new Cuban constitution, which sanctioned Washington's power to intervene in Cuban affairs. U.S. corporations owned much of the industrial and agricultural wealth of Cuba, the latter dominated by sugar production, a "monoculture" that held back economic development. The whole system came to be protected, with U.S. sponsorship, by cruel despots like Fulgencio Batista, overthrown by a Castro-led rebellion that enjoyed mass support in 1959. This historical drama climaxed with a Cuba liberated from Yankee domination, and refusing to buckle to its powerful neighbor to the north. Shouldn't we, born of a rebellion ourselves, show sympathy, not animosity, to the new Cuba?*

Soon enough, this tale of heroic little Cuba became entangled in the politics and passions of the Cold War. The Soviets came to rescue the Cuban economy from the damage of the U.S.-imposed embargo. It looked like Fidel and his band of followers, including the new icon of the global Left, Ernesto "Che" Guevara, were really crypto-Communists eager to convert their island into a Soviet beachhead "90 miles from our shores". The Left, and Left scholars offered alternative explanations for Cuban behavior. William Appleman Williams, a noted "revisionist" American historian from the University of Wisconsin, published a book which was sympathetic to the Cuban Revolution and dismissive of charges that the Fidelistas were Communists – *The United States, Cuba, and Castro: An Essay on the Dynamics of Revolution and the Dissolution of Empire.* In it Williams argued that the Revolution's primary aim was to restore the Cuban constitution of 1940, an admirably democratic document promoting land reform which was ignored in practice by authoritarians like Batista. After Williams spoke at a forum when the book was published, I noticed a moon-faced, owlish young guy about my age who seemed to be acting as Williams' wingman, answering questions from audience members while Williams was busy signing books and speaking to others. Someone told me it was Ron Radosh, a student of Williams at the University of Wisconsin. I didn't speak to him then, but not long after that encounter we started a long-lasting friendship.

Sheila and I continued to feel the political energy generated by our Cuba trip even as we began our respective graduate studies in the Fall of 1960. Our devotion to pro-Cuban activities wasn't as great as Ada's, but we contributed our share of support. We told informal groups of friends and others what we saw and learned in Cuba. We backed the "Fair Play for Cuba Committee," and I chaired a fund-raising session of sympathizers attended by the Cuban ambassador to the United Nations. We unhesitatingly denounced President Kennedy for launching the Bay of Pigs invasion of Cuba by anti-Castro *émigrés* in 1961, and blamed Washington, not Moscow, for the Cuban Missile Crisis that brought the world to the edge of nuclear war in 1962. We composed Spanish lyrics to the melody of a famous Black liberation ballad, and we gave it the title of *Venceremos,* which translates as *We Shall Overcome.* Our musical homage to the Cuban Revolution was published in the Left folky organ, *Sing Out!*. And we got a cordial acknowledgement from Pete Seeger: "Toshi [Seeger] and I certainly envy you your trip and congratulate you on it," he wrote. I often wondered, then and later, how much the FBI was on our tail during those militant days. The "Freedom of Information Act" allowed the curious to get hold of their FBI files, but I never bothered until recently. I enlisted my niece Lisa and her husband John Dellaportas, both attorneys, in the effort, but no luck so far. John reported that the FBI declared there was no file on Louis Menashe. *What*? I was insulted. Either they shredded old files, or they were just making access difficult. I couldn't believe no file existed on this radical Castro lover. Try harder, I told John and Lisa.

The Cuba infatuation even led me to think about changing course in graduate study from Russia to Latin America, or combining both. I was fluent in Spanish, an important qualification for such study at a time when my Russian was barely-existent. Russian Revolution? Cuban Revolution? They were both parts of my quixotic goal of affecting politics through academic study. There were other elements that encouraged my flirtation in a new direction. Among the four requirements as a History major at NYU was Latin America. What's more, the University also had a Luso-Brazilian Institute I could easily transition to. I even made a half-hearted effort to apply, unsuccessfully, to Columbia's much fuller and more established graduate program in Latin American studies.

I started reading in the area. I was much taken by Prescott's *History of the Conquest of Peru*, and especially by his *History of the Conquest of Mexico*, both stellar examples of old-fashioned historiography with epic and dramatic flair. I also read some of the fiction of Octavio Paz and Carlos Fuentes. Mexico was becoming for me a particularly attractive possibility for serious study. I felt the mixed-culture mystique of the place and its complicated history. And the Mexicans had a revolution there too! Modern Mexico was also the home of a trio of great revolutionary muralists, Diego Rivera, David Siqueiros, and Jose Orozco. Add Leon Trotsky to this Russo-Mexican-Revolutionary blend that was capturing my imagination. Offered political asylum by the Mexican government, Trotsky lived in a suburb of Mexico City, and was assassinated there by a Stalinist agent in 1940. The Latin America thing proved to be only a temporary infatuation, but not before it was capped by a trip to Mexico the summer of 1961, just about a year after our Cuba adventure. My cousin Mimi had settled in Mexico City and raised a family there. Sheila and I decided to visit her and have a direct look at Mexico for ourselves, not exactly political tourism this time, but still a trip with a serious purpose.

A memorable part of the trip was getting there by train. We were graduate students with part-time jobs, living on a tight budget. So tight, in fact, that we traveled the long round-trip rail journeys from New York to Mexico City and back by coach, not Pullman class. We did a lot of reading on Latin America and Mexico on that trip, and glimpsed parts of the U.S. we had never seen before, across the Mid-West to St. Louis, then southwest across the never ending Texas to the Rio Grande at Laredo, where we transferred to the Mexican railroad at Nuevo Laredo. Before boarding our Mexican train, I insisted on taking a short walk in Laredo, to honor the classic melancholy ballad that began, *As I Went Out Walking the Streets of Laredo, As I Went out Walking Laredo One day....*

An attendant of the Mexican train line led us to a car where other Yankees were boarding, but we declined the assistance and indicated we wanted to travel ordinary class, with "the people". He shrugged, skeptically. A few minutes in a very hot, very crowded car where men, women, and chickens mingled in very close proximity persuaded us out of our ideologically driven folly. The attendant smiled approvingly as we made our way, sheepishly, to a more amenable section of the train for the journey down the Central Mexican Valley to Mexico City.

We stayed at an inexpensive hotel near the *Zócalo* (the *Plaza de la Constitución*), the historic heart of the city, and checked out the usual attractions, including some striking Rivera murals at the *Palacio Nacional*. We also made the mistake of celebrating our 3rd wedding anniversary with too much wine at dinner the first evening of our stay. Our accelerating and crazily beating hearts at bedtime convinced us the end was suddenly, unexpectedly near. Why, oh why, did I ever think of Latin American studies that brought us to our deathbed in Mexico? The crisis passed. My cousin Mimi explained the next day that it was a common and natural response to the new elevation, abetted by alcohol.

Mimi Vedrenne was a member of the comfortable foreign bourgeoisie residing in Mexico. Born in France herself, she met in Mexico, and married, a soon to be wealthy French proprietor of a local metals factory. They lived with their two young daughters in the *Colonia Polanco,* an upscale outpost of the capital. Their enormous house with its entourage of servants of course impressed us even as we took note of their class standing. Forgiven; *Mimi was family.* Blood is thicker than water, my brother would admonish me. (That always reminded me of Camus' affirmation: "I believe in justice, but I shall defend my mother above justice.") We didn't get into politics with Mimi and her husband Fernand, and we enjoyed each other's company. We told them of our visit to *Coyoacán.* No, not to Trotsky's villa, the site of his assassination, but to the *Casa Azul,* the museum-converted home of Frida Kahlo, whose work we hadn't known, and whose strange, often grotesquely powerful self-portraits made up one of the memorable parts of our Mexico trip.

To get some sense of life outside the capital, we went by bus to a market town, *Toluca,* south of Mexico City. There, as well as in Mexico City, our overriding impression was of mass poverty, and a somber street mood, so different from the upbeat atmosphere of Cuba. Did I want to carve out a professional career in places like this? With depressed spirits, we decided to leave Mexico earlier than planned. At a railway stop in Mexico, hawkers approached our train windows and, as I was instructed, bargained, feeling guilty about it, with one of them for a handsome black and yellow blanket with a folkloric design. We have it still, one of the few mementos from our brief experience of Mexico. Many years later, thanks to a brilliant novel, Tolstoyan in its heft, with psychological insights worthy of Dostoevsky, and political ones recalling Orwell, I revisited Mexico and the two Coyoacán houses in its pages—Leonardo Padura's *The Man Who Loved Dogs*. Its Cuban author imaginatively recreates the parallel stories of the assassinated Trotsky and his assassin, the Stalinist true-believer, Ramón Mercader, with transfixing and accurate historical detail.

When I told my mentor, Arthur Mendel, who then handled the Russian/Soviet curriculum of the History Department at NYU, that I was considering switching to Latin American studies, seduced by the Cuban Revolution and its charismatic leaders, he splashed some cold water on the idea: "You'll be around a lot longer than Castro," he said. What he meant, I think, was: *Don't you fall for what amounts to another Caribbean strongman; he and the romantic aura surrounding him are sure to fail with time and political realities.* About the same time as that conversation I learned of the execution of *Commandante* Morgan, he of our frog-farm visit. Castro was revealing the merciless, after-the-Revolution side of regimes brought to power by Revolution. Morgan was one of thousands snuffed out by the new tyrants in Havana. What's a revolution without executions of its enemies? asked Lenin. Was Morgan an enemy of the Cuban Revolution as charged, exposed as an active counter-revolutionary agent and dealt with accordingly? Morgan claimed innocence, and sought unsuccessfully to speak personally to Castro before a firing squad dispatched him. Later studies by historians and journalists who examined Morgan's life and death portray him as a complex adventurer, a freebooter with contrasting allegiances, who may or may not have been the CIA-connected villain as the Cubans claimed. The news of Morgan's execution depressed me. Someone we recently met and admired, shot by the regime we admired. "My first *Kronstadt,*" I told Arthur Mendel, alluding to the anti-Bolshevik rebellion of former Bolshevik supporters who were ruthlessly suppressed – by the Bolsheviks—on the island fortress off Petrograd. A "Kronstadt" was a disillusion. My invoking that reference may have demonstrated to Arthur my familiarity with Russian Revolutionary history, but it was only partly sincere. My disillusion was superficial and temporary. Sheila and I (I more than Sheila) continued to cheer on the Cuban Revolution, especially in its conflict with Washington, and as for the Great October Socialist Revolution and the Soviet Union it gave birth to, well, many years would pass before that ardor was extinguished.

It wasn't Morgan's execution, nor Arthur Mendel's wry warning, that led me back from Latin America to Russia, my true love at the time, and to understand in retrospect that I had experienced but a summer (Cuban) fling. I didn't feel comfortable with some of the students and faculty I met in the Latin American studies area. Partly, it was political. I didn't cotton to their conventional anti-communist, anti-Cuban views. And in those days I judged people according to the simplistic formula, were they pro- or anti-Soviet? There was also something else, something personal, a reverse snobbery on my part, you might call it, typified by an encounter between me and Sheila and a faculty-administrator of the Luso-Brazilian program. It was in the lobby of the main NYU classroom building at the time, and I remember the well-dressed figure with pomaded hair and the scent of cologne who was trying to convince me that my Spanish was good enough to pick up Portuguese. He tried a few sentences in Portuguese, I translated correctly, and at that moment Sheila walked in to meet me. Meet my wife, I told him. He leaned forward to her, bowing at the waist, and reached to kiss her hand. He did so, but as he looked down, he jumped back suddenly as if snake-bit: he saw Sheila's torn sneakers. He became noticeably cooler toward me. No, this program and who's part of it were not for me.

Sheila framed by St. Basil's after our march through Red Square, Moscow, 1962. Photo by the author.

VI

RUSSIAN STUDIES

Sadly, it was Arthur Mendel who didn't last as long as me and Castro. He died of cancer in 1988, having left NYU to teach at the University of Michigan for many years. I was very disappointed by his departure. He was an exciting teacher who communicated a passion for Russian intellectual history, and was very familiar with the political issues roiling East and West during the Cold War. He assigned us readings in Bakunin, Chernyshevsky, Herzen, Kropotkin and other thinkers who dealt with those "accursed questions" in the "thick journals" of 19th-century Russia that agitated the *intelligentsia*—"What is to Be Done?" and "Who is to Blame?," they asked. Lenin formulated the central question of political power as *Kto-Kovo?*, "Who does what to whom?" There were also doses of Griboyedov, Goncharov, and Turgenev on the literary side. I supplemented all of these with my own texts in Lenin, Stalin, Marx and Engels. Bertram Wolfe's *Three Who Made a Revolution* was a part of my extracurricular reading and affected me powerfully. I romanticized that threesome – Lenin, Trotsky, Stalin – and Krupskaya, too, Lenin's wife. Arthur was friendly, very accessible and, moreover, understood "where I was coming from," gently indulging my Leftism. He tried to offset any affection for Marxism by reading passages from Bakunin and commenting on how infinitely richer and more insightful the thought of the anarchist aristocrat was than the materialist dialectics of Marx and Engels. Maybe Bakunin's prose was superior, but he didn't win me over. Arthur went on to write a not uncritical study of Bakunin, and once confided to me "what a *schnook*" he found him to be. I kept in touch with my erstwhile mentor for a while, and Sheila and I visited him once when he was on research sabbatical in England. We often corresponded and took differing sides on the Vietnam War in the '60s and early 70s. I dismissed Arthur for his politics as a Cold Warrior, but I really missed him at NYU.

Another Russian-history specialist in the Department was the young L. Jay Oliva, who began as a night school instructor, and enjoyed a spectacular rise up the NYU ladder as Professor, Associate Dean, Dean at University Heights, Vice President, Provost, Chancellor, and finally, President in 1991, from which office he played a vital role in boosting the university's finances and enrollments, and transforming the school onto the plane of national and international academic excellence. He once substituted for Mendel in a Soviet History course I was taking, and I immediately typed him negatively; his hostility to the USSR showed. Many years later, after *my* transformation, I had several friendly chats with President Oliva, and teased him once that maybe his familiarity with the politics of Eighteenth-Century Imperial Russia had something to do with his bureaucratic mobility and ascension to the top.

William L. Blackwell, Jr., who came to the NYU History Department in 1962 as the new Russianist, couldn't be more different than Arthur P. Mendel, personally and professionally. They belonged more or less to the same generation of Cold-War Russianists, but came from different academic universes, and I don't mean simply that one was from Princeton (Blackwell), the other from Harvard (Mendel). Arthur was looser, very engaging, loved to jest, and had an ironic sense about things. Bill was far from cold, and treated me quite well, but he was distant, and there was a tension about him. Arthur was a dynamic and wide-ranging, give-and-take lecturer. I remember a long discussion over whether Marx's vision of communist utopia would allow for police directing traffic. Bill's teaching style was the traditional lecture, detailed and formal. I assumed Bill's political leanings were liberal, but it was easier to discuss politics with Arthur, even though our views clashed. Both were extremely competent and high achievers in their respective fields – Arthur was the historian of ideas, with a moralist's interest in the issues addressed by Russian thinkers. Bill was an economic historian with dispassionate views of Russian industrialization under the Tsars. Arthur knew more and cared more about the political and intellectual background of the Russian Revolution, while Bill would place it in the developmental context of attempts at modernization by political elites. One was deep into theory; the other was economic nuts and bolts.

Where did Arthur's departure and Bill's assumption of the Russian chair leave me, and my choice of thesis and dissertation topics on the road to a Ph.D.? There were times I was painfully aware of NYU's shortcomings in the Russian/Soviet area compared to Columbia's better library and better library resources, more courses offered, and a much larger faculty boasting numerous specialists. On the other hand, at NYU I felt insulated from what I knew to be the Cold-Warrish, anti-Soviet atmosphere that dominated Russian Institutes everywhere, Columbia's included. Moreover, NYU and its History Department were very good to me; I'm not sure I would have done as well in the bigger and more competitive Columbia or other Ivy-League Russian studies environments. There was much university financial assistance via several fellowships, and after my first year I was named a Teaching Assistant by the Department. The usual arrangement was to assist a faculty historian by grading papers, leading small "recitation" sections that took off from his lectures to the large assembly, and taking care of humdrum duties like checking attendance in the big lecture hall. I was assigned to Professor Joseph Reither at the handsome University Heights campus in the Bronx. Whatever anxiety about my duties and teaching I felt that first morning at Professor Reither's opening Western Civilization lecture was instantly dispelled when a young freshman approached me to ask, very timidly, were students required to use a loose-leaf or a bound notebook for the course?

My TA and Sheila's scholarships plus her part-time work at different community centers while earning the Social Work degree at Columbia got us through our first two years of graduate work. It was the summer of 1962. Her studies were finished; her successful two years conferred on her the MSW, her "union card," as we used to say, for a professional social-work career. My card was a long way off; I hadn't even decided on a dissertation topic. But I knew it was time to visit the Great Land, even if it meant cashing in our life insurance policies. Travel to the USSR wasn't all that common in those days; you didn't just put any Soviet city on your itinerary and fly right in. There were visa requirements, and designated entry points, and all arrangements had to be handled through another of those acronymic Soviet agencies, *Intourist*. We decided to make the trip with Stanley and Betty, and map it into a wider European, Western and Eastern, journey. To make things really interesting, we hoped to drive into the USSR and maybe camp out at some grounds we had heard nice reports about. No such luck; driving into the USSR was barred that summer, or so we were told. But we did drive. From Paris to Warsaw, and back, as it turned out. Sheila's recently married sister, Carole, and her husband Seymour, were in the market for a European car. It didn't take much persuasion to convince them what a swell idea it would be for us to pick up a Peugeot 403 in Paris for them, and have it shipped back to New York. The sticker price would be cheaper in the Peugeot's country of origin, and it could be imported as a used car at a less costly tariff. They agreed to the idea, and it all worked out fine. That is, fine as far as buying the car, driving it across Europe and shipping it back is concerned. Far from fine was what we saw and experienced in Eastern Europe and the USSR. Our disappointments started early there.

First we enjoyed Paris with our good friends, the transplanted New Yorkers, Jack and Rubye Monet. They thought to blow all their money on a trip to Paris after their wedding and wound up staying for keeps, Jack as a journalist for the *International Herald Tribune*, Rubye in a variety of jobs leading at length to teaching English in a French commercial school. (Their binational, bilingual children, both born in Paris, took divergent adult paths – Juliette left for college in the U.S., and stayed, while Paul kept to France.) Our traveling foursome visited Rubye and Jack at their lovely little *rue de Bac* apartment (and had our first experience of a "Turkish toilet") after we checked in at a nearby Left Bank hotel. We picked up the Peugeot and with it, Jeff Kaplow, another young Wisconsin Lefty who was already making his mark as a historian of France. Jeff was fluent in French and knew the city and its sights. I impressed Stanley when I identified Sacre Coeur, the Pantheon, Notre Dame, *et al.* on sight. Hey, I was a student of European history and culture, I reminded him.

After Paris we drove south to the French and Italian Rivieras, spent time in Florence, Rome and Venice, then headed north into Austria. Ah, what splendid times we had in the classical tourist zones of Western Europe. Stanley and Betty did the driving. Sheila was not a driver; I had limited stick-shift experience and didn't want to log time getting used to shifting by grinding the gears in Carole and Sy's new car. That Stanley and Betty had the burden of all the driving probably sparked some of the tension that erupted among the four of us on the way back to Paris; the bigger reasons revolved around politics and perceptions. On a pleasant August afternoon we left Austria for Bratislava, the capital of the Slovak part of the Czechoslovak Soviet Socialist Republic (the only Soviet satellite to be honored with that designation; the others were "Peoples Republics" and the German Democratic Republic). Crossing into the open fields of Czechoslovakia, a SOCIALIST COUNTRY!, we were dizzy with elation, and broke into sarcarstic peals of laughter about the purported "Iron Curtain" that didn't exist. But suddenly there came into view what looked like miles and miles of barbed wire stretching as far as our horrified eyes could see. The silence in the car was terrible. We were so deflated that we didn't even comfort each other with the usual rationalizations – *Well, they have to protect their borders. They're encircled by imperialism. Cold War hostilities trigger brutal measures.* Etc. Those bromides were saved for later invocations.

We were in a hurry to get to Warsaw for a pre-arranged street-corner meeting with Leszek, a friend of a friend of Stanley and Betty, so we didn't linger in Bratislava. Someone told us it was a handsome place, on the Danube, with baroque palaces and castles from Hapsburg times, but we saw none of that. We stopped only for gas, and we experienced another depressing moment. The Peugeot was immediately surrounded by a crowd; the streets were virtually bare of traffic. The crowd, mostly men, dressed—as Sheila and I saw it – in poor, worn-out garments, gathered about us as if we were visitors from another planet. Figuratively, in political and economic terms, we were. The inter-planetary meeting was quite friendly; they were glad to see us. We communicated, thanks to our broken Russian and German (Betty was almost fluent in Yiddish), and their broken English. *Not French?* (from the Peugeot, they assumed). *Ah, Americans!* No Cold-War animosity at all, not from them, and certainly not from us—we were on their side, remember. We drove off after several minutes of shaking hands and wishing each other peace. I didn't look back, but I'm sure they stared with mixed, glad/sad feelings in our wake.

On the road we picked up a lone hitchhiker, a stocky middle-aged guy who had the look of a peasant out of the countryside we were passing through. He sat in the back with me and Sheila, and put a sack on the floorboard. The sack moved; a piglet peeked out. He grinned, and his watery light-blue eyes set in a broad bronzed face conveyed satisfaction; good luck my finding these travelers in this car. No language, broken or otherwise, effected any communication. He just kept pointing ahead, keep on going, keep on going. We were in the vicinity of Zhilina in northern Slovakia. He stopped us by a cluster of cottages, and it seemed he was inviting us into one of them. We regretted having to turn him down, but we had to cross into Poland and head for Warsaw to meet Leszek on that street corner.

Before reaching that street corner we stopped somewhere in Poland for lunch, and for our first discussion of what we had witnessed so far in Socialist Eastern Europe. That we learned the Iron Curtain wasn't just a metaphor was not mentioned; it was the recollection of the Bratislava episode that triggered some heated moments, and almost aborted our journey. Sheila, candid as always, tried to suggest, ever so softly, that things didn't look too good in Slovakia. "Whaddaya mean?!" bellowed Stanley in his piercing baritone. "Didn't you notice how poorly people were dressed," asked Sheila even more softly. "You mean the men weren't wearing ties!" Stanley shouted. Sheila: "Not just that...." She didn't finish; Stanley got up, threw down his lit cigarette and yelled, "I can't stand that kind of crap!" Betty and I tried to calm things, along the lines of let's not be jumping to conclusions, we haven't seen much yet, let's try to be quietly objective about things and try to understand what we're seeing, and above all, let's try to be civil to one another.

Stanley calmed down. Later that evening, I tried persuading Sheila to lay off Stanley on these matters. What she said was true – the sight of those people clustering around us and the Peugeot, and how they looked, was really depressing – but she should appreciate what impact this sort of revelation can have on a faithful socialist and Soviet sympathizer like Stanley. His family, his life, were enclosed in certain sentiments about socialism, the USSR, the class struggle, the socialist camp. If he were truly a hardened unthinking dogmatist, he would retreat to denial in the face of reality, as he did in our luncheon exchange. If he were less dogmatically inclined (as I was), he might discover other ways of dealing with unpleasant data (as I did). Stanley showed no hard feelings, Sheila promised me she would show more tact in these politically charged palavers, and our friendship with Betty and Stanley (our drivers!) remained strong. We drove on.

I brought a pocket Russian dictionary and a phrasebook with me. I was a Russian-language beginner, thanks to a not very systematic course of formal and informal study. My days at Monitor helped. Mischa was fluent, often chatting with his sister in Russian, and Rose could get by. *Budyet, budyet,* Rose would tell a customer asking for Monitor to release some recording or other. ("It's coming, it's coming.") Once when we all lined up in the office to stuff and stamp envelopes, Rose called it a *subbotnik*—early Soviet jargon from the word for Saturday when workers "volunteered" collective labor. In correspondence with Moscow Rose would add her fine Cyrillic script to the address on the envelopes. That script, formidable looking to the non-Russian, was really the easiest part of learning the language. (The advice I gave to all travelers to the USSR, and still do to those visiting Russia, is learn the alphabet – it's helpful in reading street and metro signs, etc., and it's not as difficult as it looks on first sight.) At NYU's University Heights campus, where I was a Teaching Assistant, I sat in on Mrs. Essman's introductory Russian course. Now here's a bit from the department of it's a small circular world. Mrs. Essman was the daughter of Aron Pressman – "Ronya" to Rose Rubin – the co-author of a popular introductory Russian-language text. Monitor put out a two-disk set of Pressman reading lessons from his text, a very helpful recording, excerpts from which I could recite by heart after repeated listening. I didn't know of the Essman-Pressman connection when I recited poetry in her class, and was delighted to meet her decades later when she turned up for my commentary on a Russian film screened at a Westchester theater. Not long after Monitor, I met Ronya again in another setting, at Indiana University, where he taught Russian in the intensive summer program, and played piano in student theatrical productions. Quite a character, Ronya. Before he left Bloomington for Moscow with students and scholars he left his exotic *Panhard* – rare for American roads – with me to drive it back to New York for him. I noticed other drivers rubbernecking in my direction as they tried to make out what I was driving.

Beleyet parus, odinokii	*A lonely sail is flashing white*
v tumanye morya golubom...	*Amidst the blue mist of the sea!*

I still recall those opening lines from Lermontov's *The Sail* Mrs. Essman introduced us to. Oh yes; one more thing: She is the mother of Susie Essman, the terrific comedienne who plays the potty-mouthed Susie Greene ("You fat fuck," is a favorite jab at her husband) in Larry David's scabrous television series, *Curb Your Enthusiasm*.

My limited Russian fluency didn't assist much in the Eastern Europe we visited; in Poland and Czechoslovakia they preferred anything but Russian. It was forced upon them as a compulsory second language by Big Brother in Moscow. For the Poles, it was the language of the historical enemy and current oppressor. At times I thought I was deliberately misunderstood by restaurant waiters when I ordered something in Russian and got something else; was it my bad Russian or their sly deception? There was the ice-cream I thought I requested for the four of us at that lunch in Poland, and got dishes of some kind of pudding instead. Later I would experience another practice in Soviet restaurants where Russian wasn't the issue: Never mind what you ordered, this is what you get.

Sure enough, Leszek was waiting for us on that street corner in Warsaw as per the advance arrangement in New York. Leszek was a marine biologist and Torun University professor that a friend of Betty and Stanley met at Wood's Hole in Massachusetts, where he was on a Ford research fellowship. He spoke a fine, slightly accented English, a cigarette never left his fingers, and he always carried an umbrella. Convinced that a socialist honor system prevailed in Warsaw, we left his umbrella in the unlocked Peugeot with some of our miscellaneous clothing. Clothing and umbrella were gone when we returned.

Leszek was the perfect host, courteous and attentive, for the few days we spent in Warsaw. After a visit to the memorialized site of the Jewish Warsaw Ghetto Uprising, we toured what was once the old, historic center of the city, where Leszek pointed out how it had been reconstructed and its architectural details restored after the war. The Germans had razed much of the city in their savage suppression of the Polish armed rebellion late in the war. Why the nearby Soviet Red Army, just across the Vistula, didn't assist the insurgents is the subject of much debate among historians – and much resentment by the Poles. And, of course, Leszek did not fail to draw our attention to what he described sarcastically as Stalin's great personal gift to the people of Warsaw, a domineering skyscraper in the wedding-cake Moscow style.

On a bus ride, several passengers noticed we were speaking English and offered us some of their sausage, which we accepted. We followed that up with mutual swigs from a bottle of vodka. We often experienced those spontaneous, open-hearted gestures on our trip to the Cold War East that offset somewhat the many disappointments we kept bumping into. At times those gestures were embarrassingly over the line. Before departing for Europe, friends had warned Betty and Sheila to watch out for the unabashed public overtures of Italian men, in Rome especially. Warsaw, not Rome is where those overtures made their appearance. "Oh yes," Betty later remembered, "the Polish men were the most aggressive and nervy in all of Europe." At a Warsaw restaurant, a guy walked up to our table to ask Sheila if she were a Gypsy, a flirtatious compliment, we supposed, on her dark good looks. At another place featuring music and dancing, a man ignored Stanley sitting at her side and invited Betty to join him on the floor. Betty declined this opportunity to advance person-to-person U.S.-Polish relations.

Thinking about those incidents much later, we chalked them up not only to the primal instincts behind openly displayed masculinity, but to deviations from the official line of hostility to the U.S. that Moscow imposed on their satellites. Could they be read as small acts of courage, even defiance, as individual efforts to pierce the Iron Curtain by showing friendliness to Americans in public? Or were we straining hard to place simple breaches of manners, or accepted traditions, into the context of our political preoccupations? The Poles, it should also be remembered, demonstrated their real resistance to Moscow with several uprisings in the decade of the '50s. Later, the big *Solidarity* workers' resistance that began in 1980 led inevitably, it could be argued, to the collapse of the Soviet satellite empire.

Our plan was to leave the Peugeot in Leszek's care until our return from the USSR about a week later. He drove us to the Warsaw station where that *Moskva?/ V Moskvu!* exchange took place on the boarding platform. Assured we got on the right train, we settled into a comfortable compartment, giddy with anticipation. Before we left the Polish capital, a uniformed customs officer checked us out. As he backed out of our compartment, he looked over his shoulder into the corridor, then turned his face to us. "Rubles for Dollars?," he whispered. We were speechless. *Ugh*! another disconcerting welcome to the Soviet dominated universe. No, thank you, Stanley finally blurted out, visibly uncomfortable, as the rest of us were by this brazen un-socialist act. The disconnect between our ideal visions and the reality on the ground was a recurring, gnawing feature of our trip we couldn't ignore, much as we would have liked to close our eyes to it. I don't recall there was much discussion then of what it meant that we had just met a corrupt ("defiant"?) customs officer on duty in socialist Poland. Would we run into similar disappointments in the socialist USSR?

That incident didn't dampen our spirits on the train; they remained high all the way to Moscow, especially after we made a few Soviet friends. At the long break for the gauge change to the wider Russian tracks, with much checking of papers, a young uniformed Soviet guard smiled at me when he inspected my passport with its many national stamps – all those countries you've been to; lucky you, he seemed to say, wordlessly. Everyone we met on the train seemed delighted to chat with young Americans, none of that frostiness that dominated the political atmosphere of U.S.-Soviet relations you might expect in personal contacts. We were traveling in the cold, turbulent wake of Congress establishing "Captive Nations Week," Khrushchev pounding his shoe at the United Nations, and his boasting, "We Will Bury You!," the U-2 incident, the construction of the Berlin Wall, the failed Bay of Pigs invasion, the Cuban turn to Moscow, and other Cold-War markers.

All that had no effect on our personal U.S.-Soviet relations. With our Russian friends we were able to communicate in pidgin versions of our languages. One middle-aged fellow commented disdainfully on the status of Polish farming, which operated on a system of private holdings unlike the collectivized agriculture of the Soviet countryside. He mimicked Polish peasants cutting hay with scythes, his way of mocking their technological backwardness – no Soviet tractors and combines there – and their underdeveloped socio-economic consciousness. Good fellow! Hip. At last, here was someone who reassured our expectations. Our confidence in Soviet socialism, if not the Slovak and Polish variants we had experienced, got a welcome boost from that guy and his mockery.

Two pretty young women, our age, it looked like, also helped bolster our pro-Soviet disposition. They were friendly Russians, all *Mir I Druzhba* to our "Peace and Friendship" offerings. Of course, they were soon eager to learn how many rubles a dollar would bring, but they didn't ask to swap some; besides, we didn't know what exchange rates the street would dictate in that kind of commerce. To their question, I quoted the official rate, which inflated the ruble wildly. Did they think "naïve Americans"? They seemed to accept my response, so maybe they were naïve, too. Or cautious about engaging in this kind of exercise in public, with Americans, no less.

In those days I was always disappointed by any Russian's attention to ordinary, mundane things, while ignoring higher political and ideological matters. Weren't Irina and Natasha concerned about the condition of the American working class, or prospects for a mass socialist party in the U.S.? Did they know their classics of Marxism-Leninism as we did? Language barriers would have stymied attempts to discuss such matters with Irina and Natasha on the train, but I soon learned to my continuing disappointment that all the future Mischas and Tanyas I was to meet weren't very interested in this stuff either. They get that -- "pap" was the word he used – in school, Arthur Mendel told me after our trip, and they have nothing but derision for it.

Anyway, we were pleased when our young friends mentioned they knew the singing of *Pol Rawbsun*. We turned to Stanley, who promptly belted out a terrific *Old Man River* to the delight of all of us. A good moment: high-minded expectations deflated by simple human interaction, but it helped that it was Robeson they named. With Irina and Natasha, Stanley and I got off the train at one of the stops for a bit of exercise. Betty later told us she and Sheila were on the edge of panic when the train seemed ready to resume the journey to Moscow without us. We lingered with the girls a short distance from the tracks, then noticed signs of train movement and hustled back. I held Irina's hand as I helped her board. She pulled it out when I held it too long.

At our Moscow arrival, we were swept into the waiting arms and itineraries of Intourist. First stop: our hotel, the Metropol. We were happy to be at this once grand, but at the time, considerably faded place, just short walking distances away from the Bolshoi Theater, the Kremlin, and other landmarks of the capital. (Several years later, traveling with our toddler, Claudia, we were again lodged at the Metropol, and found bedbugs in our room. The woman at the main desk greeted our complaint with an indifferent shrug, as if to say, what are you so squeamish about?) Betty is still fond of recalling the floor ladies at the Metropol, and how she and they got a kick out of her requesting the room key, as she carefully pronounced 484 --*chiteery-vosyem-chiteery*. How nice and quaint, each floor with a helpful concierge, we thought at the time.

Our first Moscow morning we learned of a Red Square parade that day welcoming the latest Soviet cosmonauts, Nikolayev and Popovich, who touched down August 15, 1962. The four of us wandered into nearby Manezh Square where a huge crowd of paraders assembled. We joined the crowd and discovered other foreigners like us were there as well, celebrating along with Soviet comrades. A young French *camarade* was distributing pins marking the occasion, and affixed one to Sheila's raincoat lapel. "Are you from India?," she asked (those dark good looks again). Another young woman, Russian, made eye contact with Betty, walked close to her, and whispered, *Du bist ein Yid?* ("Are you Jewish?" – Betty's "Jewish" good looks?). Betty smiled and nodded vigorously. "Do you speak Yiddish?," asked the young woman in Yiddish. Betty nodded even more vigorously. Before they could exchange some Q's and A's (in Yiddish), we were moved along by the crowd and pushed forward. What happened next took our breath away. We were heading into Red Square!

This was our introduction to that famous space. To our right the familiar Kremlin wall and towers, at the far end ahead the colored onion domes of St. Basil's; we almost danced on the cobblestones. No Soviet tanks or the newest missiles on flat-bed trucks rumbling across the Square with us, just hundreds of mainly young marchers, faces shining as in some socialist-realist *agit-prop* poster. Our faces shined, too, eyes looking up and right to glimpse the figures atop, *Gulp*! the Lenin Mausoleum. "There's the Central Committee," said Stanley (mistakenly). We couldn't tell which one was Nikolayev and which Popovich, but Khrushchev was easily recognizable, as was a liverish-complexioned Anastas Mikoyan. They kept waving and smiling at us. Around Moscow, we later noticed, there were posters of Khrushchev with his arm raised high, and the inscription, "Peace to the Peoples!" – the posters used the same shot of Khrushchev that appeared in the media back home, but with the inscription, his misunderstood "We Will Bury You!".

We walked quickly, no time to lope along and take it all in. We reached the other end of Red Square, stopped near St. Basil's to catch our breath and chat about what we just experienced. We were still agog. But Betty said that she didn't think we were welcomed by the fellow marchers around us; she noticed frowns and muttering among some of them as they pointed to us. Well, maybe they thought it was boorish of us – foreigners!—for cutting into their section of the parade, these young textile workers from the Red Dawn Factory (or some such place, we figured). Sorry, but we were pushed into the Square with them, we had no choice but to march with them, and we, if not they, counted it as an act of solidarity.

Intourist had its demands. The Mausoleum was on the agenda, as was a visit to what we were told was a typical boarding school. Sheila and I skipped the visit to Lenin's embalmed remains. Wasn't it unseemly for an atheist state led by a Marxist-Leninist party to sponsor a primitive, quasi-religious display and ritual? Stanley and Betty may have felt the same way, but as became clear during the length of our Moscow stay, they were keen on sticking to the Intourist script, Stanley especially. He thought it was the correct thing to do. Intourist didn't like us wandering off-script either. Bypassing the script was in Stanley's view some kind of deviation smacking of bourgeois individualism. But we all went to the boarding school, where Betty and I had some friction over how the kids – they were 3rd and 4th graders—were treated. Betty thought the teacher that attended to a boy who fell and scraped his knee was insufficiently caring and supportive. The social worker in her. I disagreed; the teacher patched him up and sent him on his way: what else should she do? This led to a discussion of communal rearing, in which Betty – against ideological type – extolled the virtues of familial warmth and love, and I countered with the harm bestowed on children by neurotic parents or a dysfunctional family. Our differences aside, we were all delighted by the happy, bright and lively kids, who showered us with pins and information about our astronauts and theirs. We were impressed. We took Intourist's word that the place was "typical". Much later, I knew what Soviet "typical" meant, whether factory, school, or collective farm – specially polished for visitors, with workers, students and farmers on their best, canned and rehearsed behavior. "A nation of stage managers," George Kennan said of the Russians.

Our differing styles as visitors were evident again after we ran into Jerry Silverman, an American guitarist and music teacher Sheila and I knew from the New York folk scene. Jerry told us he would be performing at a new club organized by local Communist youth, and that he could get us in. Fine, but Stanley objected; this hadn't been prescribed, and besides, he didn't like the idea that "special treatment" would get us into the place. So Sheila and I went without Betty and Stanley, and enjoyed the scene. Jerry performed some politely appreciated Russian folk songs, and concluded his set, intriguingly, with the American gospel chestnut, *Michael Row Your Boat Ashore*. We joined Jerry for the *Hallelujah* chorus, eyeing the room for the reaction of the crowd of young Communists. They sat stone-faced. We couldn't tell – Were they puzzled? Irritated? Silently applauding us? Clearly, Jerry meant it as a slightly provocative challenge, but he wasn't sure either as to how it was received.

On another occasion, we were invited by two young Americans from the mid-West to join them for what they said would be an exciting meeting after dark with some Russians they met who were eager to swap clothing for undetermined contraband. We couldn't make it, and Stanley objected, of course. For him, whatever shopping we had in mind had to be done at the big GUM department store off Red Square and at the *Beryozka* stores around town. We did shop at those venues, but not without some regrets. Sheila, in particular, thought the *Beryozka* shops, where goods were available only for dollars and other "hard currency" (*valiuta*), were marks of unseemly class differentiation – foreigners were favored over ordinary Soviet citizens who had mere *rubles* at their disposal. She also winced when we watched a Russian getting the bum's rush for trying to enter a café where Intourist had arranged a luncheon for us and other visitors. At GUM, I bought some 35mm film for my camera, then discovered next day the roll wasn't right for my Ricoh. I expected a simple exchange or a return of money at the GUM counter I bought it at. Fat chance. The unsmiling woman at the counter refused my request, with a loud and clearly articulated *Nyet*! I dropped the roll on the counter and walked away, dispirited. Several shoppers looked on with, I thought, sympathy, but didn't intervene on my behalf: *That's the way things are here.*

We left Moscow, with collectively mixed judgmental feelings ranging from, let's say, approval and qualified approval to unqualified disapproval. Stanley, Betty, and I were at the front end of that scale, while Sheila stood at the other end. Stanley thought things were just fine, Betty thought not so fine, but was easy on the criticism, while I gently expressed some doubts and disappointments, but covered them with the pro-Soviet rationalizations I hung onto for years – as nations go, the USSR was quite young, it was badly disfigured by the enormous trauma of WW II, the imperialist encirclement meant valuable resources had to be expended on defense, *valiuta* shops were an economic necessity, etc., etc. Back home, especially if I faced hostile questioning, I had only praise for what we had experienced – What an efficient and handsome subway system! What a spectacularly impressive architectural ensemble at Red Square! What friendly people! What clean streets! When Sheila's Uncle Herbie noticed the unsmiling faces in the street scenes we photographed, and took them as a sign of dissatisfaction among ordinary Soviet citizens, I of course bristled and argued it was a cultural thing having no political significance. Sheila was discreetly silent during such exchanges, but she would have none of Stanley's approvals or my rationalizations: she was profoundly disappointed and disliked the place, period. She even traced some intestinal or cardiac symptoms she began experiencing after Moscow – "jiggles" she called them, incomprehensibly – to the stark imperfections of the purported socialist society she had expected. As usual, she was more honest and clear-headed than me, and reacted more emotionally to our disappointments.

Tensions were building between the two couples over respective political impressions, but we managed to keep them in check as we made our way out of the USSR and Poland. We picked up the Peugeot from Leszek in Warsaw and headed for another prearranged meeting, this time with friends of Stanley's family in Prague, where yet other disappointments would surface. At the Czech border we watched patiently as a Polish customs guard inspected our baggage and then the Peugeot interior. He seemed satisfied, but looking into the trunk, something caught his attention. *Uh-oh*!: he noticed and reached for that small engraving I picked up in a Warsaw bookstore, and that I thought I kept carefully hidden under some clothes, having anticipated some questioning. The print depicted a country scene, undated, and captioned in French with something like *In the Environs of Pinsk*. Not only was it a charming memento of our stay in Poland, but I imagined it to be the work of some French artist accompanying Napoleon's armies in their invasion of, or retreat from, Russia in 1812. Maybe even worth something. The guard looked it over and headed for the office. He returned and made it plain I couldn't take it out of the country; it belonged to the category of national treasures to be kept within Polish borders, he explained calmly. My first gambit in the hope of dissuading him from confiscation: But it's clearly French, not Polish! That didn't move him at all. My second: The scene is not even in Poland, it's Pinsk, I said. That aroused him: *Pinsk is Polish*! he affirmed in a tone that brooked no further discussion.

It made no difference that Pinsk was located then in the Byelorussian SSR (now Belarus), not Poland. The guard surely was aware of that, wasn't he? I thought of those historically disputed regions along the Polish-Russian frontiers that changed hands violently over the centuries, and concluded the guy was invoking a Polish nationalist's reality of a Polish Pinsk over the current geographic/political reality of a Soviet Pinsk. Besides, we Americans wouldn't know otherwise if he said Pinsk was Polish. The guard gave me a receipt for the print, and assured me it was my property, that I could "have" it anytime I returned to Poland, while I remained in Poland. I kept the receipt. Several years later, we hosted a visiting Polish academic in our Brooklyn apartment, and told him of the engraving encounter. "Do you still have the receipt?" he asked. Yes, of course; I fetched it and handed it to him. He looked it over and asked to take it back with him to Poland where he would try to retrieve the print for me. Sure. How noble, I thought; thanks to him I might see that dear precious and historical work of art again. "Good luck!" I said as we led him to the door. I never saw or heard from him again.

There was another border caper, this time on the Czech side. Betty and Sheila were involved in that one. They giggled as the Czech officer asked what the *tampons* he found in Betty's bag were for, dangling one by its string. With the assistance of some very tactful gestures they explained, and he sent us on our way with a tactful smile.

Belle Chapman of the "Belle and Abe" Stanley primed us for, welcomed us to their handsome, spacious apartment in the center of Prague, not far from the hotel she booked for us. Abe was recovering from a heart attack in a local hospital, so we didn't see him. (We met him much later, in Brooklyn.) Belle and Abe were good friends from the Bronx of Stanley's parents. Personal and political friends – we never did know for certain about Stanley's parents, but Belle and Abe were surely Party members. They, like many others in their orbit, fled overnight for Mexico when Julius and Ethel Rosenberg were arrested for atomic espionage in 1950. They feared their own arrest for they thought, in the exaggerated fears of the time, that "fascism had come to the U.S.," and massive repression of the Left was in the offing. Thanks to the international help network organized by the Party and Soviet and satellite agencies, they were settled in Prague as comrade-victims of the Cold War.

Belle, a lively, 40-ish, woman who kept her Bronx accent, was an engaging hostess, as were her two daughters and Czech son-in-law. Prague had a grayish tonality, but its Baroque architectural beauty overwhelmed the gray. The big attraction, however, was Belle herself, and what she had to say about experiencing life in the Czech "soviet socialist republic". As her daughter, Ann Kimmage, recalls in her memoir, *An Un-American Childhood*, Belle "did not disguise her bitterness and disillusion." She also remembers the "Atmosphere of secrecy" and the "presence of strangers who visited at unpredictable times and for varying lengths." We were among those strangers, but not on any suspicious mission. For us, in candid words that she said Stanley's parents would never be able to handle, Belle described harsh living conditions, class differences and unevenly distributed privileges, ideological rigidity, "bourgeois" attitudes, neighbor against neighbor, even anti-Semitism. The notorious Slansky trials earlier were clear evidence of that. She did say, unapologetically, that the bloody Soviet-bloc suppression of the Hungarian Revolution in 1956 was correct because everyone "smelled fascism". (That ever handy political mantra.) Betty, Sheila and I listened in disconsolate silence. Stanley took Belle's unpleasant report with "proletarian" fortitude; he trusted Belle's political savvy and honesty and he knew whatever faults existed in what was later called "really existing socialism," were inescapable results of hard struggles against imperialism.

For all of Stanley's emotional strength, Sheila and I couldn't help wondering if these regular disappointments were taking their toll on him, and were perhaps the main reason why our trip out of Iron Curtain territory remained frightfully tense all the way back to Paris. Betty understood Stanley's hurt, and stayed "on his side". There were long, long silences on the road in our Peugeot 403. The Promised Lands we had reached were responsible for nearly rupturing our friendship.

Back home, we sent Leszek a gift of gratitude, an umbrella to replace the one he lost to the thief or thieves who came upon our unlocked Peugeot in Warsaw. Betty had left Belle some of her clothes, and later we sent her as she requested, a big package of feminine wear, things like under garments and nylons, pre-washed so they would look used. A year after our trip, Belle and Abe were glad to be repatriated, having negotiated their return to the U.S. with their daughter Ann, according to what conditions and agreements between them, Prague and Washington we never learned.

Some people are enthusiastic, even smitten, over their first visit to the USSR, usually those who expect to find the worst of Cold War imagery there. Look! People are amiable and want peace, just like us! And they seem to move freely in the streets! The place doesn't feel "totalitarian"! Other visitors, like those of us with high hopes for finding socialism, were bound to be let down. Aside from some depressing signs of economic backwardness and political controls, where was the revolutionary fervor? It was natural, but simple-minded, even childish, for me and Sheila to expect Moscow, 1962, to resemble Havana, two years earlier. Of course we would be disappointed. Maybe Petrograd, 1917 would have matched Havana for the passion we wanted.

Stanley and Betty never visited the USSR again. I, naturally, went many times in the years to come, for professional reasons, not for love of the place. I managed to drag Sheila to Moscow for my second trip there (and her last) in 1968, the very week Soviet bloc tanks and troops crossed into Czechoslovakia to crush the "Prague Spring" that promised "socialism with a human face." It was just a brief visit, a special deal offered by a travel agent in Paris where we were living for the summer, and we brought little Claudia, just over a year old, with us, along with a social-work friend of Sheila's who was thrilled by the idea of a trip to the USSR. We had no time for political probing and pulse taking. Moscow seemed quite calm, and we weren't aware of the historic protest by a handful of dissidents on Red Square. An African student we met called the Soviet invasion "an act of naked imperialism." Back home, defensive as usual, I invented the usual rationalizations – Moscow was right not to accept any backsliding from its Czech "ally," a united front against NATO was essential, and Prague's reforms might open the door to hazardous steps like leaving the Warsaw Pact.... That sort of thing.

There were several endearments in our short Moscow stay of 1968. Even Sheila was pleasantly surprised. We often went out walking with little Claudia, who had taken her first steps several months earlier in Paris, behind the cathedral, so we called the event The Miracle of Notre Dame. Invariably, with the slightest chill in the August air, Muscovite women would lean down, without requesting permission – what do foreigners know about proper care of children! – to better button or zipper Claudia's cardigan.

We always tipped the driver when we rode in cabs – a bourgeois norm that was gratefully accepted by the proletarian cabbie.

There was one exception – a woman driver shook her head when we offered her some rubles above the charge. "It takes a woman to show us what's right!" Sheila commented.

Intourist placed the three of us at the Metropol, and Sheila's friend Carol at the distant Ukraine, an uncomfortable separation for her, mainly; Carol was already complaining about everything from conditions at the airport to our uncomfortable taxi. At the Metropole desk, a young woman greeted our request to keep us together with sympathy, so unlike the response by another clerk about our bedbug problem. This episode would count as a living lesson in how bureaucratic systems are subverted by simple touches of common sense. The nice clerk got on the phone. Someone at the other end made her frown; the request was obviously denied, but she continued. I understood her expressive Russian, and especially her expressive face: "But Sasha, they're close friends from America, and she's never been here. She worries about being separated. Please, Sasha." Carol got her room at the Metropole.

Thus the structures of a rigid bureaucracy, of the totalitarian state itself, could be, in many aspects of daily life, lubricated to make life livable. Cutting corners, doing transactions under the table ("on the Left," Russians say), greasing palms, ignoring a regulation or two, venting with anti-establishment humor around a kitchen table (jokes, *anekdoty*, Russians call them), or just sweet-talking like our Metropol desk clerk – all such efforts helped Soviet citizens in their daily struggle to survive in the Union of Soviet Socialist Republics.

Even when those structures were creaking with age, and a new generation was bringing palpable change, old rigid habits remained. At my Moscow hotel in 1984 I asked at the Intourist desk about tennis courts – I always traveled with a racquet. The woman on duty was puzzled by the request and had to make a phone call first. She then instructed me to go to the *Luzhniki* sports complex and wrote out an elaborate memorandum for me to take to the *Diryektor* there, asking that he permit the *Amerikanets, L. Menash,* to use a court. I rode the metro to Luzhniki and searched there for the Director's office. I asked a young guy I spotted where that might be. "What for?" he asked. For permission to play, I told him. *Are you kidding*? *Just go out and hit*! And he pointed me to the courts. There you have it: a small example of young, fresh winds blowing away old ways.

There was an even happier ending to the story. All the courts were taken, so I waited for a vacancy to practice my serve, or until one of the players put down his racquet. Soon I saw someone leaving a court and I trotted up to the partner who remained. *Khotitye igrat' s'omnoy*?, I asked him in my careful Russian. ("Would you like to play with me?") "I'd love to," he answered in perfect, only very slightly accented English. That's how I met Oleg, the beginning of a relationship lasting many years to the present, from Moscow to New York. I hit with him for a while (we were roughly at similar levels), after which he told me he had just played with a member of the Swedish table tennis team in town for a tournament and for whom he was serving as guide and interpreter. Later he would do the same for Billy Joel during his Russian tour. Oleg was a brilliant linguist, skilled in several tongues, and also an extremely smart and ambitious young man whose talents were able to flower and profit in the radically altered environment of Gorbachev's *perestroika.* Before emigrating to the U.S. Oleg had headed the accredited Moscow office of Pepsi Cola, charged with distributing the beverage throughout the USSR. Pepsi had negotiated a splendid barter deal by which *Stolichnaya* vodka – "Stoli" – was marketed in the U.S. Still feeling constricted in the new post-Soviet Russia, Oleg left, settled in New York, married Julia Sloan, a management specialist from the Mid-West, and he now works successfully as an independent International Business Development Consultant.

From the 1960s through the mid-1980s I made several trips to the USSR, to Moscow and Leningrad to be exact, punctuations to my graduate studies, later to teaching and publishing. There were always constants no matter the passage of time or Soviet leaders, from Khrushchev through Brezhnev, Andropov and Chernenko. The metro was always clean and trains ran on time, but curtains and heavy drapes in hotel rooms never closed or opened smoothly. Restaurants didn't always have what the menu listed, and waiters and waitresses were rarely eager to serve you with a smile, or serve you at all. "Not my table," I often heard from them. Apartment building hallways, especially in those pre-fab units on city outskirts thrown up hastily in Khrushchev's time, were smelly and dirty, and their elevators or floor buttons couldn't be counted on to work. But the smallish apartments were always pleasantly decorated, with colorful rugs tacked over beds and sofas, straight-edged wooden furniture featured functional if not elegant mahogany sideboards along the walls that held china and glassware behind their glass doors. Residents of those places were always gracious to visiting foreigners, shoes off, please, and generous with food and drink. And never shake hands across the threshold; do it when you step into the apartment. I got the point after many unsuccessful attempts to shake my host's hand as I walked in. Only when he or she had beckoned you inside did you exchange handshakes. When I was working on a documentary I learned of another popular belief Russians lived by. On my way to the railroad station by cab to head for Yaroslavl to do some interviews, I suddenly remembered I left my address book, with the names and numbers of interviewees, back at the hotel. Do we have time for us to go back to the hotel and still make the train? I asked the driver; I left something important behind. Yes, he answered; we went back, I got my book, and we headed for the Yaroslavl station. "You know," the driver told me, "if you were Russian, you would never turn back to retrieve something, even if it was important." I checked with several Russian friends who confirmed the cabby's observation. Oleg was emphatic about it. "If a guy's job *depended* on a file he had prepared for presentation at a board meeting, and he forgot it en route to the meeting, he would NEVER go back for it. He would rather take his chances by winging it at the meeting, and accept the consequences."

You wouldn't know Russians constantly complained about shortages from the volume of food they put on the table for you. Some of my most agreeable Soviet hours were spent in those apartments. If I didn't visit or travel by metro I took taxis and the cabbies always asked, after recognizing me as American, "Is it true that unemployment exists in the U.S.?" Surely it did and always has, but back then I was only too eager to support official Soviet propaganda in its claims about the harsh reality of an American capitalism that cared little for workers in the quest for profits. But the cabbies' question underscored something else I got to understand – their suspicion about the official assertions they were fed. The modern Soviet public was not some inert, easily manipulated mass swallowing propaganda whole. Skepticism about what came down from up high was wonderfully expressed in the punning folk formula, "There's no Truth (*Pravda*) in the News (*Izvestiya*), and No News in the Truth."

People always stared at me, marking me as a foreigner, from my clothes most likely. Some even stalked. In the (paranoid?) suspicions of the time, were KGB agents on my tail? Not all my encounters were as felicitous as my meeting Oleg, or led to relationships that lasted. At the *Tretyakov Gallery*, devoted to Russian art, a young woman, in her teens I think, followed me from room to room, looking anxious but keeping uncomfortably close. I finally turned and asked her politely if I could be of any help. She fumbled a friendly answer and suggested we walk out together. Small talk ensued, she was kind of puzzling, and I felt uneasy with her, so I wished her well, and gave her a key chain I had with me. She reciprocated with a bracelet, and Alyona and I parted. Later, I thought she might have been a nervous hooker on a first outing, or just a fidgety country girl in the big city hoping to meet, actually meet, a foreigner. She never said that, but that's exactly what a young stalker in a bookstore told me after I asked *him* could I be of any help. He apologized profusely, and told me he meant no harm; he just wanted to exchange a few words with an American. Much later, when telling my Soviet-*émigré* students about these and other encounters over the years, they had no doubts at all that as a foreigner I was under KGB surveillance; to think otherwise was simply an American's naiveté about the hyper-vigilant nature of the Soviet system. The KGB has a long reach and never sleeps, they insisted.

At the Lenin Library, a helpful clerk announced to me, proudly, I thought, and with a broad smile, that I was the first American she had assisted. There were other pleasant meetings with Muscovites and Leningraders in those years, some by arrangement, some by accident. Most were fleeting; we never saw each other again. Alyosha was a friend of a couple of my Soviet studies colleagues who had spent some research time in Moscow on the Exchange Program (IREX). Young, very bright, fluent in English and in American literature, Alyosha located for me some Soviet recordings of patriotic songs I was seeking, especially those popular during the Second World War (*The Great Patriotic War*, in Soviet parlance). Anything I can do for you in return, Alyosha? Let me have your raincoat, he answered promptly. It was one of my favorite garments, a snazzy blue with a belt and a hood. I handed it over to him on the spot. Ah, Alyosha, I never knew your intention: Did you sell it off for a handsome price, or did you keep it and draw the envy of your friends when you wore it?

These were the 1970s, during the Brezhnev years, part of what was later designated *zastoi,* the period of "stagnation". Shortages were the norm, and anything foreign had a particular attraction, especially if available directly from foreigners. Igor spotted me on the *Nevsky Prospekt* in Leningrad one afternoon, and didn't hesitate to approach me. I think he asked if I had a smoke. No, but I had some time for him; he was pleasant company, and we spent several hours together ruminating on comparative contemporary lives in the USSR (not so good), and *tam* ("there," the U.S.) – we have problems, too, I told him, my customary line in those days. In a sign that things were loosening up somewhat at the time, whatever else was stagnating, he invited me to his apartment to meet his parents and neighbors for dinner. Mama laid out a never ending spread from *zakuski* and *borshch* to roasted chicken for me, accompanied by vodka and a popular Armenian *konyak.* The men in my numerous visits like that one rarely if ever assisted, aside from pouring the drinks and conducting the toasts. I always got up to help with clearing, and was usually shooed away, with a surprised, not ungrateful look. Once, I was asked by the woman of the house, "Hey, don't you have a wife at home?!"

I did a slow fox-trot with Igor's mother while everyone watched. Igor was a pop-music fan who knew Western repertories, The Beatles above all. Many young Russians, I discovered, learned their English from Beatles songs. I had my tape recorder with me plus several cassettes, including Carole King's *Tapestry,* a big hit with Igor. One of my more emotional moments in the USSR came when he and I parted late that evening after dinner. I played *You've Got a Friend* at the Moika River embankment, not far from the Astoria, where I was staying, and explained the lyrics to him. Yeah, he said, but we'll never meet again. Who knows, I said. He was right. I left Carole King and my tape recorder with him.

Before that trip, Sheila and the young Claudia, 6 years old at the time, saw me off at JFK. Claudia cried uncontrollably in Sheila's arms when I walked to the passengers-only area. A bad case of separation anxiety, I thought then. But there was something else about her behavior that puzzled us when I returned. Sitting behind me in the car going home, she suddenly reached over to pull my hair. Maybe just a playful, slightly odd sign of affection and satisfaction, her way of welcoming Daddy back? I asked her about that before-and-after behavior many years later when I was putting some thoughts down in a journal. She had some hazy memories of it, but she remembered I was going to *Russia*, and that I might never come back. OK, an intense anxiety about separation, not unusual in very sensitive children like Claudia. Was there something about *where* I was going? And what about pulling my hair when I returned? "I wanted to find out if it was really you," she said. "As if I had been kidnapped, and you were seeing a body-double?," I asked. "Something like that," Claudia said.

I, nor the adult Claudia thought that at six years old she was attuned to prevailing concerns about travel to and in the USSR, much less about how sinister agencies like the KGB might relate to foreigners, Americans especially. But I can't help thinking that through some weird osmosis the young Claudia had internalized some of the fearful political atmosphere of the time. Her particular syndrome may have been a clinical novelty of the era: *Separation Anxiety, Cold War Specific.*

Stanley, Betty, and Sheila with Leszek. Note Leszek's ever present cigarette and umbrella. Warsaw, 1962.

Sheila and nursery school kids exchanging pins, Moscow, 1962. Photo by the author.

VII

THE DISSERTATION: Me and Gooch

Sheila's studies at Columbia University's Graduate School of Social Work included a course with Richard Cloward, an innovative sociologist and popular lecturer there. His influential text, co-authored with Lloyd Ohlin, *Delinquency and Opportunity*, was an important theoretical foundation and a main inspiration for "Mobilization for Youth" (MFY), established on the Lower East Side of Manhattan in 1961. MFY was an ambitious community based program that attracted the Kennedy White House's attention and its funding too, on the assumption that offering job training and remedial education to the young, along with family, group and individual counseling, were ways to head off what used to be called "juvenile delinquency," and even to fight poverty. Echoes of MFY would be found in Lyndon Johnson's "Great Society" and the "War on Poverty".

Sheila's connection to Cloward got her a job at MFY right after her graduation from Columbia in 1962 with a Masters in Social Work degree. She was one of hundreds of MFY employees that saturated the Lower East Side in the 1960s, numerous social workers among them, all fired up with the certainty that social progress came from this kind of direct community action. Lefties of many different stripes were naturally a big contingent of the MFY leadership and staff. Our comrade Stanley was an early hire, as were other friends and classmates of Sheila's who shared radical perspectives. At one point the whole program was endangered amidst media charges of "Communist influence".

I, meanwhile, was finishing course work at NYU, writing a Master's thesis, thinking of a dissertation topic, and preparing for comprehensive written and oral exams. Then, as later, I felt that

Sheila was the one engaged in real political activism, doing radical work on a practical level. *Brava, Sheila*! And she was getting paid for her "politics". Her salaries at MFY, then at other agencies, plus my Teaching Assistantship followed by several awards saw us through my graduate years.

The NYU I attended was not the powerhouse university it is today, from physical as well as academic points of view. My courses in the period 1960-1963 were in drab classrooms occupying a building of distinctly un-academic visage at the corner of University Place and Waverly Place. The building adjoined and resembled the 10-story neo-Renaissance structure, now the Brown Building, where the awful Triangle Shirtwaist Factory Fire had taken place in 1911. That building now houses NYU's Silver Center for Arts and Science. No campus, but we did have Washington Square Park across the street, and the whole of Greenwich Village at our doorstep, at a time when the sounds of the folk-music revival and later the folk-rock revolution were heard in the area's cafes and clubs. *Was that Bob Dylan I saw on 4th Street one afternoon*? I'm not positive. I spent a lot of time in the ground-floor reading room of the Library—no imposing Bobst Library then—and almost an equal amount of time at the Chock-Full-O-Nuts across the street on Waverly Place.

The Head of the History Department was the soft-spoken and courteous Baird Still, a specialist in the field of Urban Studies. Assisting him was John Fagg, the Department's Latin Americanist, also soft-spoken and courteous. I enrolled in several of Professor Fagg's courses, covering Latin American History from pre-Columbian times to the present. Latin America was one of the four areas I picked for the Ph.D. degree, which required choices from a menu divided into two sections. From Group A, I chose "Europe, 1500-1815," and "Europe Since 1789," along with Latin America. Remember, I was vaguely attracted to the formal study of history and politics south of the border after our exciting Cuban experience. From Group B, it was "Russia." More in retrospect than at the time, I felt the Department's emphasis on widening horizons instead of focusing in depth on a single area short-changed my training in Russian studies, however much I may have enjoyed and benefited from courses on Modern and Early Modern Europe. After Arthur Mendel left, there were no vivid personalities, no charismatic lecturers for the courses I took. The biggest luminary on the European side of the Department was Leo Gershoy, a French Revolution specialist. His lectures were chatty and engaging, not very formal, and he had a fine sense of humor that informed his sympathetic exploration of the Revolution. Another of the Department's prominent Europeanists, not as well-known as Gershoy, but a respected scholar in his own field, was A.William Salomone. Italy and modern Italian history were not just his professional specialties, but his personal passions, always on display in his classes and lectures when he seemed to channel Mazzini or Garibaldi. He told us he named his daughter Italia. My first published article in a scholarly journal spun off from one of Professor Gershoy's courses. I examined how historians presented the term "Baroque," and discovered a muddle of elegant but contradictory definitions that overlooked the material dimensions affecting the art and architecture of the age. The article pointed to my proud credentials as a budding "Marxist historian".

As for my prime interest, I stuck to the pre-Revolutionary period over the Soviet end of Russian History. It was partly out of my own inclination and partly from what was available in the Department. I stayed away from the Sovietology courses offered in the neighboring Political Science Department, and took Bill Blackwell's courses on Russian economic history after Arthur Mendel departed. In their very diverse ways, Blackwell and Mendel led me to concentrate on the Revolution of 1905, the "dress rehearsal," as Lenin described it, for the big Revolution of 1917 that toppled tsarism and brought the Bolsheviks to power. When I consulted various Department faculty members about their ideas for suggested thesis and dissertation topics, the answers I got were remarkably uniform. Look into, they said, "alternatives to the Revolution," or, "alternatives to Bolshevism." There were solid academic reasons behind that advice. So much work had already been done on the 1917 Revolution and on the Bolsheviks that I should be examining other themes; research on the master's and doctoral levels should explore new ground, or new ways of looking at familiar topics. There may also have been extra-academic considerations coloring their recommendations, or so I thought at the time. They – Mendel, Blackwell, Gershoy, Salomone, *et al.* – held no brief for the Bolsheviks and the regime they established, hence scholars would do well to deny them any claims to historical legitimacy and inevitability by showing that real alternatives existed. That the Bolsheviks were able to seize power was an unfortunate fluke. With a few exceptions, that was the pre-eminent view operating in the Cold War groves of academia during my graduate-school days.

Before the thesis and dissertation, there were comprehensive written and oral examinations to undergo. In three years of reading I had accumulated yards of 5-by-7 note cards in addition to the in-class notes on lectures I kept. I resolved to review them all before heading for the written exam, the passing of which qualified you for the orals. At a certain point I felt I wasn't making enough progress in getting through the notes and note-cards. I spent too much time reading "outside my field," as a friendly critic told me when I mentioned that I set aside the massive notes-review project to read, and be dazzled by, Thomas Mann's *The Magic Mountain*. Then there were those exciting political events of the time, constantly distracting me and Sheila from graduate endeavors. The terrifying Cuban-Missile Crisis unfolded shortly after we returned from our Paris-to-Moscow trip. We blamed the Kennedy Administration's Cuba policies for bringing it on; Moscow was responding justly to an ally's defense needs. The Kennedy assassination and what followed shook us up. Lee Harvey Oswald the sole assassin? Jack Ruby *his* sole assassin? Nonsense, we thought; clearly, a large, frightening conspiracy from the Right had been launched. First, we made sure our passports were in order. Next, Sheila and I reminded each other that if a real threat loomed while we were separated, with round-ups of the Left a possibility, we would meet at our pre-designated spot – the Clock at Grand Central station, no less, to plan our "escape"! Surely, the network that got Belle and Abe to Prague would do the same for us. Or some such idiocy animated us at the time.

But the real threat, not the politically paranoid non-existent one, was the written exam I faced – and I hadn't finished reviewing ALL my note cards on the eve of the test. Sheila had to virtually push me out the door of our Brooklyn Heights apartment when I was overcome with panic and told her maybe I should postpone taking the exam. *Thanks, Sheila*! I had no trouble invoking shards of what I had read and absorbed those three graduate years in my fluent answers to the questions covering my chosen areas, Europe at different periods, and Russia. Three areas only were on the exam; Professor Fagg exempted me from the Latin America part. I seem to remember questions focusing on Nationalism, a popular scholarly theme of the day, and also about conservative thought in modern Russian history—that "alternative" again. I passed and looked forward to the dreaded orals. Don't worry, Arthur Mendel wrote me, your questioners will be as bored as you are anxious; you shouldn't have a problem convincing them of your competence.

I passed the oral exam "With Distinction". I hadn't experienced a panic attack before it like the one that beset me the morning of the written exams. I just felt confident and ready; a shot of whisky before the exam also helped. Alcohol was something I learned to rely on, in moderation, for the tremors I anticipated before some important public performance. There are many different expressions of anxiety associated with what might be called, inexactly, stage fright—sweating, flushing, speech impairment, twitching. I have none of those; mine is pronounced hand tremors. They conflict with what I think of as my natural cool, so I seek help. Neurologists and the medical literature confirm what I discovered on my own in my early twenties, that alcohol is an effective form of self-medication for Essential Tremor. A potentially hazardous form, for obvious reasons, but it certainly works temporarily to control those shakes which in my case have always embarrassed me since that classroom eye test long ago. Alcohol has been an ally against tremors when the occasion calls for it, but I'm pleased and grateful to note that it never led to alcoholism. Long after graduate school, Beta Blockers were the medical treatment of choice prescribed for my Essential Tremor. They have helped, but in the short run, a glass of wine does the trick; Red, please.

That shot of whisky which calmed my demeanor at the oral exam may have also been responsible for a memory lapse, that *nominal* amnesia so common in our older years. During a lengthy disquisition on classical economic theories by European thinkers, I cited figures from Ricardo to Marx, but kept realizing as I talked that there was a *name* I was forgetting. Just as I was explaining how the free market was capable of correcting itself through the mechanism of....One of the Inquisitors interrupted: Who was the most prominent champion of that theory? I, sheepishly, in a whisper: "Sorry, I've forgotten his name." Adam Smith, perhaps? said someone else. Before I could say anything by way of recovering, everyone laughed; it happens all the time at these things, said Professor Minna Falk, another Department Europeanist. And that was it. They all congratulated me. I ran out onto Waverly Place where Sheila was waiting; she could tell it went well, no need to explain. Big relief, big hugs.

I had written a Master's Thesis based mainly on secondary literature, some in Russian, most in English, on one of the prominent organized political groups to emerge from the 1905 Revolution. The Constitutional Democratic Party, known by the acronym, "Cadets," was led by the outstanding historian and public intellectual, the liberal Paul Milyukov, and was an example of those "alternatives" to the Bolsheviks that Department faculty kept advising me to examine. I can't find it now, and the Department doesn't hold on to Master's Theses beyond a couple of years, but I can at least tell you the title, *The Cadet Party in 1905-1906: An Explanation of the Failure of Russian Liberalism*. Sheila typed it for me; I can still picture her now, working at night from my hand-written legal-size pages at a portable, non-electric Underwood under a lamp on an end table in our cozy top-floor apartment on Henry Street in Brooklyn Heights. My "Explanation" borrowed heavily from the critique we Marxist radicals leveled at American liberals – that they belied their own values by their politics of accommodation with existing structures dominated by capital and its agents in "the ruling class". The Cadets failed, I argued, because they were too timid in their demands, did not join their cause to the revolutionary socialist parties, and allowed Tsarism to survive the mortal threat to its existence generated by the mass upheavals of the day.

With an M.A. now under my belt, it was time to aim for the Ph.D. and pick a topic for a doctoral dissertation. The standard parameters applied – my choice had to be a subject that hadn't been mined in the existing scholarly literature in English, or, if already existing, to be presented with a novel reinterpretation. Other requirements: Research based on primary sources, the more drawn from archives, the better. Naturally, all this meant facility in Russian, if not spoken fluency, certainly reading ability. As to subject:

Bill Blackwell's studies in Russian economic history described the fascinating phenomenon of industrial enterprise on the part of those dissidents from the Orthodox Church known as Old Believers. Often these entrepreneurial sectarians were still enserfed or bought themselves out of serfdom. The Guchkovs were one such Old Believer family of successful textile industrialists whose founder was a peasant serf from Kaluga, south of Moscow. His most famous descendant, generations later, was Alexander Guchkov, a leading figure in the politics of Imperial Russia during the final years of the last Romanov, the ill-fated Tsar Nicholas II. Guchkov, in fact, was one of two figures dispatched to the royal railway car near Pskov where the Tsar was moored to seek Nicholas's abdication from the throne in March, 1917. Note this thread of high historical drama with its strong Russian flavor – the descendant of serfs requests and receives the written abdication of the last Tsar. Why not something on Guchkov for your dissertation, Blackwell suggested—he knew my interests lay in political, not economic history. I agreed. After some consideration of research options, we both concluded I should stick to the Revolution of 1905, a subject I had worked on, and examine Guchkov's role in it.

Normally, at this point in the academic course of things, I would have applied to IREX, the International Research and Exchange Board, a State Department agency that was sending Russian and Soviet area scholars to the USSR for research and study. Living in the USSR for a stretch and working in Soviet libraries was a must for any serious area specialist. Moreover, archival work was increasingly possible at the time, the mid-'60s, as the Soviets were beginning to loosen up on access. Certain topics and figures were off limits, of course, especially those belonging to the Soviet, post-1917 period. But even aspects of the Tsarist epoch could be barred to exploration. Since I wasn't an IREX scholar, I once tried using a *blat* ("pull," "influence") connection to get into an archive for further post-dissertation work on Guchkov. I got in touch with Timur Timofeev, an invitee to the Socialist Scholars Conference in1967, and someone I go to know a bit in Moscow. Timur, the son of Eugene Dennis, longtime head of the American Communist Party, was raised in the Soviet Union and was an established Soviet scholar of the working class, even headed up an institute. He turned me over to an aide when I asked about archival access. Politely, and with an apologetic look the assistant turned down my request: "Louis, you know how sensitive archival matters are in our country……" This was in the 1970s.

About the same time, before he left Moscow, Bill Rosenberg asked me to copy some materials from a pamphlet for him at the Lenin Library. I quote from my letter to him about my experience. "Alas. Remember that square-jawed, tight-lipped, grey-haired lady who processed copying requests? She took an extra careful look at the pamphlet, and after much leafing through pages handed it back to me with a curt, 'statistics not allowed.' I played dumb and innocent but she was adamant and said I could take it up with the Director. I figured I better not, since maybe they don't think it's cricket for me to be copying stuff for someone else, or some *schmucky* unfathomable reason like that. So I waited till someone else was on duty at the copying desk. A couple of days later I handed the pamphlet to a seemingly more amenable woman. She *was* more amenable; she accepted it 'conditionally,' saying she would have to take it up with others. Next day she said, sorry, no go. This time I was the hurt, incredulous foreigner who had traveled thousands of miles to obtain material like this. To which she answered, dead panned, 'statistics concerning the first years of Soviet power are not allowed to be reproduced.' A physicist from Sverdlovsk I was friendly with from many trips to copy-land together later commiserated: he raised his index finger to his temple and made circular motions with it to describe the state of things."

Moscow always considered the past, whatever the subject, a touchy matter that could have political vibrations in the present. Some things were just too hot to handle even for Soviet scholars, much less foreign ones. The official line on historical subjects was constantly changing; yesterday's heroes of the Revolution could be easily un-personed or demonized according to who was in power exercising what programs today. As the fine Soviet joke told by historians had it, the past is difficult to predict. Or, more pungently, the trouble is you never know what will happen yesterday.

Back in the '60s I wasn't about to propose a project on Trotsky, but one on Guchkov might pass muster, wouldn't it? Yet several reasons kept me from applying for an IREX grant. Bill Blackwell, my mentor, didn't encourage it – in an unguarded moment he once said to me, "who wants to spend much time in the Soviet Union?!" That sounds like an odd thing to say for a historian of Russia, but it was entirely understandable; the land of the Soviets was overall a disagreeable place. I remembered the joke that probably came from the satellites: A Polish worker, say, wins a prize of one week in Moscow for his workplace excellence. Second prize: *Two* weeks in Moscow.

Sheila certainly shared Blackwell's feeling. I, on the other hand, thought IREX and Soviet hosts would provide decent living conditions, at Moscow State University usually, plus offer the opportunity to advance research and let me soak in the Russian Idea, the Russian Mystique, the Russian Soul, the Soviet Experiment, call it what you will, not to mention getting to meet Russians like the young women whom we befriended on that first train trip to Moscow, or that guy on that same trip.

I didn't press the issue with Sheila. A double bind: She would have to come with me but against her wishes, or I would be guilt-ridden if I went alone and left her for several months. Stories abounded about broken marriages because of the long research trips or the inevitable extramarital affairs with Russian partners. So I decided against applying for an IREX grant. Besides, I still felt uncomfortable about my Russian, and thought I might consider IREX when my fluency and comprehension improved. There was one good way to do that: I spent a summer in Bloomington, at Indiana University's Russian program, where I rubbed shoulders with the IREX cohort honing their linguistic skills before heading for the USSR. Speaking, reading, and writing in Russian for two months – anyone admitted to the program had to sign a contract agreeing to full-time Russian; no English allowed – helped bring me up to speed. That summer I also met Stephen F. Cohen, later a luminary in the field of Soviet History and Sovietology. The word about him quickly circulated on campus that Moscow had turned him down for a research visit. His proposed project centered on the unfortunate Nikolai Bukharin, who had suffered, like scores of Old Bolsheviks and heroes of the Revolution, a fall from grace and ultimately a date with Stalin's executioners. Clearly, Bukharin was one of those historical subjects on the Soviet no-no list. Cohen managed without an IREX trip, and later published a well-received biography of Bukharin. The Soviets regularly denied some of his visa applications until the Gorbachev period, when official views of Bukharin, and much else, shifted. Moscow hadn't always recognized who their real friends were. Steve and I maintained a cordial relationship for many years based on our sympathetic views of the USSR, and our mutual anti-Stalinism. We were of quite different backgrounds, and travelled contrasting professional routes, but for those reasons I came to regard him as a kind of mirrored other, a counterpart of the person I might have been had I stuck to purely academic bearings.

Thanks to the Bloomington summer, my Russian may have improved immensely, but domestic matters kept me from seeking an extended IREX stay in the USSR. With both our Masters' degrees and my written and oral exams out of the way, we decided the coast was clear to raise a family. Not so easy; not without emotional and physical distress. Sheila miscarried once and soon after developed an originally misdiagnosed, excruciatingly painful ectopic pregnancy. Fortunately, the condition was identified before it could become life-threatening. Dr. Robert Porges performed successful surgery, saving one of Sheila's fallopian tubes. We picked up where we left off, and Claudia was the result. She wasn't named for anyone in the family, alive or gone, but for the name of the character I met in Mann's *The Magic Mountain*, the sultry, mysterious woman from the Caucasus, *Klavdiya*. She was an appealing figure, but It was the sound of that Russian name I really adored. Claudia, the English equivalent, was close enough, and met with Sheila's approval, especially since one of her beloved fictional characters from her teens was the "Claudia" from Rose Franken's stories, *Claudia and David*. Later, we lifted the "David" part (for other reasons, too) for the name our second child. Before Claudia (*Klashenka* in the Russian diminutive) was born in 1967 – May 3rd, not planned that way, but it was also Pete Seeger's birthday—Sheila and I traveled to various locations on the hunt for my friend Guchkov.

We enjoyed that hunt. No Soviet archives or libraries for my research, but an abundance of archival and printed materials on Russian history and its personages were on hand in places other than Moscow and Leningrad. I delved here in New York into Columbia University's Archive of Russian and Eastern European History and Culture, and of course, at the New York Public Library into its rich collection of Slavic materials. I spent many, many hours in the special reading room there, where the intense Viktor, who looked like one of those feverish students in Dostoevsky's fiction, got you the requested books and articles, and occasionally engaged me, furtively, with some provocative question on contemporary politics, usually Jewish themed. At the University of Chicago I examined the Samuel N. Harper Papers for the period 1902-1916. At Cambridge University it was the Papers of Sir Donald Mackenzie Wallace, for 1905-1909. Each, from extensive direct experience in Russia, had pioneered the study of the late Romanov Empire in the United States and Great Britain, respectively. In Paris it was the *Bibliothèque National* and several other libraries and institutes for their holdings on Russian affairs and history. From a couple of helpful fellow students also working on their dissertations, I even had some microfilmed documents from historical archives in Leningrad and Helsinki, Finland.

At the *Bibliothèque National,* one of my targets in its collection was Guchkov's newspaper, *Golos Moskvy* ("The Voice of Moscow"), available there on microfilm. I was seated but a few minutes at the microfilm reader when a librarian tapped me on the shoulder, excused herself for interrupting me, and told me "this gentleman" – standing next to her was a tall young man, my age, I guessed (late 20s), dressed formally in suit and tie, academic looking – "would like to speak to you." He bent down to ask me, "Are you Lou Menashe?" *Gulp*! Who is this guy, and how the hell did he appear here knowing my name? This guy was John Hutchinson, a Canadian doctoral student at the University of London working, naturally, on the Octobrist Party, and looking for, naturally, the *Bibliothèque's* holdings of *Golos Moskvy*, but in the same year, on the same day, at the exact *moment* I was engaged in that same enterprise! I couldn't help experiencing that slightly creepy but not unpleasant mystical feeling of some pre-ordained coincidence that drew me and John together in the *Bibliothèque National* on that morning. I've had, we've all had, several of these weird coincidences, but this one could compete with the most unique. Years later, looking for some metaphysical explanation for these occurrences, I read Jung's essay on what he called "synchronicity," but, disappointingly, it offered no satisfaction. Turning to the simple logic within the chain of causation, John's appearance at that *moment*, is explicable – a doctoral student of my time, looking for an un-mined topic picks the Octobrists, perhaps suggested by faculty to "consider alternatives to Bolshevism," as I was encouraged by my faculty, learns that an important "primary source," an Octobrist newspaper, is on hand across the Channel in Paris, and decides to go there. He's seen my name in some Russian studies publication tracking works in progress, and when he is told that microfilms of *Golos Moskvy* are in use by someone, he guesses, who else but Lou Menashe? Clearly not so mystical. Still.... Later I'll describe another astonishing synchronicity, that one involving a Moscow apartment.

John went on to write a dissertation on the Octobrist Party, 1905-1917, with a more-or-less conventional political focus – the parties, the Duma, the "public men" of the time. I took as my subject, the Party and its most prominent figure, Alexander Guchkov, but limited the frame to the 1905 Revolution. I felt somewhat abashed about my chosen subject when I started researching. There didn't seem to be anything "Marxist" about covering a conservative monarchist party and its leader during the crisis facing the Romanov dynasty in the turbulent period, 1905-1907, and I looked to be a "Marxist" historian. Revolution was certainly a "Marxist" subject, but the Marxist historian's methodology had to explore social structure, economics, class and class conflict as the real sources of historical content, and certainly not have it center exclusively on a personality, no matter how large an individual—like Guchkov, for example. His political rival, the liberal "Cadet" and famous historian, Pavel Miliukov, called Guchkov, appropriately, a *Bolshoi Chelovek*, a "Great Man," in an obituary appreciation. Before I began my work on the Octobrists, I got to know Jeffrey Kaplow, mentioned earlier, at NYU – Jeff was an instructor in European history after completing, and publishing his Princeton University dissertation on social structure in an 18th-century French province during the revolutionary period. I was envious. (Jeff was another graduate of the University of Wisconsin, Madison, which seemed to turn out New Left activists, my future comrades, from an academic assembly line.) But there came a breakthrough; no ordinary historiography for me, after all. As I reviewed the list of members of the Octobrist Party, with their brief biographies, I noticed how many were, in the archaic designation the Tsarist regime still categorized each of the strata in Russian society, *Kuptsy*. "Merchants": but these were not hawkers at shops and bazaars from pre-modern economies; they were bankers, industrialists, financiers, owners of commercial firms animating the modernizing Russian economy of the early 20th century. *Bingo*! I had my Marxist subject, the Russian *bourgeoisie.*

The result of my research and writing was the dissertation, *Alexander Guchkov and the Origins of the Octobrist Party: The Russian Bourgeoisie in Politics, 1905,* a pioneering work in English language studies of the promising "new class" of an increasingly capitalist "new Russia" blasted off course by the Bolshevik coup of 1917. My epigraphs for the study pointed to the themes I explored:

Now, what manner of men were these newcomers, creeping in silently to conquer the world? (From a work by the German economic sociologist, Werner Sombart.)

May God give us a bourgeoisie! (a hope expressed by the Russian writer, Vassily Botkin).

These "newcomers" were far from silent in 1905, they comprised what Botkin wished for, and one of their leaders was the formidable Guchkov. There was much promise in the capitalist path they were clearing, but all were overtaken by forces and events more powerful than them.

Sheila didn't have to type my draft of the dissertation, as she had for the Master's Thesis. That job fell to the typists at the pool where I was teaching, as of the Fall, 1965 semester, the Polytechnic Institute of Brooklyn, known far and wide for its excellence in engineering and science as "Brooklyn Poly". Here was one of those pleasant perks of academic life that I experienced at the start of my career. More comfortable benefits would come, but I felt that a strictly *academic* life of scholarly research and publishing was not my real calling, and I never tried climbing to the top of the profession. I enjoyed teaching, was good at it, won a student award for it, but I lacked that donnish *je ne sais quoi,* and also that *sitzfleish* of the true, the authentic academic scholar. My dissertation might have had more than a marginal impact, personally and professionally, if I had chosen to have it published by a university press, the normal sequence for a worthy doctoral thesis. Instead, I sought a commercial publisher, and remarkably quickly Doubleday responded; they liked the dissertation, they offered a contract, and I gladly signed. I had a wildly ambitious scholarly work in mind that might also have popular appeal – something that obviously attracted Doubleday. The Guchkov family history would offer a platform for a broad examination of Russian economic and social life from early modern times to the 20th century, throughout which a new capitalist class was gestating and maturing, culminating in its political debut in 1905, with a coda on the debacle of 1917. I did a considerable amount of research and some writing on the proposed book, but there was no way I could do a satisfactory job and meet the several Doubleday deadlines given the domestic, political, and academic responsibilities I was undertaking in those excitingly distracting 1960s; I abandoned the project and returned the advance. That scholarly commitment and respect for serious historical writing was always there, but my true calling, I thought, lay elsewhere; nearby, but elsewhere.

Except for a difference of opinion between me and Professor Edward Tannenbaum at the dissertation defense, I held my ground successfully. He didn't care for the term *bourgeoisie* in my thesis title. That's outdated *Marxist* language, he sneered dismissively. I understood his charge as part of the academic territory in those days when anti-Marxism was normal as a kind of ideological adjunct to the politics of the Cold War. It was one reason I saw academic life as inhospitable, but back then I was determined to fight those Cold-War attitudes from within the academy as well as outside of it. My reply to Tannenbaum didn't invoke what I thought to be the patent accuracy of Marxist social analysis and vocabulary. Instead I used an argument on chiefly *historicist* grounds: the actors in my study used the term themselves—see Botkin's epigraph above. Other members of the defense committee, including my sponsor, Bill Blackwell, backed me up, and the thesis title stayed.

One of the pleasures of working on Guchkov – my friend *Gooch,* I came to call him – was the contacts I made, and the hidden history they uncovered for me. From reading the political literature of the time as well as the writings of later journalists and historians, you learned that Guchkov had a pronounced adventurous side with a taste for personal dueling (with pistols), and liked to turn up in theaters of war. He joined the Boers fighting in South Africa and suffered a wound that left him with a limp for life. Trotsky's acid description of him: "a liberal with spurs". But there was even more color in his life.

In Paris in 1964, that same season of the John Hutchinson synchronicity, I placed a *petite annonce* in one of the Russian *émigré* newspapers asking for any information relevant to research on Alexander Ivanovich Guchkov. The response was swift and copious. A journalist at the newspaper office gave me his widow's telephone number – she's still alive?! I blurted out. She, Mariya Ilynishna, was very much alive, a tall, willowy and spry woman of 91, who came from the famous Ziloti musical family. We chatted in her not very upscale apartment, in French and Russian, and she was most helpful on Guchkov family history, and on her own background. Rubye Monet was there with me to help with French, if necessary. Guchkov's widow didn't tell me about Lidiya Csaszar; another source led me to her. She was, as I discreetly put it in the thesis, Guchkov's "companion" during his *émigré* years in Paris, and had a daughter by him.

There was an older daughter, from the Guchkov-Ziloti marriage, Vera, named for her godmother, the diva of the stage, Komissarzhevskaya. Vera Traill (1906-1976) got in touch with me herself when she learned I was peering into the Guchkov story. She was born in St. Petersburg, and settled in London, capping an adventurous life that in its way rivaled her father's. I regret that we never met, but we carried on a lively correspondence for a few years. She had fled with her parents to the Crimea after the Revolution, then was schooled in Berlin and did her university studies there. Her first marriage was to another *émigré*, Peter Suvchinsky, who was active in the tangled politics of the numerous post-Revolution exiles populating European cities. Vera was also a close friend of Prince Dmitri Mirsky, a brilliant literary critic with whom she shared an interest in Soviet culture and sympathy for the Soviet experiment. You know she was a *Communist*! *émigrés* were always sure to inform me. Both Vera and the Prince were in the USSR in the '30s; she worked at the *Moscow Times* as a translator, and there she met and later married Robert Traill, killed in Spain as a volunteer for the Republican side during the Civil War. She did not share the fate of her friend Mirsky; who died in the Gulag in 1939, a victim of Stalin's Great Terror. Vera was told to leave the USSR after Mirsky's arrest in 1937, and settled in France, bearing a daughter from the Traill marriage. She was a capable writer and translator—when I was in touch with her, she sent me some of her work, asking if I could place it—and kept her hand in *émigré* political affairs, some of them murky and lethal. I imagine she could have fit in as one of the characters in Nikita Mikhalkov's Oscar-awarded film of intrigue during high Stalinism, *Burnt by the Sun*.

Pictures of Guchkov show a stolid fellow, not particularly good looking, with *pince-nez* glasses, a tidy beard and closely cropped hair. You wouldn't know it from his photographs, nor from scholarly and journalistic accounts of his life and career, but as Vera told me, somewhat proudly, I think, daddy was a prodigious womanizer. Many illegitimate children were the result, as were emotional scenes with his wife Mariya. Vera once mentioned to her father that Andre Malraux boasted of X-number affairs. How vulgar, Guchkov commented. That he had so many? asked Vera. No, that he counted them, answered daddy. This was all fascinating stuff that I learned about after completing my dissertation, and it belonged to another kind of study, certainly not in a doctoral thesis of that time.

A decade and a half later, the early 1980s, as I was developing an interest in writing history and criticism about Soviet films, I interviewed the director Andrei Konchalovsky, in New York to publicize his fine historical epic, *Siberiade*. I mentioned my work on Guchkov and told him I thought he could be the subject of a wonderful historical film. He knew who Guchkov was, and agreed his career might make for an interesting movie, but "too bad he was a member of the Provisional Government". Konchalovsky knew that Soviet guardians of the film world would never sanction a film honoring a reactionary member of the government the Bolsheviks overthrew. After the collapse of the Soviet Union, though, pre-Revolutionary figures of the Tsarist political establishment like the tough Interior, then Prime Minister, Peter Stolypin, were "rehabilitated ," and I was not surprised to learn that a documentary film appeared on Russian television about that *"Bol'shoi Chelovek,"* the hard-headed constitutional monarchist of the Duma years, the would-be conspiratorial dynasticide when it looked like Nicholas II and Rasputin were leading Russia to ruin, the descendant of serfs who received the Tsar's abdication in 1917, the Minister of War in the first Provisional Government, and after the Bolshevik coup an active "White Russian" fighter-in-exile against the Soviet regime—Alexander Ivanovich Guchkov.

Figures like Stolypin and Guchkov, who stood for socio-economic development within a regime of order and strong state controls, attracted the attention of the new men of power in Vladimir Putin's authoritarian establishment. Putin even told of his admiration for Guchkov in the TV documentary. What an inconceivably strange road Russia has traveled since I wrote a thesis that was set in the darkening shadows of Tsarism.

"Gooch"—Alexander Ivanovich Guchkov, 1862-1936.

VIII

SCHOLAR? ACTIVIST? SCHOLAR-ACTIVIST?

In my quest to do battle on behalf of socialism and the USSR (they went together in my mind then) and for decent, peaceful relations between Moscow and Washington, I intended life as a scholar-activist. But this was the period – starting from the mid-sixties – of the Vietnam War and the massive protests against that war, and also of what looked like the unfolding of a possibly mass socialist movement in the U.S. So there was as much activism as scholarship, and I didn't neglect my teaching and other academic duties in addition to writing and publishing. Besides spinning off several articles from my Guchkov dissertation, my early publications résumé did not include studies in refereed journals, those stepping stones to professional eminence – and tenure. My writings appeared in the less academically weighty but serious publications of the Left – *Liberation*, *Ramparts* (both defunct), the Marxist journal, *Science & Society*, among them. I wrote from a kind of opinionated middle-ground, where journalism meets scholarship, neither scholarship nor journalism alone, technically speaking, but an advocacy sort of writing informed, I hoped, by the historian's sensibility.

Through Monitor Records – Monitor again! – I got to know John Simon, a friend of Rose Rubin's. In New York's liberal and Left circles John was "John the Good," while the other John Simon, the acerbic conservative culture critic, was "John the Bad". My John, "the Good," a good Lefty who became a star editor at Knopf, told me I should get to know the people, a bunch of Lefties, in the Economics and History Department at the Polytechnic Institute of Brooklyn where a teaching job might materialize. Eugene Genovese, later the renowned historian of the slave South, taught there before moving on to Rutgers, and I knew Gene from a Marxist political study group. He told me at an annual meeting of the American Historical Society, where graduate students before and after completing their Ph.D.'s all went looking for jobs, to get in touch with Helmut Gruber, the Department Head at Poly at the time – you can't miss him, he smokes a pipe and he's sort of Oriental looking, Gene said. Helmut, of Austrian-Jewish parentage, had blue eyes and dirty-blond hair, but he did have the broad, flattened facial features that likened him to an Asian male. A student once referred to him as "that Chinese gentleman." I found him clustered around some colleagues, mentioned comrade Gene, laid out my credentials, and told him I could teach Russian and Soviet History. Serendipitously, the instructor responsible for teaching that area at Poly announced she was leaving at the end of the 1964-65 academic year. Without much more than chatting with Helmut, arranging for transcripts to be sent from NYU, and promising to complete my dissertation in reasonable time (I did, two years later), I got the job as her replacement at the Assistant Professor level. So began my four decades at "Brooklyn Poly," the center of my academic life, and also the setting where some political issues played out.

At that same AHA meeting where I was job hunting, I met another job hunter who became a life-long friend, Ronald Radosh. His first wife, Alice, told us afterwards that Ron reported "meeting this great guy, Louie Minoso!" You recall I first caught sight of him earlier at a Cuba-related event. For a long while Ron and I remained *political* comrades as well, until he swiveled 180 degrees to the Right. Sharp political differences, on the Left or Right, often led to rifts that resembled messy, ugly divorces. I've never been a party to those outcomes, and Ron and I have kept our friendship, even when some of his writings have tested its limits for me. Substitute "politics" for "country," and I concur with E.M. Forster, who said if "I had to choose between betraying my country and betraying my friend, I hope I have the guts to betray my country."

Ron and I were introduced at the AHA conference by my fellow NYU graduate student in History, Daphne Stassin, who knew Ron from undergraduate days at the University of Wisconsin in Madison. Ron and Alice, Sheila and I were two close couples who liked to throw dance parties, participate in anti-Vietnam war actions, and shared interests in films and folk music – Ron played superb guitar and 5-string banjo, having studied the latter with Pete Seeger. Ron and I used to meet for our bagged lunches in the staff cafeteria of the New York Public Library's main branch on 42nd Street, sandwiched between my working in the Slavonic Division on the dissertation, and his ghost-writing (with a portable typewriter) articles for NAACP head, Herbert Hill, along with work on *his* dissertation. Ron already had a political reputation from his Wisconsin days, and he was a demonically fast writer. As a red-diaper offspring, Ron was very hip from an early age to the main roads and nuanced byways of Left history and contemporary Left politics. His anti-Stalinist, anti-Communist Leftism came to be leavened by the theoretical views of *Studies on the Left*, the influential "New Left" organ founded by the ardent socialist (and very wealthy) James Weinstein in Madison.

In these matters Ron was a mentor and I was just an amateur studying at his feet. I knew Russian history, though, and especially revolutionary history, so I could handle more than my own in discussions about Trotsky and Lenin and Leninism and their possible relevance to American radical politics. (No one was interested in Guchkov.) Both of us, not just us, were much affected by the work of Isaac Deutscher, the brilliant Polish-Jewish – a "non-Jewish Jew," he called himself – Marxist of Trotskyist political background who settled in England and wrote important, widely read biographies of Stalin and Trotsky. He was at work on a biography of Lenin when he died in 1967. In clear, stylish English, not his native language, he offered an elegant rationalization for the brutish phenomenon of Stalinism. Without minimizing his crimes, Deutscher emphasized Stalin's achievements as war leader and modernizer, driven by the desire to overcome Russian economic backwardness, whatever the cost. In the latter regard, Deutscher's analysis was an elaboration of the familiar trope, "You have to crack egg-shells to make an omelet." We accepted the legitimacy of that argument in those days. Much later, I preferred the wry counter-argument that might well have come from the long suffering Soviet citizenry, "So where's the omelet?"

The years 1965-1968 were politically charged nationally and internationally, but also energizing for me at home, at work, and on the streets. Sheila was an instinctive modern feminist *avant la lettre*. Not a *radical* feminist: she didn't believe in, for example, "smashing the family". But household duties and care for the infant and toddler Claudia were to be shared by husband and wife. She wouldn't have it any other way, but she didn't have to press me into this service; I wasn't called on just to "help," I was committed to taking on all responsibilities with her. No exaggerating when I often described myself as a "house husband." Both of us were working full-time, so we did have to retain some assistance. I wanted to hire a Russian speaker with whom I could exercise my fluency in that tongue, and maybe even expose Claudia's young ears to the language of Pushkin and Lenin. We settled instead on Mrs. Strauss, a warm Orthodox Danish-Jewish woman who kept her promise to "take good care of your daughter." Care and warmth were needed, along with hospitalization and proper medication, when at seven months the infant Claudia developed a frightening disorder affecting the skin and other body membranes as part of a very serious condition, Stevens-Johnson Syndrome. Fortunately, Claudia's doctor was the venerable Brooklyn Heights pediatrician, Dr. Virginia Weeks, who happened to be a specialist in researching and treating the disorder. Thanks to her and the steroids she prescribed, Claudia pulled through without any of the serious impairments—to the eyes, for example – that the Syndrome could inflict.

Living in Brooklyn Heights meant work at Poly was but a walking distance away. Arriving at the Department those first days in the Fall of 1965, I was immediately conferred with dual citizenship – in academics and politics. My three course load had me teaching Russian History, a survey that included the USSR, plus two phases of Western Civilization. I later broke up the survey into two courses, a "Russian" and a "Soviet" part. The Western Civ array would disappear in favor of accommodating what we sought in those days, *relevance*. Hence, a "Contemporary World History" course where we could explore the hot topics of the day, from Hanoi to Moscow, as they affected Washington. Together with Department Head, Helmut Gruber, our Marxist anthropologist, Eleanor Leacock – "Happy" to her family, friends and colleagues – prepared a proposal to the Carnegie Corporation for an inter-disciplinary program that would introduce Poly students to the theory and practice of the Social Sciences. (The Department had shed its "Economics and History" name in favor of the broader, "Social Sciences".) Carnegie approved the proposal and granted the Department an award that provided for administrative assistance and release time for faculty. Helmut picked me as one of the participants in the program, and we eventually co-edited an ambitious multi-volume set of readings to assign in our newly developed courses covering social theory from Plato to Saint Thomas Aquinas to Herbert Marcuse. It was exciting to be involved in this high-minded educational project, and a learning experience for me as well – I knew Marx, a bit of Plato, but Aquinas? Yet I've often thought that at the outset of my faculty appointment the project side-tracked me from what should have been my main line if my goals were strictly academic and professional as a Historian of Russia, working hard, that is, on an innovative study of the pre-Revolutionary Russian bourgeoisie, something I had to abort, because other causes and tasks drew me, and I just couldn't do it all.

All Department members took our teaching very seriously, and teaching at a school where engineering students were the main constituents added a sense of mission to our course preparation and classrooms. We wanted to widen their general outlook on society, culture and history, not to mention "correct" their political understanding, all done with rigor and, we insisted, intellectual honesty. We thought we were *educating*, not *indoctrinating*. But there was no getting around where the Department, its core, actually, stood amid the radical political currents then blowing in the wind. I discovered that the Department housed some of the practical-slash-theoretical political activity of its core – Helmut Gruber, Historian and Head, David Mermelstein, finishing his dissertation in Economics at Columbia, Marvin Gettleman, American Historian (and fellow City College alumnus), Happy Leacock, and Shane Mage, a brilliant, if sometimes loopy economist with a Columbia dissertation under his belt that supported Marx's theory of the declining rate of corporate profit under capitalism.

They constituted the busy nerve center for the first annual Socialist Scholars Conference, the brainchild of Eugene Genovese, Warren Sussman (a Rutgers Historian of American Culture), and some other academic comrades. Gene and his close friend and colleague, John Cammett, were Gramscian Marxists, convinced that socialist political hegemony in America derived from a prior infusion of socialist values into the culture at large, and dominating it – no storming of barricades or dictatorship of the proletariat in this vision. Instead, a "long march through the institutions". (The phrase is often attributed to Antonio Gramsci – it certainly has a Gramscian spirit -- but was coined by the German student activist, Rudi Dutschke.) John's political biography of Gramsci was very influential in those days. I was an enthusiastic joiner of the Core, no persuasion necessary. Soon enough, from Department offices, I was making phone calls, duplicating flyers, stuffing envelopes, contacting "socialist scholars," in preparation for the two-day meeting at Columbia University. It got lots of attention and was well attended, a harbinger of bigger things and bigger hopes to come. The following year, 1966, the 2nd Annual Conference brought a huge turnout at the old Hotel Commodore – we needed a proper site, just like other big meetings of "bourgeois" scholars and professional societies. And I was its Chairman.

IX

SOCIALISM ON THE HORIZON

I believe Irving Howe offered the melancholy observation that the idea of socialism in America would always remain suspended on an ever-receding horizon. In those days, the mid-'60s and for a while thereafter, it seemed to many of us that socialism in the United States was not an abstraction somewhere off in the distance, but an idea ready for testing in the streets, in the academies, in local communities, in the press and media and even, we thought, at the ballot box. We were carried away.

Thousands showed up for the 2nd Annual Socialist Scholars Conference. The Conference came out of the academic intelligentsia, tenured faculty or faculty on the road to tenure, graduate and undergraduate students, but it also attracted enthusiasts, old and young, from non-academic walks of life. Never mind the "scholars" part of our title. A big diverse SRO crowd packed the main ballroom at the Commodore to hear the keynote address, "On Socialist Man," delivered by none other than Isaac Deutscher, a respected voice as historian, biographer, and also commentator on Soviet affairs from a non-Cold War perspective. He brought as well a kind of Old World, Old Radical, Old Trotskyist set of credentials to the proceedings, precisely what the State Department didn't like about him. I and my colleagues spent many difficult hours on the phone and in writing trying to persuade the Department to grant Deutscher a visa; certain Cold-War practices, like keeping Commies, ex-Commies, or fellow travelers away from our shores persisted. Or maybe Washington just enjoyed watching them twist in the wind a bit. On the eve of the Conference Deutscher was deemed no threat to national security, and his visa came through.

At his hotel the evening he arrived, he offered us some of the Scotch he brought with him, and saluted our efforts, particularly in the anti-Vietnam War movement clearly swelling up across the country. We, in the paranoid, slightly delusional style of the Left (marking much of U.S. politics, not just the Left), told Deutscher a big repressive counter-attack might be directed at all radical movements by the Johnson Administration. We might even have invoked that reliable catch-all "fascism". No, not in the land of Jefferson, said Deutscher. I remember Genovese smirking, shaking his head as if to say, you've got a lot to learn Mr. Deutscher.

His opening night, plenary-session address at the Conference was not particularly notable. His title for it, and we didn't object, "On Socialist Man," would not have sat well with the feminist movement which wasn't in high gear yet. More memorable was Deutscher's reaction to Shane Mage's memorable comments. We didn't ask other panelists of the evening to show us their planned remarks in advance. If we had, I think some of us in the SSC steering committee might have tried to dissuade Shane from what he planned. We expected that Shane's erudition in Marxism, along with his experience in the American Trotskyist movement would offer some welcome commentary on Deutscher's traditional appeal to socialist values. *Ha*! No prophetic Marx, Lenin, or Trotsky or even Marcuse pointing the political way forward for Shane. His message was dipped in acid, its prophet was Timothy Leary. Shane's prescription, *Turn On, Tune In, Drop Out*, drew embarrassed looks from some of us on stage, a few puzzled titters from the audience, some clearly approving applause, some indulgent laughter, and much general discomfort as to how to react. Mixed reactions from a mixed crowd of Old and New Lefties. No mixed reaction from Deutscher; he could barely contain himself at this call for political retreat back into individualist, self-induced nirvana. "*Drrahgs! Drrahgs!*," he shouted in his wonderful Polish-cum-British accent. Other European revolutionaries had turned to drugs, he pointed out, and such developments led nowhere, only to self-destruction.

On succeeding days, there were many panels, many speakers exploring many topics following that evening, but I would guess that anyone attending the 2nd SSC would have a vivid memory only of Mage's quiet bombshell and Deutscher's thunderous response.

It's certainly one of the few things I remember. Many Socialist Scholars Conferences followed, with other Chairs, other sessions with their notables—at one of them Herbert Marcuse decried the idea of "flower power"—even as the anti-Vietnam war movement ballooned, diverting many scholars from their desks and libraries onto the streets for marches and demonstrations, in Washington and at home. At SSC planning sessions after the first couple of conferences many participants felt the Conferences had lost their "relevance," that key word of those days, and demanded a practical political answer to *What Is to Be Done?* Someone actually posed Lenin's famous question at one of those sessions, seriously. The SSC deserves a place in the history of American left-wing activity, an important place. Smaller versions than the original ones in the '60s continued to appear, down to recent times. In his memoir, *Dreams from My Father*, Barack Obama mentions dropping in at one of them when he was a student at Columbia in the 1980s. That intellectuals, the academic kind or otherwise, could stimulate debate and kindle theoretical and practical insights into socialist possibilities by meeting regularly outside of political formations, remained an appealing idea.

I shared the energy of those early SSC days. Mine flowed along two main lines, Russia and Vietnam. The classroom was a natural venue for both, but there were other ways to deliver my contributions. When I worked at Phonotapes, described above, one of the satellite organizations associated with the Sam Goody firm, I got to know and occasionally collaborate with Moses Asch, son of the famous Yiddish writer, Sholem, and a big personality in his own right. Moe was certainly big physically, a mustached bear of a man, but big and important also for founding and running Folkways Records, devoted to recording for the public the sounds of the world in the 20th century. That ambitious description was not a false marketing device; what came to be the enormous Folkways catalogue of titles included everything from music from everywhere to the spoken word to sounds of tropical rain forests. While I was completing my graduate degree, at work on my dissertation, Moe told me he had a bunch of Soviet recordings of folk and other popular songs connected to the Russian Revolution and Civil War. Would I select several to be included in a Folkways album, and provide program notes for them? *Sure*! Guchkov can wait. The result was, to give it its full title, *History of the Soviet Union in Ballad & Song. Volume One: Songs of the Revolution & Civil War*, with "Introduction and Notes by Louis Menashe". It turned out to be one of the most satisfying projects I've worked on, before or since. For weeks the words and melodies of songs both lively (*Smelo Tovarishchi, V'Nogu – Boldly, Comrades, In Step*; a favorite of Lenin's) and mournful (*Vy Zhertvoyu Pali – You Fell Victims;* sung and played as a funeral hymn) danced in my head as I plunged into serious research on the composers, lyrics, and backgrounds of each *Ballad and Song*.

I'm still proud of my efforts, but I wish I could take back that first sentence of my introductory notes. Forgive me, I was just a grad student straining for literary effect concerning a much written about historical event: *In March, 1917 all the exposed, twitching nerves of Russian social life twitched at the same time to bring the autocracy down*. Ouch.

Moe and I talked about preparing follow-up recordings after "Volume One". I thought of several possible themes, and did some cursory probing and collecting. "Volume Two" could have been "Songs of Industrialization and Collectivization". A Third Volume could have been devoted to "The Great Patriotic War of the Soviet Union," as World War II was commonly known in the USSR and in today's Russia. The Russians and peoples of other nationalities comprising the Soviet Union boasted superb musical talent, and turned out terrific "ballads and songs" and tuneful *chastushki* (nonsense ditties), relating to significant events and personalities. Many of them made it to the West – remember the sweet-flowing lilts of *Meadowlands* or *Katiusha*?—thanks in part to the recordings of the *Red Army Chorus and Band*. But I never could set aside time for those follow-up ideas in the very hectic '60s. "Volume One" would stand alone. But unlike so much ephemera I published, or books I edited or contributed to that were remaindered or pulped, or went out of print, "Volume One" has stood the test of time. Moe made it Folkways policy never to delete a title from the catalogue, no matter the sales volume. It was in keeping with the idealistic aims he kept for the Folkways project. After his death in 1986, the Asch family donated the entire Folkways catalogue, numbering over 2000 titles, to the Smithsonian Institution's Center for Folk Life and Cultural

Heritage, provided the recordings would remain in print forever. You can now find and buy, in the format of your choice, *History of the Soviet Union in Ballad & Song: Volume One* on the *Smithsonian Folkways* label.

The '60s were hectic for me and Sheila in no small part because of the Vietnam War, and our opposition to it. There were big marches in Washington, smaller ones in New York, "demo's" of all kinds at all kinds of places, and of course the Vietnam "Teach-Ins". We took little Claudia to many of these events, on my shoulders or in her stroller. The teach-ins kept me busy in lots of ways. There was Folkways again as a venue doing double duty – contributing important "sounds of our time" for posterity, and as an instrument of anti-war protest. The teach-ins were a remarkable politico-educational phenomenon propelled by the anti-war sentiment sweeping the country, inside and outside of the academies. I "Edited, Compiled and Annotated" the *Berkeley Teach-In: Vietnam*, 1965, a two-record Folkways set offering excerpts from addresses by speakers at what was probably the largest teach-in event on a campus ever, certainly dwarfing the original specimen born at the University of Michigan on March 24, 1965. With the typical swagger I nourished in those days that combined my identity as political activist with my serious, academic credentials, I introduced the printed notes for the set with *Ten Theses on the Teach-ins*. [!] Here's a sample, from *Thesis 2: The teach-ins were not conceived as ordinary forums where the case for each side might be aired, but as platforms of informed and coherent protest at a time when one side (the government's) virtually monopolized the flow of information to the public, and when the limits of acceptable opposition in the press and in congress were…too narrow*. Another, from *Thesis 5: The teach-ins issued from an acute moral revulsion unparalleled in the history of American military involvement….*

I cited napalm and atrocities, and quoted Graham Greene on how "the long slow slide into barbarism of the Western World seems to have quickened."

I even provided a "Brief Chronology" in the printed notes, "One Year in the Life of the Teach-ins," and concluded with "References and Suggested Readings". All in all, I thought I had prepared a comprehensive booklet—which also included printed excerpts of the addresses on the recordings—that did the Berkeley participants and the movement proud, and that maybe might even impress a Tenure Committee someday.

The Berkeley teach-in featured a glittering array of personalities associated with that campus (Mario Savio, of "Free Speech Movement" fame, for example), in addition to politically minded celebrities (Dr. Spock, Norman Mailer among them). Even more glitter marked *The Original Read-In for Peace in Vietnam,* recorded at Town Hall in 1966 and issued by Broadside Records, an offshoot of Folkways. I co-edited the record and booklet with Rosalind Wells, another politically engaged member of the New York intelligentsia. The *Read-In* was chaired by the drama and film critic Stanley Kauffmann, who told the capacity audience that "we protest…not only the death, mutilation and suffering of Americans, Vietnamese, and others; we protest the corruption of this country, the lying, obfuscation, and distortion that are being foisted on us as American principle." The organizers of the event noted, quixotically, that President Johnson "could not afford to ignore the dissent of those who are best equipped to make articulate the unspoken doubts and fears of the population." That evening, the "best equipped" included A-list artists and writers like Maureen Stapleton, Tony Randall, Jules Feiffer, William Styron, Robert Lowell, and Susan Sontag, to name only a handful of the assembled glitterati.

The satisfaction from my "doing something" about the war in those days was matched by my having worked on those recordings. It was exciting to be a part of the world of recorded sound, to be bold-faced in the credits, and to have an enduring place in the noble Folkways legacy. But I was embarked on an academic career, and that had to involve a book. Enter again, from stage Left, the teach-ins. With my friend and colleague – we were now both teaching – and political comrade, Ron Radosh, we circulated a proposal to do a book on the teach-ins, documenting their origins and development, and writing as two historians-participants of the movement. A serious, even scholarly, book, with some political heft. Several publishers showed interest, and we went with Frederick A. Praeger, an unfortunate choice, as I explain below. The result – another exciting project for me! our first book!, and our gift to the "movement"! – was *Teach-ins: U.S.A. Reports, Opinions, Documents* (1967). The subtitle was modeled on that of another scholarly-cum-political book, a best-seller no less, edited by my colleague Marvin Gettleman, *Vietnam: History, Documents, and Opinions on A major World Crisis* (Fawcett, 1965), a volume we cited and described as "a kind of *Robert's Rules* of the teach-in movement." For future historians of American opposition to the Vietnam War, or of campus-based political activity and innovation, *Teach-ins: U.S.A.* was and remains a valuable resource. It earned respectable reviews at the time from different quarters for its presentation of living history. Ron and I were invited to radio talk shows to discuss the book and the issues it raised. *Best seller it was not.*

For one thing, "Vietnam" was nowhere in the title or represented in the cover art, which simulated writing on a blackboard. From the title and cover, the book could be mistaken for some bland, apolitical volume on—general education? campus social life? teacher training? But another, much more powerful disincentive to sales struck. Scarcely did the volume appear on bookstore shelves when a story broke about Praeger acting as a publishing conduit for the C.I.A. Our book promptly disappeared from those shelves. In our eagerness to get the book published, we were blindsided by the publisher. Praeger himself was an Austrian *émigré* who served in U.S. intelligence and military government during and after World War II. The publishing house he founded specialized in anti-communist writings, especially those emanating from Eastern Europe and the Soviet Union. Among notable Praeger titles were *The New Class* by Milovan Djilas (1957), and Alexander Solzhenitsyn's *One Day in the Life of Ivan Denisovich* (1963). Given those profiles – of the man and his publishing house—why would Praeger publish a book by two radicals that had a clearly anti-Washington axe to grind over the Vietnam War? Was it a case of co-opting or de-clawing a potentially important volume in the battle of ideas and policies regarding Vietnam, one with a strong anti-war message? One of our editors at Praeger perhaps gave the game away when we complained about the failure to market the book as a documentary indictment of Washington's war in Southeast Asia, and we emphasized the mistake of omitting "Vietnam" from the title. If "Vietnam" were in the title, he replied, we wouldn't have published the book. Praeger himself, in a brief pre-publication meeting we had with him, said the teach-ins impressed him as academic forums of "inter-disciplinary" activity. A piece of disingenuous flim-flam by this former intelligence agent? Or a sincere assessment of the teach-in, as the jacket blurb put it, becoming "a permanent feature in American education – an exciting, always volatile manifestation of free expression and the blending of academia with public life."?

As a movement in its own right, part of the anti-war repertory, the teach-in faded, overtaken by other forms of protest. The Menashe and Radosh families continued anti-war activities, signing petitions, preparing newspaper ads, and we participated in many marches and demo's, so long as they were peaceful. Meanwhile, Ron and I went on with our teaching and writing. I may have set Guchkov aside at times, but he was never forgotten. The Praeger book jacket identified me as Assistant Professor of History at the Polytechnic Institute of Brooklyn, and "author of a forthcoming study of the Russian bourgeoisie in the revolution of 1905." That "study" never *forthcame,* but about the same time *Teach-ins: U.S.A.* appeared, my article on Guchkov, the "Liberal with Spurs," was published in the journal, *Russian Review.* The article was the subject of a story in *Novoye Russkoye Slovo* ("The New Russian Word"), published in New York, and read widely in the *émigré* community. Newsstand operators had a quaint name for the paper. I once asked for the paper at a stand near the New York Public Library main building on 42nd Street, using the Russian name. "Don't carry it," came the reply. "Ah, here it is," I said as I was about to walk away. "Oh, you mean "*The Hobo News,*" he corrected me. In this amusing transliteration, the Cyrillic "n" and "v" of *Novoye* were taken as the Latin "h" and "b," while the "o's" sounded much the same in the respective alphabets. Hence: the "hobo" of the *Hobo News.*

The newspaper story generated the same flurry of *émigré* activity in New York that my notice in search of information on Guchkov did in Paris a few years earlier. *Gospodin* Ivanov, an imposing, splendidly mannered, perfectly bald *émigré* who helped me keep up with my Russian at Berlitz, offered "*Congratulations, Professor Menashe,*" when he greeted me one afternoon. He held his lit cigarette, in a cigarette-holder, of course, in one hand, while the other held a copy of *Novoye Russkoye Slovo* turned to the Guchkov story. Letters and phone calls to me soon followed, most memorably from a Georgian Prince (or so he identified himself) who invited me to lunch. Swarthy, elegant, wearing a camel-hair coat, holding his other glove in his leather-gloved hand – I didn't have to check his credentials to recognize the airs and look of a Georgian nobleman. He was intrigued by my work, and asked for research leads on his own study of the period I wrote about. "I warn you, Professor," he said, as we parted, a sly glint in his eyes, "I'm a very dangerous man." Did he mean, I wondered, that he was still fighting the Bolsheviks?

Encounters like that were precious for the Russianist or Sovietological side of me, and I wish I had cultivated more of them, but other demands kept intruding.

The war in Vietnam escalated and escalated, and the home-front wars against Washington, with Nixon in the White House, expanded accordingly. The Nixon decision to send troops into Cambodia ignited campus-wide protests. At Kent State in Ohio one such protest resulted in the deaths of four students and wounds to nine when national guardsmen with live ammunition in their weapons opened fire on the demonstrators. Faculty and students responded across the country with classes – and final exams – suspended; there were shutdowns of entire campuses. At Polytechnic a raucous faculty meeting pitted our cadre in Social Sciences against many conservatives in the engineering and science faculties. But so powerful was the revulsion at the war that we numbered many allies in those departments as well. Many protested out of concern that their sons, or grandsons, might be sent to what came to be dubbed the Vietnam quagmire. It's true that since the draft-by-lottery was in effect, much opposition to the war derived from that fact; card burnings and self-exiling to Canada by many young men reached epidemic proportions. But there were other, entirely sincere and valid political objections to the bloodletting in Vietnam and Cambodia aside from the self-serving ones. Our faculty meeting ended with a vote to suspend classes and shut the school down.

Some of us, acting as vigilantes to enforce the faculty vote, prowled the hallways to make sure no one was violating the decision to suspend classes. David Mermelstein and I, in an act that filled me with shame not long after (and still does, today), entered the classroom where an instructor was carrying on despite the ban; we took seats, and tried to stare him down into compliance. He was visibly uncomfortable (I always notice hand tremors), but wasn't cowed, and we walked out; at least we had behaved peacefully, if not graciously. Who were we to try to metaphorically strong-arm him into submission? And he was probably right to regard our behavior as an attempted violation of his sacred rights of academic freedom and the autonomy of his classroom. The war had brought us to such encounters. The nation, not just the faculty was sorely divided.

In a less bullying mode, if somewhat flamboyantly, maybe even at times a bit ridiculously, I exercised my oratory in those days. The vote to shut Poly down came after my impassioned plea to faculty colleagues – while we debate, the carnage goes on! I shouted. The same day, I led a group of students to join a big protest crowd assembled at the steps of Brooklyn's Borough Hall, a short distance from Poly. Someone handed me a bullhorn and from the top of the steps I led the crowd until my voice cracked in loud, repeated chants of the slogan popularized by young draft resisters – *Hell No, We Won't Go!, Hell No, We Won't Go!* .... For several minutes I had experienced the power of oratory to move a crowd. There were times when I felt I was really at the top of my teaching form, and left a strong impression on students assembled before me in the classroom, but it was nothing like that sense of electricity charging between me and the crowd before me at Borough Hall that day. All right, so it wasn't Petrograd or Havana, just Brooklyn, and I wasn't Trotsky or Fidel or even Mario Savio. Still, moments like mine were taking place all over the country, and collectively they had a tremendous political impact. Along with other ensembles of opposition to the war in every corner of American life, they played a part in pressuring the White House to wind the war down.

There were other "actions" that eventful spring. At Poly, commencement was allowed to proceed, but our band of anti-war students and faculty were determined to "bring the war home" to the graduates and their families and guests. There were some politically sophisticated and committed students among the Poly undergraduates protesting the war. I used to have political discussions with one of them, a Trotskyist, a member of the Socialist Workers Party. I got two separate calls from the F.B.I. about him. Sorry, but I decline to provide any information about my students, I told both the agents. Thank you, said one, politely; the other, not so politely, "so you don't want to assist the government of the United States, Professor?" said the other.

The 1970 commencement took place outdoors, fittingly enough beneath the Brooklyn War Memorial of Cadman Plaza Park in downtown Brooklyn. Those outdoor grounds became a temporary war zone when we suddenly appeared, marching down a central aisle with a makeshift coffin bearing the names of the Kent State victims. We were immediately assaulted. Some graduating students simply resented our spoiling their commencement. Others were angrily opposed to our position on the war. Shouts and curses filled the air; fists and kicks flailed as some faculty tried to separate the battlers. On our side was the student John Cirafici, a veteran of the Vietnam War, in which he served as a Ranger; John knew how to use strategically placed leg kicks against students who were assaulting us. Parents rose from their chairs and screamed curses at us. One woman singled me out: "Go to Russia! Go to Russia!" she yelled at me. It happened I planned a trip there that summer, so I yelled back, "I'm going! I'm going!"

The old mind-set of the Cold War underlay the woman's invective. In her eyes we weren't protesting the Vietnam War, we were simply "communists". Or, if we were anti-War protestors, our actions served the Kremlin. And if we didn't approve of our government's policies, why don't we just get out of America and go to Russia. That attitude or views like it surfaced often among students in my classes. My response, always careful to frame it respectfully – opinionated passion was reserved for teach-ins and public meetings – relied on arguments familiar among critics of the War, especially from the Left, in those days. The Viet Cong, the enemy U.S. troops faced first, were national liberation fighters, not instruments of "international communism," while their supporters in Hanoi and the North Vietnamese Army sought the unification of North and South into one independent Vietnam, not the creation of another Soviet satellite, nor another "falling domino" to communism. Ho Chi Minh, the popular North Vietnamese leader, was more a Vietnamese *nationalist* than a communist, and certainly not a Kremlin stooge. As for the Soviets, I had come to understand their international behavior as dictated by national self-interest, not as promoters of revolutionary communism, whatever their official rhetoric.

They did not look kindly on independent-minded communists like Tito or Mao. They assisted the Vietnamese battle against the U.S. with considerable arms shipments in line with policies of global *realpolitik,* not necessarily from motives of revolutionary solidarity.

Several of those assertions might be properly tweaked years later, but they came to be accepted by a big slice of public opinion and by U.S. policy makers as reflecting new global realities that replaced the old, now simplistic perceptions of the Cold War. The mass anti-War movement had something to do with altering attitudes toward nationalism, communism, the Soviet Union, and Third World struggles to overcome economic backwardness and political fragility. On the Left, the existence of a mass movement embodying not just anti-War sentiments, but potential for political action on behalf of socialism juiced us up with hope. We felt we occupied the high moral ground about the Vietnam War even as mass rallies, marches, and teach-ins demonstrated the possibility of real movements of political alternatives. Socialism, anyone?

Meanwhile, absent that socialism, I, along with other "radicals with tenure" (in the critical but very expressive phrase), continued our opposition to the War with whatever (peaceful) means were at our disposal. The massive "Christmas Bombings" of North Vietnam, December, 1972, occasioned the idea for a sit-in at the U.S. Mission to the United Nations. Radosh and Mermelstein were active members of an ad hoc group of action-oriented oppositionists named after the Pupin Building at Columbia University, where classified Defense Department research drew protests. I joined the group and signed up for the sit-in. Ron, did too, but with his bladder problems, he worried about having to sit long without a bathroom visit. He managed; we all did. A dozen of us walked in, tourist like, and we chatted amiably with a friendly receptionist before we all in a flash sat down on the pre-arranged cue. Police arrived, as did media cameras and journalists; we were hauled into paddy wagons as we shouted slogans and gave our raised-fist salutes to the cameras. After many hours lying on a floor behind bars we were released for a future trial. Ron and I rushed to his place where Sheila, Allis (also an American historian and anti-War activist, soon to be Ron's second wife; they met at the Pupin demo's), and Jane Prince, an English friend in from London, were waiting for us. We watched the evening television news, of course: "There's Lou Menashe!" said Jane. Yes, raised fist and all. In the McLuhanite world of that time it wasn't "real" if it wasn't on television. We were so satisfied. But what I remember most was the look on the face of the friendly receptionist when we suddenly sat down. I was abashed and felt sorry for her. *Some radical!*

Opposition to the war led to a zealotry that turned violent. Ambrose Bierce likened zeal to "A certain nervous disorder afflicting the young and inexperienced." Bombs were set off at government and university installations by the angry young. "Weatherman" personified a murderous rage that could lead nowhere when what we needed most was peaceful change growing from a sense of political reality. It seemed that the end of the Vietnam War eliminated the single issue that had released so much political energy. Different kinds of energy, and much patience, were now needed to inaugurate a comprehensive, reality-based movement for socialism over the long haul. Many of us often cited that dictum about the need for that "long march" I mentioned earlier. I no longer believed in the Soviet model, which had tarnished the idea of socialism. Much later I had to grudgingly admit that maybe for many solid and enduring reasons – the American culture of possessive, competitive individualism, for example, or associating the socialist idea with totalitarian practice – socialism as ideology and as a politics didn't seem to fit U.S. conditions. But I never went as far in my assessment about chances for U.S. socialism as Stalin reportedly did in his statement about Germany, that socialism fit there like a saddle fit a cow.

My attitudes toward the USSR remained defensive; the Cold War was still on, after all, and I would continue to brand the U.S. as the party to blame for Soviet anxieties. However powerful the Soviets had become, they still felt threatened by an unflinching "capitalist encirclement" led by Washington and its NATO allies. But more and more I realized what awful failures inhered in the Soviet brand of socialism, what awful consequences flowed from the Bolshevik coup of 1917, led by men, no longer young, but very zealous, afflicted by Bierce's "nervous disorder." But something else was slithering into my Russophilia.

"Lenin is Always with Us": Sheila and Louis with toddler Claudia, who had just turned 1. The Kremlin, Moscow, 1968.

X

THE WORM

From Leningrad on one of my research trips to the USSR in the 1970s, I wrote to Sheila of my experiences and mood. "There have been a couple of nice moments here and there," I wrote, "and a couple of good finds at the Library. But too often I'm afflicted with sort of emotional hot flashes, particularly at night. Loneliness. Too much vodka with dinner. Self-doubts. Confusion about my work. Not enough sleep. A bit of Mystique coming from the literary overtones of the city – Dostoevsky's lonely, agitated intelligentsia, Gogol's meek and helpless Akaky Akakievich, Pushkin's Bronze Horseman chasing a hallucinatory young man driven mad by the death of his fiancée.... Get it? In short, I'm looking forward to Moscow."

But Moscow only brought me more anxieties. Late one night I left my hotel near the Kremlin – the monstrously conceived "Rossiya," since torn down – to amble along the quiet cobblestones of Red Square. The dense brick walls of the Kremlin and the Spassky gate and clock-tower loomed above me to my left, the Lenin mausoleum ahead. Full moon. Even though Saint Basil's behind me and the Kremlin walls were brightly lit, the whole scene felt dark and oppressive and I felt small and experienced a chill on that warm night. It wasn't just the massive architecture at night that overwhelmed me – by daylight it has a more agreeable majesty. But that imposing ensemble of fortress and cathedral and Mausoleum bordering a huge cobblestoned space may have played a part in my uneasiness: From that night on, I developed an agoraphobia that struck whenever I crossed Red Square. I preferred to avoid it or if I didn't, I hugged its sides, walking quickly along the façade of the GUM Department Store, for example. What an odd development for someone whose introduction to Red Square a decade earlier was ecstatic. I later learned that Nikolai Bukharin, an Old Bolshevik victimized by his old buddy, Stalin, suffered a similar Red Square malady.

Bukharin had good reason to come down with some kind of nervous disorder in those days of the Terror. Unlike Bukharin or many anxious foreign tourists who always imagined the KGB on their trail, I wasn't terrorized, but I was suddenly very alienated from my Russian surroundings. My Russophilia was at risk. Never mind that Moscow was not terribly pleasant on any comfort scale. Never mind that Soviet socialism had already disappointed me. Something else grabbed me hard and shook me up, the sensation that I would never *understand* Russia. More: I suddenly experienced a fear that I would always be a stranger in this alien corn. It wasn't just the language, which I knew I could not truly and fully master. Arthur Mendel once told me he wouldn't dream of having a serious conversation with a serious Russian intellectual without first having read all of Tolstoy in the original. A hyperbolic assertion, no doubt, but certainly an achievement to aim for. No, I would never read all of Tolstoy's many volumes in the original, but couldn't I feel comfortable among the people who spoke his language? And the culture and land of those people – all that Chekhov, and onion domes, and *zakuski*, and birch forests, and balalaikas, and warm hearts and hospitality, and chilled vodka—wouldn't experiencing those things as an historian and frequent visitor be enough to satisfy my quest for identity as an authentic Russianist?

No. Often when I introduced myself as an historian of Russia and the Soviet Union, Russians assumed my family heritage was Russian. As if it were a case of "who else would want to specialize in this place?" Another sign of that sense of inferiority I frequently encountered among Russians. To their surprise I explained otherwise; there was no family connection to Russia. My background took in Spain, Portugal, Turkey, Greece. I felt considerably more at home in those places than I ever did in Soviet Russia. It wasn't the discomforts of the USSR, the shortages of basic things, the tensions enveloping contacts with ordinary Russians, the felt burdens of a heavily bureaucratic police state, where regions and cities were off-limits to foreigners and proper *dokumenty* were required for the most ordinary transactions. No, I experienced the same alienation in the freer, goods abundant, and more open *post-Soviet* Russia.

Back to that anguished night. The *worm* of disengagement from my first love and chosen career had begun to gnaw at me. For several nights after the moonlit walk I had to knock back more than one shot of unchilled vodka at the Rossiya – North Section, 11th floor, room 132—to help me sleep. *Unchilled* because my room had no refrigerator. Reading the supply of Maigret novels by Simenon that Sheila bought for my trip helped at bedtime as well. As did listening to dear little Claudia singing Woody Guthrie songs on a tape I took with me. *I'm gonna write myself a letter....* She sang, with feeling. Meeting Bill Rosenberg and sharing thoughts about our mutual discomforts in Moscow also assisted my getting through those troubled days and nights. (Bill went on to a distinguished career in Russian studies at the University of Michigan, joining Arthur Mendel there.) Maybe Tyutchev, the great Slavophil poet, was right. It might be hopeless for me to try to *understand* Russia. But *believe* in her, as he insists? I couldn't do that either.

There were other psychic elements at work besides what I've described above. I harbored some confusion about who I was professionally, and what I was doing extracurricular. Despite many cozy academic perks, did I really have the temperament to devote hours, days, years in libraries and archives? I hung on to Guchkov and Company throughout decades of ambivalence, spending time in both the Lenin Library in Moscow and the Leningrad Library named after Saltykov-Shchedrin. But there was a constant pull in the direction of political action and *relevant* publishing. At meetings of Slavists I may have been known as a Guchkov and *kupechestvo* specialist from my dissertation plus several published articles on the subjects. In other circles I was the Lenin dude. Stanley Aronowitz, a New Left luminary, once asked me, "When are you going to write the definitive work on Lenin?" For the *Nation* magazine I wrote a piece, "The Greening of Lenin," that attracted the attention of Phillip Rahv, co-founder in 1934 of what became the leading literary-political journal of the anti-Stalinist Left, *Partisan Review*. I was flattered, but didn't follow up on his invitation to write more on Lenin. That would come later for other publications. The "Greening" piece took off from a short, posthumously published work by

Isaac Deutscher, which he had intended as the opening of a major work on Lenin to complement his acclaimed study of Stalin and the ambitious trilogy on Trotsky. Both works, on Stalin and Trotsky, were major influences on my thinking in those days. Deutscher's *Stalin*, because it offered a way to accept Stalin's "rough stuff" (as Pete Seeger charmingly put it) as necessary for modernizing backward Soviet Russia in a purportedly socialist direction. The Trotsky trilogy, because its elegant prose endowed the victim as martyr with anti-Stalinist *prophetic* dimensions; each of the three titles has Trotsky as "Prophet" – *Armed, Disarmed,* and *Outcast*. I gradually grew suspicious of Deutscher's work to the point, eventually, of seeing more hagiography than impartial biography, in his portrait of Trotsky, especially.

By "greening" Lenin, I meant to picture him in a more benign light, disengaging him from the Stalinist authoritarianism that was conventionally seen as the inevitable Leninist legacy. I was contributing to the "revisionist" views that began to percolate in the late '60s and early '70s about Lenin's own purported "revisions," as revealed in fragments he composed before his death, and in the so-called "Testament" in which he is critical of Stalin and calls for his removal as General Secretary of the Soviet Communist Party. Moshe Lewin's *Lenin's Last Struggle,* based largely on the fragments, was a bellwether for this new trend. More "greening" revisions about different aspects of Soviet history would follow as a new generation of scholars took issue with inherited anti-Soviet interpretations borne of the Cold War.

"Greening" was a popular meme in those days, from the bestselling book by Charles Reich, *The Greening of America* (1970). Its subtitle bares his intent: *How the Youth Rebellion is Trying to Make America Livable*. Reich, by emphasizing everything from bell-bottom trousers to supposedly new forms of consciousness, partly drug activated – Consciousness Three or "Con III" became a familiar byword—elevated the counter-culture championed by the young to transformative heights. Time has shown what little effect Con III and summers of love had on American politics and the social order, but Reich's enthusiastic brief (he was a Professor of Law at Yale) on behalf of a novel path to change had many on the Left mesmerized: Who needed Lenin's vanguard party? The "dictatorship of the proletariat" was devised for other times, other places.

Sheila and I and our immediate circle were beyond the mythic dividing line captured in the phrase, "Don't trust anyone over 30," but we were close enough to the music, the "vibes," the ambience, the experiments of the period to try something of the new flavors ourselves. We lived on Columbia Heights, in Brooklyn Heights, near Montague Street, not the Montague Street of Bob *Dylan's Tangled Up in Blue* – his was in New Orleans, I think – but we heard *music in the cafes at night, and revolution was in the air*. We would start and live in an urban commune. We were too attached to our extended families and jobs to go off and break ground in, say, New Hampshire or Vermont, as so many of the young were doing. Park Slope in Brooklyn, astride beautiful Prospect Park, became our frontier. With other like-minded friends in the anti-war movement sharing similar communal ideas, we agreed to begin a search for space for our "Vanguard Commune". Three families launched the plan, the Menashes, Radoshes, and Ciporens. Miriam and Freddy Ciporen were friends of Alice and Ron from – where else? – the University of Wisconsin at Madison. Miriam was teaching elementary school at the time; she was an affable, buxom brunette, from the Bronx originally who laughed heartily and repeatedly at Freddy's one-liners and anecdotes, as all of us did. Freddy, an adjunct historian at several local colleges, was a master at imitating the accents and rhythms of Anglo-Yiddish in hilarious stories drawn from family experiences. His comic side belied a scholarly appearance, what with his pipe, spectacles, a bald head topped with a fringe of gravity-defying hairs that stood upright. He reminded me of the Karl Radek I knew from old photographs – Radek was another Old Bolshevik victim of Stalin's terror. Freddy, like all the politically committed Wisconsinites, was a devoted socialist and active anti-Vietnam Warrior. Once, after we saw and discussed a Truffaut film, Freddy wanted to know, "Don't the French know there's a war on?"

We looked forward to a single kitchen in our commune, meals taken together regularly, all house chores and costs distributed equally, and, most alluring of all, shared child-care. Claudia was 3 at the time, Alice and Ron were parents of Laura (7), and the infant Daniel (1); Miriam and Freddy were soon to conceive Jeremy. We weren't radical communards, out to smash the family and open-up monogamous relationships; the three families would remain intact, each autonomous within a collective setting. I had been to Soviet communal apartments and knew their reputation. What had been one of the central dreams of the Bolsheviks—negating the bourgeois nuclear family's individualized home arrangements by introducing living spaces defined by egalitarian and communal norms – often turned nightmarish, as communal apartments became dens of squabbling and disorder in close quarters. *Another Soviet dream gone sour.*

Our commune would be located in a spacious Park Slope brownstone, selling at very affordable prices in the early '70s, and be governed by mutual affection and shared commitment to a politics that might inaugurate an American socialism. We found a place on 6th Street, down a block from Prospect Park. If Stalin was determined to build "socialism in one country" in the USSR, we would continue our project of building socialism in the U.S.A. by introducing its ideals into one neighborhood. From our communal base, we envisioned stirring up strong community involvement in bringing socialist values to education, housing, sports, and the anti-war movement. We even located a brownstone next door for three like-minded families who would buy and inhabit it as a commune. We would be, we boasted, "building socialism in *one neighborhood*". Stalin succeeded in nationalizing the industrial economy and collectivizing farmlands. An abstract definition of socialism – eliminating most private property -- would have it that the USSR was socialist by the mid-1930s. Soviet propaganda and communist supporters everywhere trumpeted that motif. But what kind of "socialism" was it that rested on violence, terror, dictatorship, and the totalitarian model of social organization?

Flash Forward

Our commune blueprint was attractive on paper, but collapsed for want of wedded unity among the original would-be practitioners. The 60s atmosphere of loosening marriage ties shot down the unions of first, Alice and Ron, then of Miriam and Freddy, while Sheila and I held firm after surviving many discussions, discussions only, of "open marriage" and sexual experimentation. Our communard founders and many other couples in our circle were not "stickers," like us, to use the term coined by my mother-in-law, Bea. We re-dubbed the *"Vanguard Commune"* as *"Rearguard Realty"*. The same fate ultimately befell the commune next door, *"Sideguard,"* we called it, though its communards really practiced the communal idea – one kitchen, in the best definition – for a much longer period than our feeble, short-lived experiment. Their families broke up; lovers replaced husbands and wives, new faces displaced the old, death intruded – Rachel Fruchter, an ardent movement feminist and founding communard, was hit and killed by a van while she rode her bicycle in Prospect Park. Alice Radosh, instrumental in devising our original communal idea, began a relationship with another movement figure, David Gelber, which broke up the Radosh marriage. (With David I canvassed for George McGovern in the 1972 election that Nixon won by a landslide. It was my first – sobering – political action in Park Slope). Alice was on her way to a doctorate in psychology; she and David comprised one of the original "Sideguard" communal couples. Today, Sideguard and Rearguard, *né* Vanguard, have become condos and co-ops, converted from the original communal or would-be communal spaces. You might trace the political/ideological trajectory of our section of the Left from inception to demise of its communal idea. Sheila and I are Rearguard survivors; I'll discuss who replaced Freddy and Miriam below. Elayne Archer, a writer and educator, is the lone survivor of the original Sideguard. After her marriage dissolved, she met and married Cliff Rosenthal, who, interestingly enough, started as a Russianist, with a Columbia degree, and later headed a major Credit Union office in New York. *Tesnii mir*, say the Russians for small world (literally "tight or close world"). With another Columbia alumna and friend of mine, Barbara Engel, Cliff had co-edited the book, *Five Sisters: Women Against the Tsar*, featuring the journals of five Russian revolutionary women who "went to the people" in late 19th-century Imperial Russia.

New arrivals to Park Slope during the '80s and beyond to the 21st century consider us "pioneers". Barack Obama lived for time a few blocks away from us, on 2nd Street. *Was that Obama I thought I saw running one morning in Prospect Park?* We were pioneers, in the sense of helping revive a neighborhood that had visibly declined after WW II; we and others like us took over vacant brownstones in stages of disrepair, and worked hard to restore them, anticipating the gentrification that made Park Slope the magnet it is today for families of professional and other elite backgrounds. Ah, the irony. Radicals prepared the terrain now occupied by the gentry. We were political pioneers, too. Many a movement get-together came to our place; our spacious parlor floor was designed, we said, for "dance parties and political meetings". Over the years diverse "movement" gatherings took place here or next door – by groups opposing the Vietnam war until it ended in 1975, later by political formations with larger ambitions than anti-war protests, like the New American Movement, a national organization with a democratic-socialist and feminist orientation . I was a charter member of NAM's Park Slope chapter. The chapter and the national organization had short lives. We hung out at the Mongoose Coffee House, like other such establishments across the country, a center of anti-war activity. Mongoose, however, had a remarkable after-life: it helped spawn the Park Slope Food Co-operative, to this day one of the nation's largest and most durable co-ops. A sign of its distinction: people from Manhattan cross the river for its goods! I and Freddy joined and spent many hours working there until our commitment flagged. Oscar Wilde had a point: socialism requires too many spare evenings.

With my night of terror on Red Square in Moscow and the distractions of left-wing protests and politics at home, little wonder that my professional commitment to Russian/Soviet studies was tested in those days. Another domestic development demanded attention as well, lots of it: David Gene Menashe was born in 1976. He was named after my father; the Gene came from the "G" in *Gertrude,* Sheila's lovable and quirky Aunt Gertie, the piano teacher, and from *Eugene* Debs the great American Socialist and sometime serious presidential candidate. And don't forget the "David" from Sheila's unforgettable *Claudia and David* stories. There was another "Eugene" in the naming decision, *Gene* Bruck, my boss and mentor from Phonotapes, one of the Sam Goody/Moe Asch enterprises I once worked for. He and his talented artist wife at the time, Joan, later Joan Diamant, were both graciously and immensely helpful in getting me and Sheila started in married life, whether it was finding an apartment or learning about antique furniture to fill it. Gene is gone after a long decline, as is Joan, who passed away, vigorous to the last, at 91. Both remained our loving good friends over the many years.

David's birth coincided with the birth of another Left organ, the bi-weekly newspaper, *In These Times,* founded and edited by Jimmy Weinstein as a democratic socialist publication of the New, non-Marxist-Leninist, Left. Its tagline was *With Liberty and Justice for All,* and Jim defined its mission as seeking to "identify and clarify the struggles against corporate power now multiplying in American society." Jim was a close follower of Soviet affairs, who recognized the need for understanding what went wrong there, and didn't dismiss the idea and hope that the Soviets would develop a more human face for their brand of socialism. He also knew the Bolshevik Revolution and the Soviet experiment that followed it had little relevance to U.S. conditions and to a movement for socialism here. Those were my views too. *In These Times* was designed mainly to report and comment on the American scene, domestic politics and economy, especially, but there was room for international relations, and keeping an eye on the Soviet bloc in the Cold War confrontation was important. Jim asked me to contribute on Soviet affairs for the newspaper, and I agreed.

I wasn't trained as a Soviet historian, I certainly wasn't a Sovietologist nor its subset, Kremlinologist, but I thought Jim's paper was a fine undertaking, and I would do my best to inform its readers about Soviet goings on and their historical background. My general perspective? Critical but sympathetic, if you know what I mean. The dark Stalinist past had given way to a promising future, inaugurated by Nikita Khrushchev's denunciation of the tyrant in 1956. Khrushchev was soon eased out of office, and a carefully modulated backsliding took place, not quite a return to Stalinism, but still a disappointing reliance on political repression and backward economic and cultural policies. It was Brezhnev's USSR I wrote about, the times later described by the Gorbachev reformers as the "period of stagnation." I kept track of the new and heroic dissident movement, offered a mild defense of the Soviet invasion of Afghanistan, and wrote my first pieces on Soviet cinema – a critical review of *Moscow Does Not Believe in Tears,* and an article based on my interview of Andrei Konchalovsky, whose colorful historical epic, *Siberiade*, played successfully in New York. For a symposium on Warren Beatty's *Reds*, which had sent the Left into raptures of appreciation toward Hollywood for its sympathetic portraits of the Bolsheviks and their revolution, I offered my against the grain assessment – *Reds* gave me the *Blahs*. I thought it followed clichéd story lines, and had what I thought was a distorted picture of Lenin as a sort of pompous, professorial ideologue. That drew a rebuke from a reader, who quoted Louise Bryant's description of Lenin, obviously a source for the *Reds* screenplay and its portrait of the Bolshevik leader. Another rebuke: this one from William Mandel, a well-known translator from, and apologist for, all things Soviet. Mandel wanted to know why I would be critical of a film seen and loved by millions in the USSR. Good question, and one I would have to address in my future writing on Soviet cinema – do I examine those films from universal esthetic standards, or my own subjective ones, as against placing them in some Soviet historical, even political context that makes artistic considerations a secondary matter? I tried to do both in my work on Soviet and post-Soviet cinema, which later became my prime professional specialty; I would write as both film critic and historian, emphasis on the latter.

Odd how I remember vividly those letters-to-the-editor which criticized my articles, more vividly than the many letters of praise the articles got in the newspaper. Those were probably from Lefty readers, Old and New, who appreciated my sympathetic tone regarding the USSR. Steve Cohen commended my sympathetic writing on the fate of Bukharin. In those days Steve was instrumental in getting *samizdat* literature out of the Soviet Union to the West, and bringing forbidden Russian language materials in. As a valuable "scholar-activist" in the Soviet sphere, Steve was providing immense and much-needed help to the dissident movement inside the USSR.

Another critical letter to *In These Times* complained that I engaged in observations about Soviet current affairs without real on-the-ground, insider reporting from Moscow. True enough, but I saw myself more as a historian than as a political correspondent or commentator, and I wrote that way. In any event, my association with the paper trailed off and eventually ended, for no special reason. *In These Times* continues to publish, transformed as a monthly, in magazine format and committed to the same mission articulated by founder Jimmy Weinstein.

Other organs of the Left claimed my attention, but unlike *In These Times* they turned out to be firefly publications – they lit up at first, then faded and had short lives. One of them, heralded at the time, was *Marxist Perspectives,* a major enterprise of Eugene Genovese who, as a good Gramscian and respecter of scholarship, conceived of a Marxist journal free of Left tendentiousness and sectarian combat that would appeal to American academics and the wider community of intellectuals. Gene's reputation by this time, the late '70s, thanks to his path-breaking research and writing on the culture of slavery as a creation of both the slaves and their slave masters, carried great weight, and the journal attracted much attention. The cute headline of a *Wall Street Journal* story: "What's Black, White And Red All Over?" After circulation quickly climbed to 5,000, Cambridge University Press agreed to take on publishing and marketing the journal when, suddenly, with warning signs not apparent to most of us, it shut down. For reasons that have never been clear. Rumors at the time had it only that Gene and his wife Elizabeth Fox-Genovese were involved in some acrimonious intra-editorial disagreements with others. What Gene created, Gene took away.

After a couple of issues, I was brought in as Communist Affairs Co-Editor with Elizabeth ("Miss Betsy," to Gene). I secured a piece by my close friend at the time, Joel Agee, a pre-publication excerpt from his fine memoir of growing up in East Germany, *Twelve Years*. I also got and translated an article by Roy Medvedev, one of the few prominent Soviet dissidents, who, unlike the great writer and truth-teller, Alexander Solzhenitsyn, and the celebrated physicist Andrei Sakharov, "Father of the Soviet Hydrogen Bomb", was a devoted Marxist and still honored Lenin and the Bolshevik Revolution. I was glad to have made some contributions to the journal, but something I wrote, and its fate, highlighted for me once again the road not taken.

I had prepared a long, ambitious article, a derivative of my doctoral work on Guchkov – Gooch again, still! – enriched by the additional research I had done in Moscow and Leningrad libraries, on the history of the Guchkov family as a kind of paradigm for understanding 19th-century Russian socio-economic and political development. The family's origins lay in serfdom, and its last generation before the Revolution commanded great wealth and political prominence. I thought it was good enough for the *American Historical Review*, the leading professional journal in the field, and so did the several readers who refereed the article. A lower level editor supervising my submission and readers' responses who was filling in for the responsible editors at the time, wasn't sure about green lighting the article for publication himself, and suggested some revisions. I lay the article aside as I considered some options. Why not offer it to *Marxist Perspectives*? Genovese was certainly committed to publishing serious scholarship on diverse themes from, ahem, a *Marxist Perspective*, for his journal. Already some people were complaining about several of the articles in the early issues of the journal, that they were too academic, not lively and "political" enough. Well, my piece was written in an academic, but accessible style, and I thought that any work that illuminated the pre-Revolutionary background of Tsarist Russia should inform the political and historical understanding of the American Left. So I gave "The Guchkovs of Moscow" to Gene, who liked and welcomed the piece, went over it carefully as scholar and editor, and I looked forward to seeing it in print, when POOF!...... I forget who phoned me with the bad news. End of *Marxist Perspectives*; my Guchkov opus there sank with it.

I sent the Ms. to one of the leading scholarly periodicals in the Russian area, *The Russian Review*, which had earlier published my article on Guchkov. I received a kind rejection note from the Editor, without any comments from referees. My hunch then was that if one's work was not based on recent findings in Soviet archives, its chances for publication in refereed journals were slim. I resented that, too, and it confirmed my feeling that a traditional, purely scholarly involvement in the Russian/Soviet circuit was not my path. It's not that I thought I wasn't good enough for serious work and production in the profession. I had already demonstrated that I could pass muster. Or that I thought there was active bias against Left-oriented work. It was more like, why bother with trying to publish in academic journals when I could always contribute reviews and essays to "un-refereed," but no less serious publications of the Left? My first published book review, while I was still a graduate student, was for such a journal, *Science & Society* (subtitle: *An Independent Journal of Marxism*); more contributions to *S&S* from me would follow.

When *Marxist Perspectives* was closed down, several of us associated with the journal formed the East Coast "Collective" for the San Francisco based *Socialist Review*. In those days, "Editorial Board" was considered an old-fashioned, even "bourgeois," designation, missing the flavor of "participatory democracy" that the term "Collective" carried. Leonard Quart was part of the group of New Yorkers making up the "Collective," and we became quite close as friends and comrades. Len is a multi-talented writer and historian in different areas, most prominently in film, and brings exuberance to whatever subject he's on, in writing and conversation. At the Staten Island branch of the City University of New York, he also occupied, like me, that twilight zone of college teaching *sans* traditional scholarly ambition, favoring informed "popular" writing as a public, not an academic, intellectual. Len was an editor and prolific contributor at the independent magazine, *Cineaste*, widely respected in film circles. When I turned to film, *Russian film*, to be exact, and I too became a frequent *Cineaste* contributor, our friendship was once again sealed by association with a Left-leaning publication.

I didn't publish anything for *Socialist Review*, which began to concentrate on "identity" issues, but my two long essays on Lenin and Solzhenitsyn appeared in its immediate forebear, *Socialist Revolution*, another journal founded by the indefatigable Left publications impresario, Jimmy Weinstein. Earlier, Jimmy had been an originator of *Studies on the Left*, a major influence, in the first instance, on students at the University of Wisconsin, Madison, then on a wider readership when it moved to New York, with its signature attacks on "Cold War Liberals," and against "Corporate Liberalism." Those terms were introduced – in Madison—by Jimmy's frequent publications collaborator, Marty Sklar, the brilliant theorist and avatar-hero of those who welcomed his innovative (but difficult to read) writing about possibilities for American socialism in the context of mature global capitalism. *Socialist Revolution*, San Francisco based, was a logical successor to *Studies* as the anti-Vietnam War movement generated radical political moods, among the young, especially, and kindled hopes for a socialist – Revolutionary! – movement on a national scale. The title transition from *Revolution* to *Review* marked the downward evolution of those hopes.

Lee Baxandall, another Wisconsin alumnus and *Studies* associate, chided me about my "Greening" piece on Lenin when it appeared in *The Nation* – according to you, Lee said, Lenin was "some kind of flower child." Not quite, but I did intend a softening of Lenin's image, in keeping with the developing revisionist views I alluded to earlier cultivated by a new generation of Russian-area scholars, especially as those views applied to the "revisionist" speculations ascribed to the ailing Lenin before his death. The idea was that if the leader had lived, the course of Soviet development might have been markedly different from the bludgeoned Stalinist path. As for countering the prevailing interpretation that the Lenin-led Bolshevik Revolution was a naked, *minority* grab for power, a *coup d'état* executed behind the backs of the people, the new revisionist outlook, by contrast, stressed the radical mood of workers, peasants, and soldiers (peasants in uniform) as the *mass* foundation for launching the Bolshevik leap to power in Petrograd, October, 1917. Hence, the Bolshevik Revolution should be seen as "legitimate," as a popular, authentically democratic political act. In my provocatively titled lead article in the journal, *Socialist Revolution*, "Vladimir Ilyich Bakunin: An Essay on Lenin," I tried to undermine mainstream views of Lenin, by some on the Left as well, as an elitist Marxist intellectual disdainful of the working-class, an organization man who exalted a hegemonic party as the exclusive revolutionary instrument. Those accepted views seemed to be supported by the famous passage in Lenin's 1903 polemic, *What Is To Be Done?* concerning "spontaneity" (bad) and "consciousness" (good). My article shifted the ground away from the 1903 context, and argued that in 1917, Lenin's "anarchist" mood embraced mass moods and impelled the daring Bolshevik coup. Just read Lenin's *State and Revolution*, I argued, to capture Lenin's thinking during those fateful days.

My article drew (understandably) critical responses from New Left libertarians, but the New American Movement made it required reading, and its Cambridge Chapter invited me to lecture at

Harvard (!) on translating the *true* Lenin for U.S. socialists. I never made it to Harvard in my scholarly capacity as a historian of Russia and the Soviet Union, but I entered through a back-door there as the Lenin specialist of the New American Movement. After Lenin, I took on Solzhenitsyn. If I intended to enhance Lenin's reputation, my intent, for *Socialist Revolution* readers, was to take down Solzhenitsyn's. No questioning his courage in challenging the Kremlin, nor some of his literary talents, best evinced in *One Day in the Life of Ivan Denisovich*. As chronicler of prison camp horrors in *The Gulag Archipelago*, Solzhenitsyn's contribution to our knowledge of Stalinist civilization is immeasurable. But, I argued, with a certain insolence—who was I to thumb my nose at this extraordinary figure in the literature and history of our time?—Solzhenitsyn's grasp of Marxism and his views of the Bolsheviks were quite primitive; moreover, they betrayed some of the very smug *Soviet* attitudes he railed against.

These and other reviews and essays in Left journals and newspapers earned my credentials as the "Russian specialist" in the Movement. I cite them here, not to plug my reputation, or recall their value—some hold up, I think, while others make me cringe from their arcane "movement" language and quest for political "relevance"—but as evidence of how I did not pursue the scholarly, academic goals mapped out by my work on Gooch and the Russian pre-revolutionary bourgeoisie, in favor of addressing and enlightening my comrades who were not especially interested in the Moscow *kupechestvo*. In this regard I differed from Steve Cohen, a comrade at the time. We shared similarly *simpático* views of the USSR, and I thought his Bukharin biography pointed to one of the proper, less ultimately tragic, policy alternatives to Stalinism. But I cultivated a comradely audience *outside* the academy; Steve's emphasis was working *within* the profession. His regular pieces as "Sovieticus" for *The Nation* suggested, however, that he was comfortable in both venues. My venue(s) were more "movement" oriented than his.

The "Red Jet," Davey, swinging for the fences, at the Parade Grounds, Brooklyn, 1984. Photo by Joe Zarba.

XI

NEW DIRECTIONS?

The strictly academic path should have taken me to the USSR for the library and archival research afforded by IREX and other funding sources. But other concerns, domestic issues among them, tended to keep me in New York, not Moscow. Adjusting to our new lives in Park Slope, and caring for Claudia and David topped the agenda. Freddy and Miriam's departure from "Rearguard" created an opening for another family to join us; they would have the downstairs duplex, we would stay above, even as we retained the cooperative arrangements. We had built a connecting door between the two apartments, facilitating mutual access for both families. Word of the vacancy got around, and soon enough Elizabeth (Liz) Phillips and Mark Naison "applied" for it, having heard about the place from another Park Sloper and Left historian, Judy Hilkey. I knew Mark from the movement, and from his reputation as a fiery radical; he was part of the "Mad Dog" faction of SDS at Columbia, and was always called upon to serve as muscle and enforcer for movement rallies and actions. I didn't know Liz, but I had been to one of the popular parties she and Mark threw in their Upper West Side apartment. Liz had calmed Mark down a lot; he was teaching at Fordham when we "interviewed" them for the vacancy, and at work preparing his Columbia doctoral dissertation for publication, on the Communist Party in Harlem during the Depression – Mark specialized in Black studies. Liz was an editor at the Feminist Press when we got to know her, later a devoted public school teacher who ascended to Principal of P.S. 321, which became under her leadership the superb institution coveted by all Park Slope parents for their children. We liked each other at the "interview," and the deal was swiftly done. Thanks to a loan from my mother, we bought Miriam Ciporen's share of Rearguard (Freddy had consigned their unit of our co-op to her) and promptly sold it to Mark and Liz at no profit to us. With them we were now, in the legal language of property ownership, "tenants in common". That had a nice, almost socialist ring to it.

Moreover, both Sheila and Liz were pregnant at the time. David's birth preceded Sara's by three months, and they grew up together in a close friendship helped along by our sharing dinners together once weekly, maintaining that connecting door between our respective apartments, and from their parents' baby-sitting and child-caring built into our "tenants in common" arrangement. Prodded by Mark's encouragement and tutorial skills—Mark was a strong propagandist for all sports, and cultivated a fierce competitive streak – David and Sara challenged each other for mutual benefit in neighborhood tennis and baseball. Mark and I coached their Little League baseball team, the "Red Jets," sponsored by Saint Saviour's Catholic Church, located across the street from our Red enclave—Peaceful Coexistence between normally hostile neighborhood factions and classes is an endearing feature of Park Slope. David's *Unassisted Triple Play* stands out vividly from all those games in Prospect Park, for me and Sheila, anyway. While I wrote on Soviet Affairs for *In These Times*, Mark contributed a column on sports, a reflection of Jim Weinstein's hope for a well-rounded socialist and popular newspaper that didn't confine itself to just political discourse. Jim was once a Party member himself, and had to remember the old Communist newspaper, *The Daily Worker*, which featured a regular sports column by Lester Rodney. Mark suggested I contribute to a special edition on "Culture and Class" for the *Radical History Review*, where he was a member of the New York editorial – yes—"Collective," and again I wrote one of those revisionist pieces that took off from comparing the contrasting views of John L.H.Keep (in his *The Russian* Revolution*: A Study in Mass Mobilization*) and Alexander Rabinowitch (in his *The Bolsheviks Come to Power: The Revolution of 1917 in Petrograd*). Keep represented the mainstream anti-Bolshevik outlook, with its emphasis on Leninist *manipulation* of mass moods through the Party's purported organizational wizardry, while Rabinowitch emphasized how much those mass radical moods affected Bolshevik behavior and Lenin's own options and not the other way around. Again, the traditional view stripped the Bolshevik Revolution of its "legitimacy," while the new outlook conferred on it the stamp of a legitimately democratic action of the masses.

I titled the piece "Demystifying the Russian Revolution" because I called for attention, in the case of 1917, to complex historical circumstances, to the people caught up in them, and to their interplay. Lenin's or Trotsky's writings were only partial, and often misleading, ways of explaining events. I also pointed out, in an ironic gloss, that the academic mainstream's conclusions emphasizing Leninist theory along with Bolshevik Party discipline and organizational savvy as masterminding events in Petrograd also mirrored the claims of another mainstream—Soviet historians and official Soviet *agit-prop*. I concluded the article by naming the new, young, revisionist scholars and cited their published and unpublished works; they were offering well researched counter arguments to mainstream views – William Rosenberg, David Mandel, Diane Koenker, George Phillips, Robert Devlin among them. They were applying the social-history methodology championed by the older, very influential Leopold Haimson of Columbia's Russian Institute. My article, with its sharper polemical edges considerably sanded down, could have been placed as a review-essay in some scholarly journal. But, as usual then, I preferred addressing my crowd, not the academic community.

While I was writing for the Left in diverse movement organs, Sheila was working for the needy from different platforms, first at Mobilization for Youth, then at several other agencies based in the Lower East Side and the South Bronx. It was hard not to notice her in her field. She earned a reputation for her great warmth among co-workers and for her empathy to the down-trodden. She also knew how to get the job done for her clients whatever community she worked in, whether it had to do with housing, health, employment or family issues. She applied the lessons she learned from her field work to training future social workers when she joined the faculty of the NYU Graduate School of Social Work, one of the prestigious places for social-work education in New York. (Later she would teach in the Graduate School of Social Work at Columbia

University, an even more prestigious place.) Another position soon beckoned, however; head-hunters with an innovative idea had her in their sights. Through the joint efforts of the Columbia Graduate School of Social Work, the Columbia University Law School, and the legal department at DC 37, the Municipal Workers Union, and with the financing of the Ford Foundation, a pilot program was launched that would provide *free* legal assistance to DC 37 members in any civil case they confronted. The plan originators understood that legal problems often had personal and family consequences beyond issues of the law, and they decided an important adjunct to the team of attorneys would be a social work unit. Enter someone like Sheila as its Director. We debated long and hard when she was offered the position. Leave NYU and all the academic perks behind? For a program that may not have any staying power? Take on a daily job when we knew Sheila would log in more hours than 9-to-5 called for? The expression didn't exist then, but 24/7 is probably how Sheila would work. She took the job, never regretted it, and that's exactly how she worked. Teaching at NYU (and later, at Columbia) had its personal rewards and a sense of professional contribution to social work theory and practice, but at DC 37's Municipal Employees Legal Services, or "MELS," division, Sheila, with her union-girl genes, felt she was in the trenches, engaged directly with the working class, many constituting the working poor. They benefited from her operating style; compassion always, but bare knuckles when it came to fighting landlords and bill collectors, or even attorneys in her own division.

The "pilot" succeeded well beyond expectations; the program became a mainstay at DC 37 and a sometimes imitated model across the country. Sheila would serve there for three decades. Her full-time efforts in those early years, my full-time teaching at Poly, writing for the movement, joining this or that study group or new political organization complicated our two-children domestic life plus our comradely child-care obligations (there was now an Eric Naison-Phillips, Sara's little brother, downstairs), and derailed any idea of extended research time in the Soviet Union. There could be more digging on Gooch and the *kupechestvo,* and I also thought of breaking new ground for a study on the origins of the soviets, the working-class committees that sprang up during the 1905 revolution, when I realized there was next to nothing done on the subject in English. Such a work, history from below, historiographically fashionable at the time, would be in keeping with revisionist trends, and not just in the Russian area. But it was just a thought, as it turned out, even if I received an ACLS grant to begin such a project. I couldn't head for Moscow and Leningrad for long periods and leave Sheila with her hands full. But, let's face it, I didn't much care for spending lots of time there either. What a frame of mind for a Russian specialist!

Was it time to throw in the towel on Russian studies, or just understand and admit what my limits were as a serious academic historian of Imperial Russia and the Soviet Union? It didn't help that my warmth for the USSR as "socialist model" had long ago faded. The Chinese, to whom many on the Left looked to for constructing authentic socialist alternatives to the Soviet pattern, offered a confusing and often repulsive picture – the cult of Mao, the demented "cultural revolution," the millions dead from various political and economic campaigns that made Stalin's massive crimes almost minimal by comparison, the turn to a kind of state capitalism while institutionalizing a repressive Party: No, the Chinese were no model. It was amusing and irritating to witness defenses of Mao and Chinese communism with the same kinds of rationalizations many of us once used in defending the USSR.

But "Eurocommunism" and the promise of a reformed communist movement in the West with truly popular appeal quickened our pulses. We even arranged a meeting at Ron Radosh's Upper West Side apartment with Santiago Carrillo, once a loyal Stalinist, then a leader of the Eurocommunist section of the Spanish Party. With guarded hopes for this promising development, I contributed an essay to the volume, *The Politics of Eurocommunism* (edited by Carl Boggs and David Plotke, 1980), with its hopeful subtitle, *Socialism in Transition.* My piece looked at "Eurocommunism and the USSR," and asked if this meant the "End of the Bolshevik Tradition in the West?" Yes, was the answer, it soon became apparent – a real break with Moscow was a pre-condition for communist or socialist vitality. I ventured this formulation: "Eurocommunism can be a historic second wind [for movements inspired by the Bolshevik Revolution and the USSR] leading either to political triumphs or exhaustion and demise." Not too long after that sentence was published there was no doubt as to which of the "eithers" proved true. The Gorbachev *perestroika* eruption was, you might say, the Soviet form of Eurocommunism, and it failed there, too. More on that later.

My political and ideological moorings were frayed by the early '80s, but I still had my teaching, and my commitment to the Department. And I was still in the business of educating Poly students about the USSR and its historical backgrounds. These were the Reagan years, and the rhetoric of the "Evil Empire". I had to work hard to kindle and keep student interest, and explain why my views were softer to the USSR than official attitudes coming from the White House. The Poly student population numbered predominantly engineering and science majors (engineering especially), who had heavy technical-course loads that left little time for the social sciences and humanities, much less for studying the fall of the Russian Empire, or the fate of Leon Trotsky. Certain innovations did work. I organized debates on important issues, around the Bolshevik Revolution, for example, or the collectivization of peasant farming. Students volunteered for sides; those who spoke up on behalf of the Bolshevik seizure of power against those calling for the Menshevik program of a unity government of all the socialist parties. Or the "Stalinists" who wanted immediate collectivization, by force if necessary, against the "Bukharinites" arguing for gradualism in agriculture and in industrial development. Literature also helped; I could rely on the exceptionally rich and accessible works of the Russian literary giants. Turgenev (*Fathers and Sons*) or Goncharov (*Oblomov*) illuminated aspects of culture and society in 19th -century Russia. For the Soviet period there was Solzhenitsyn; not just *One Day in the Life of Ivan Denisovich*, but *First Circle* and *Cancer Ward*. But what really got their interest (and improved their understanding, too) were the treasures of Soviet cinema, from the silents on revolutionary Russia (*Mother, Potemkin*) to the moderns on The Great Patriotic War of the Soviet Union (*Ballad of a Soldier, The Cranes Are Flying*), or on mature Soviet society (*Moscow Does Not Believe in Tears, Autumn Marathon*). Such films grabbed their attention and supplemented the texts I assigned in ways that humanized the subjects as only cinema can. Peoples of the USSR – Russians and other national groups—as *people*. Never mind that the films were often perceived as "propaganda" by skeptical students; but that too could be a terrific topic for discussion – on the meaning of propaganda in general, or on the conflicting aims of art and politics in the USSR.

More than anything else, however, was the impact of Soviet cinema on me; those films threw me a lifeline that kept me happily afloat for the duration of my academic career. As for attracting attention to Soviet themes, there was no need to try very hard for the new population filling my classrooms in the early '80s, students from the Soviet *émigré* invasion.

Russian *émigré* students meet the Lumbees. I'm at center (with sun hat); Claudia and host John Rimberg to my right. Pembroke, North Carolina, 1986. Photo by Jack Monet.

XII

YES: A NEW DIRECTION

I and my colleagues, not just those in our "Red" Department, were always grateful to the Polytechnic administration, under whichever President, for allowing us to go our own ways at our own chosen speeds in the classroom and in research, or in our politics, for that matter. Naturally, there was more pressure on the Engineers and Scientists than on us to bring in research funding, but even among chemists and transportation engineers, many admitted they were pretty much left alone by various Deans and Provosts. They and Poly limped along without bagging huge research contracts. Tenure and promotions could be a problem. Actions in those areas could show exactly who was boss. Tenure was a relative breeze for me, but I ran into some trouble advancing to full Professorship. Difficult to say why, since I was approved for promotion by the Tenure and Promotions Committee, but blocked by the Provost. Or was it the President? Or was it just one of those years when administrators felt the door to too many promotions had to close?

Or was it, after all, that our political activity on campus was considered unseemly. I don't think that was it exactly, but I should point out what we "scholar-activists" were up to in those days. No more Vietnam War to protest. In good time Washington established full diplomatic and economic relations with a united Vietnam. I now wear shirts and tennis shorts "Made in Vietnam," and we often dine at the Park Slope restaurant, "Hanoi". *Hanoi.* Remember how that was once a dreaded name in government and media discourse? But back in the '80s, the Reagan administration was not only reviving Cold-War rhetoric, it was putting much muscle into U.S. foreign policy in the Third World. There was covert assistance to the jihadis fighting Soviet forces in Afghanistan, as well as engagement, covertly or overtly, in Central American upheavals. The Civil War in El Salvador and the fear that another Vietnam was in the making brought radical academics into action. I, together with Poly colleagues Marvin Gettleman and David Mermelstein, plus my old comrade Ron Radosh and the journalist Patrick Lacefield, gathered important documentation and opinions for the volume, *El Salvador: Central America in the New Cold War* (Grove Press, 1981). We thought the U.S. public was in the dark about El Salvador and the historical backgrounds that led to the Civil War there, and our volume filled a need; we soon learned that all journalists covering the war on location included our book in their luggage. There was even a revised and updated second edition (1986), but with Radosh missing from the Editors. He was by then well along his political journey to the Right. It was a slow-moving journey with several notable road markers pointing the way rightwards. He was put off by some of his fellow political tourists during a trip to Cuba. Ron was appalled when he learned about the lobotomies local surgeons commonly performed for mental illness, but someone in his group defended them as "socialist lobotomies." His journey accelerated with the publication of his provocative book, *The Rosenberg File* (with Joyce Milton, 1983), which argued, unimpeachably, as later revelations proved, that Julius Rosenberg was indeed engaged in espionage for the Soviets. The response from the Left, Old and New – from his erstwhile comrades, that is – was predictably hostile and quite fierce. Radosh, the traitor, the heretic, the renegade had sided with the inquisitors who sent the innocent Rosenbergs to the electric chair. In his memoir, *Commies,* Ron cites that response as one prompt to recalibrate his political bearings. Moreover, he went on to "consider the ultimate heresy: perhaps the Left was wrong not just about the Rosenberg case, but about most everything else. Perhaps....the entire socialist project was wrong." Whatever fully accounted for the change of colors by Ron and others – there is something formulaically pat, even melodramatic for effect in that explanation I quoted – Ron, post-'80s, became a scourge of the Left, and a prolific exponent of conservative politics in domestic matters and foreign policy. We continue in our friendship despite serious political differences. Not all relationships survive political disagreements, a result I can't abide, as I mentioned above. Rupturing a friendship is so....*Leninist*. Ron lost many friends over the Rosenberg book and his Right turn. I've never forgotten one of our comrades telling David Mermelstein that if he voted for Rudy Giuliani over David Dinkins in a New York Mayoral election, "It would mean the end of our friendship."

But about the El Salvador book. Once again, I had spent much time off my main Russian track, in favor of a form of political engagement that also qualified as a serious academic effort. Sure, in taking up the Salvador theme, I was also addressing Soviet-American relations – "the new cold war" – hence I wasn't totally off track. I don't think Poly administrators looked askance at what the Reds in the Social Sciences Department were doing off campus. In general, they had surprisingly benevolent attitudes towards us. Dean Eli Pearce once boasted of the "distinguished Marxist" Department at Poly. Had he checked carefully when he made that statement, he would have discovered that Mermelstein and I had ceased wearing that label; I think only Gettleman kept it – forever, actually. Leacock and Mage were gone, while Gruber had always fit the mold of the theoretical Marxist, not the practitioner.

In-house radical activity, not politically tinged publications is what I was alluding to above in speculating about the reasons for hitches in the promotions process. There was the time the "Fifth Floor," i.e., President George Bugliarello and his officers, decided to award William J. Casey an Honorary Degree. Casey was CIA Director during the Reagan presidency, and known as an aggressive champion of applying pressure on the USSR, whether it was supporting the Islamic warriors in Afghanistan or assisting Solidarity's struggle against the communist regime in Poland. Bugliarello, a Civil Engineer by training, moved easily in the corridors of University-Defense Department affairs; his affection for the CIA, and Casey, personally, was part of that territory, some of us surmised. Nancy Tooney, of the Chemistry Department, and I spoke up against the award at a faculty meeting. To no avail; Casey got his degree, over our objections that he hadn't demonstrated any contribution to scholarship or higher education.

Another battle shaped up over the "Shockley affair". We won that one, but I admit now to some reservations about our campaign and our victory. William B. Shockley was a Nobel-Prize winning physicist (one of three responsible for developing the transistor), who was invited to speak at a special Poly convocation marking some science or engineering anniversary. Shockley accepted the invitation, gladly, since it gave him the opportunity to speak, as he informed the inviters, on the subject of race and intelligence. *Uh-Oh.* Shockley was by then well known as a proponent of eugenics, and claimed that testing showed Blacks in the U.S. had genetically inferior I.Q.'s. Was this someone to whom Polytechnic was officially offering a public, university platform for expressing what we considered racist views? The organizers of the convocation had been blind-sided. They had simply sent out invitations to all Nobelists in the science and engineering fields. Who knew that this guy would accept so as to air his, in the eyes of the Poly community as a whole, repulsive views clothed in purportedly scientific data? It became clear the organizers were embarrassed by Shockley's acceptance of their invitation, but once he was invited and he accepted, they felt honor bound to swallow their objections and let the invitation and his acceptance stand. Moreover, the thing had become for much of the faculty a free-speech issue, and a matter of allowing the academic *agora* to openly determine the rights and wrongs of a controversial question.

That's not the way some of us in our Social Sciences Department saw it. Shockley was handed a loudspeaker for racist views and Polytechnic should not be extending its hospitality to a racist. As for his credentials, his Nobel was for electro-physics, not for scholarship in human intelligence. Eleanor Leacock, our prominent anthropologist, led the charge. "Happy" – the name her father, the distinguished critic, Kenneth Burke, had given her from an early age – Leacock had researched and written widely on education and intelligence, and, as a Marxist, would be skeptical of any conclusions derived exclusively from innate, not socially determined characteristics. Happy was also politically active in matters of race relations and civil rights; her husband, Jim Haughton, was a militant who worked at getting building-trades unions to expand their Black membership. She could certainly argue as a social scientist that Shockley was really practicing a form of pseudo-science to peddle racist nonsense, and that it would be beneath the dignity of the Polytechnic to extend its good name and space to him. We in the Department of course agreed with her, and so did large numbers of the engineering and science faculties. But large numbers also looked at the affair from the countervailing free-speech angle. Tempers flared at the faculty meeting held to take up and vote on this academic hot potato. "Who decides?!" I remember the Mathematics Professor Harry Hochstadt standing and shouting at us during the debate when the subject on the floor was defining free-speech parameters. Harry, like quite a few Polytechnic faculty, was a refugee from Nazi Austria, and ordinarily a friend of our Department. But he was super sensitive about any restrictions on freedom and open debate, especially in the academy. Happy, however, had another arrow in her quiver. What, she asked the Administration, did they think the reaction of "the community" might be to inviting a racist to speak at the school? The "community" she had in mind were the many people of color – African Americans and others from the Third World – who populated the residential neighborhoods nearby. Picket lines? Violence? Bad publicity, at the very least? There was no evidence to back Happy's claim that the "community" would intervene, but the argument seemed strong.

In a close vote at that special meeting, the faculty came out for rescinding the invitation to Shockley. But, in the end, the "community" threat is probably what swayed the Administration most when they decided to cancel the Convocation. So we were victorious, but was it a mistake to keep Shockley away? That's what I've come to think, not as an ACLU purist that regards free speech as an absolute. Rather, I think we should have let him come, and then let him have it. Surely, Happy and others could have taken him on and beat him at his own game of using intelligence test data to generalize about race. And Polytechnic could have claimed some academic high ground for not having throttled debate on controversial issues.

At the time, I savored the victory along with Happy and other academic comrades. I also felt proud to be at the Polytechnic, where such issues and debates could take place and fire us up then, and later, during the conservative tides of the Reagan years, and where our Department had some respectful standing in the eyes of administrators and the general faculty at this engineering and science institution. Behind my Polytechnic pride there lay the conviction that in my teaching I was reaching out to working-class and lower middle-class students who were probably far more conservative than the faculty. We imagined there was some link between engineering studies and political conservatism, or perhaps just political indifference. That made our teaching all the more challenging. I may have been envious of some of my contemporaries at Princeton (Steve Cohen) or University of Michigan (Bill Rosenberg), or University of Colorado (Barbara Engel) as they prepared undergraduate and graduate students interested in politics and history, even majoring in Russian politics and history, but toiling in the lesser heights brought me some moral satisfaction. At least that's the way I rationalized it. No radical academic should be teaching at an elite university, I remember a member of my Park Slope NAM chapter instructing us. I took that to heart. Besides, we could be big fish in the smaller ponds. For my second go at reaching for the promotion to full Professor, I impressed the Tenure Committee with my portfolio of published work, teaching honors and committee assignments. They also got favorable evaluations from distinguished scholars in the Russian/Soviet area. Steve Cohen was one of them. He wasn't effusive, but complimentary enough. This time, the Administration approved the Tenure Committee's recommendation, and I joined the ranks of the full Professoriate. Administrators may have disapproved of my outspoken, on-campus radicalism, but I wasn't one of those *crazy* radicals (some with tenure) who dotted university campuses across America; here in Brooklyn, I was a solid Polytechnic citizen.

Around the same time, the early '80s, the Russian language could be heard in Polytechnic hallways. The Russians were coming. In small Soviet *émigré* numbers at first, then in big clusters, and finally in post-Soviet swarms after the collapse of the USSR. There is an old Soviet joke: *How many Jews want to leave the USSR*? Answer: *250,000,000*. Vast numbers of the Soviet population would have liked to cross the borders to freedom in the West, but few were allowed that privilege. Among Soviet nationalities, Jews—considered a nationality according to Soviet law—were among the lucky few. Others were Armenians and those of German descent. Permission to leave did not come out of the humanitarian hearts of Soviet officials. Enabling Jewish families to join relatives abroad was the official, euphemistic, reason for letting them go. In reality, Jewish emigration was used as a valve regulating Cold-War temperatures affecting U.S.-Soviet relations. In the warmer atmospheres of detente in return for certain concessions, grain shipments from the U.S., say, the Kremlin could "reward" Washington by relaxing restrictions on Jewish emigration. That was the case in the late '70s, in the Carter and Brezhnev years. When things turned frosty after the Soviet invasion of Afghanistan, and with Reagan in the White House, Moscow tightened the valve.

His image remains undimmed in my memory, that student who was first to introduce me to the new Russian-Jewish wave from the USSR. At the start of the semester for my class in the History of the Soviet Union, I asked, as I always did, to help clear the traditional introductory-class tension, for only those who spoke Russian to stand up. Usually, of course, no one did; just a joke, I would explain. Except this time one guy did stand up; I think his name was Leonid, a tall young man with reddish-brown curly hair who looked around at me and the class, half-proudly, half-uncertainly. He caught me by surprise, but from then on I grew to expect a sizeable Russian caucus in my courses on Soviet history. The *émigrés* flocked to my classes, a chip on their shoulder: What does this Professor know about the place we just *escaped* from? Memories of those Veras and Leonids are indelible. My classes sparkled from our weekly jousts. I was still in my sympathy-for-the-USSR phase, and they outdid traditional Poly students for conservative politics and strident anti-Leftism of any sort, whether the target was communist, socialist, or just liberal. Sergei Poliakoff countered my abstract definitions of socialism with his reality version: "Socialism means shortages of sand in the desert!" Val Berman greeted me, grinning from ear to ear, in the elevator one morning in January, 1985 with his triumphal: "Reagan was re-elected, Professor!" Divergent opinions aside, to my presentation of commonly accepted historical facts, they weren't shy about challenging me with their own critical commentary and "corrections". I described Lenin's return to Petrograd in 1917 and his increasingly radical appeals for mass opposition to the Provisional Government. To which, Alyosha: Professor, you didn't mention that Lenin was a German spy. To my account of Lenin in his last days, commonly accepted that he was a stroke victim, the same Alyosha didn't hesitate: Professor, Lenin died of syphilis. Proof, Alyosha? "It is well-known, Professor." Dmitri rejected my analysis of the Red Army's victory over the Wehrmacht. Professor, he said, echoing a conclusion often affirmed in the West, the German invaders could have won over the Soviet populace if they had behaved less murderously. I was always ready for that one in discussions of WW II. I had heard it often enough from my American students, but it surprised me – maybe it shouldn't have—coming from a student raised in the USSR. My standard reply, and the one I gave to Dmitri: *If my aunt had balls, she'd be my uncle.* The class, the Russian caucus included, laughed; so did Dmitri. (I noticed an unsmiling Vera Polyachek leaning to a neighbor to ask for a translation of what I said. She got it and laughed, too.) Where was the logic in expecting the Nazi invading army to behave other than in the Nazi murderously way to the Slavic *Untermenschen*?

Overall, the attitudes of my Russians were, roughly: This Professor seems to know his pre-Soviet, Tsarist history pretty well, but he's very naïve about the contemporary USSR and he sugarcoats its past. A benevolent mixture of respect and condescension defined their view of me. Describing my trips to Leningrad and Moscow in class always drew Cold-War-flavored queries from my non-Russian students – Was I free to walk the streets? Was I followed? Were my phone calls tapped? Well, regarding phone calls, it's true I was sure to use public phones far from my hotel when I wanted to reach someone in those pre-Gorbachev days, to protect me and especially the recipient of my calls from the eavesdropping KGB. As for walking the streets and being followed, of course I could walk feely, and no one followed me. When one of these exchanges took place in the presence of the *émigrés*, it produced loud guffaws from them. *Of course you were followed*! they yelled in unison. Were they right? Maybe the KGB did keep tabs on me, though I argued they wouldn't want to waste their time following me around. I couldn't convince the Russian caucus of that. Whether they were right or not, their reaction was another example of the streak of high regard for Soviet power and achievement that they harbored, even as they *hated* the system. "You can't *breathe* there," Val told Poly students in class one day. But the Soviet army had no match, Kalashnikovs were the best automatic rifles, the Kremlin could always out fox the White House, and no security agency could compete with the KGB. They also resented impressions Americans had of the USSR as a totally backward land. Several in the caucus told me how irritated they were by Americans asking if there were refrigerators in the USSR. They also disliked the film, *Moscow on the Hudson*, for its scene of robotic Russians standing in line at night for toilet paper. Strong doses of Soviet pride and patriotism were mixed into their anti-Sovietism.

For all their criticisms of Soviet socialism, they were prime examples of some of its benefits, in education, especially. I don't refer to their obvious technical proficiencies in math and science; I spotted Russian surnames regularly on the Polytechnic Dean's List. Their knowledge of world, not just Russian, literature was impressive, and they could speak and understand the analytic language of Marxism as if it properly described the natural way society works – the terms, *bourgeoisie, proletariat, capitalism, ruling class, class struggle, state power, imperialism* needed no amplification from me. When I asked for a definition of the U.S. policy known as the "Open Door" in Asia, Sasha from Moscow answered at once: "The Open Door is insuring that Third World countries are open to the flow of U.S. capital." I couldn't have said it better.

Some of their criticisms were sophisticated and drew my grudging acknowledgment. Sergei, who offered that definition of socialism at work in the desert, also pointed out that communism as envisioned in the formula "from each according to his ability, to each according to his needs" in a society of full abundance would result in degeneration, with the erosion of incentives to work. Yevgeny criticized the Bolshevik power seizure as premature, and he cited Engels (*Engels*!) on the tragedy of a revolutionary party assuming political authority before its time. "The working class in Russia in 1917 was too small," Yevgeny adds, "and too uncultured. So the Bolsheviks ruled by coercion." It's a view I came around, eventually, to support. There was advice, too, from the Russians. One piece I'll never forget came from Dina Yershova before one of my trips to Moscow one spring. With that vaguely condescending but endearing look I grew accustomed to, she recommended I not speak Russian – Russians get suspicious when Americans speak the language, she explained. "So don't be a *spasibo* big shot!"

Those encounters with the Russians, in and out of the classroom, made teaching a more satisfying experience for me. I looked forward to the friendly jousts, and even learning from them. They were instrumental, I think, in dashing some of my lingering fondness for Soviet socialism, and in better appreciating the discontents eating away at the foundations of Soviet society. At the time I tried my best to persuade my young anti-Soviet *émigrés* to indulge in some sympathy for the land they left behind. Soviet Russia, I argued, was the victim of inherited economic backwardness and unremitting hostility from the capitalist world. That produced Soviet rule marked by "bureaucratic distortions," to use a Trotskyist term, which sullied socialist practice. Above all, I insisted, one shouldn't judge *socialism* by its Soviet incarnation. That was my credo then. My Russian caucuses didn't swallow it. I would have trouble with it, too. Later.

Now on my résumé I could identify myself not only as Full Professor of History, but also add "*Spasibo* Big Shot". I disagreed with Dina, though she was expressing that common feeling among ordinary Russians, amped up by official alarms, that—watch it!—all foreigners, and especially Americans, might be in the service of intelligence agencies hostile to Soviet interests. Such attitudes were certainly revived in Putin's Russia. In my contacts with Russians they usually showed surprise, with even a bit of gratitude, that an American spoke any Russian, and complimented me accordingly. That Spring of Dina's warning I agreed to assist Bob Devlin, a Russian historian at Adelphi University, on one of the trips led by him and his wife that shepherded students on visits to the USSR. They, and many other academics, organized such ventures for personal and professional profit, and for adding experience on the ground to students' class work. I didn't especially like the idea of handholding, but it was time for another visit to the USSR, all expenses paid, and it was an interesting moment: Yuri Andropov had just died, and the new *GenSec* was the colorless (and ailing) Konstantin Chernenko, who wouldn't last long in that final phase of societal "stagnation" before Gorbachev's *perestroika.* Educationally, the trip taught students just how friendly and appealing Russians were, but also how far behind they were materially. One of their measures related to food. "I can't believe they don't have hamburgers!"

someone said. I would have picked bananas as a woeful lack. The Adelphi undergraduates were always pleased to impress the young Russians they met with the electronic gizmos they all carried. A young woman watched wide-eyed as a student showed off his portable electronic keyboard: *Chudo* ("a wonder"), she exclaimed.

I used the occasion to get in touch with Roy Medvedev, admired by the American Left for his avowed Marxism and sympathy for Lenin and the Bolshevik Revolution, virtually unique among prominent dissidents, and for his majestic anti-Stalinist study of the Soviet experiment, *Let History Judge*. On someone's recommendation, Steve Cohen's maybe, I brought with me a bagful of stationery for him – small and large note pads, index cards, ballpoint pens, and the like. Another comment on Soviet shortcomings. He accepted them gratefully, but with a touch of I would expect nothing less from my American comrades. Much later, visiting his office at his home, I noticed how neatly he organized his massive collection of research notes. I couldn't tell if my stationery was among them. With Bob Devlin we chatted at length on how politically depressing things were. He was especially saddened by Yuri Andropov's early death and disappointed in his successor Chernenko. Oddly echoing some journalists in the U.S. who saw the former KGB Head as sympathetic to the West (he was said to like Scotch and jazz), Medvedev thought Andropov was quite intelligent, and would have been open to the kinds of domestic reforms and foreign policy initiatives unlikely in an inert Chernenko regime.

Back at Poly, my *émigré* cohort was eager to hear about my trip, ready to pounce on any benevolent report. Of course I kept from them my own increasing disenchantment, that worm eating away at my affection for, and defense of, the place. No, things looked better in the '80s than my last trips there in the '70s, I told them, noticeable on arrival. Things that immediately meet the eye like conditions at the airport, the look of autos, people's clothing, and hotels seemed much improved, as did warmer, but still distant, attitudes of ordinary Russians towards visiting foreigners. The *émigrés* greeted all that with disdaining grins. Sergei, the articulate scold, spoke up. The young American whose economic index emphasized the absence of hamburgers, had his counterparts in Sergei and his fellow Russian-caucus members. They measured Soviet economic levels by a meat index. "Did you see any meat, Professor?" asked Sergei with a *gotcha* squint. I fumbled an answer about eating plenty of meat at restaurants, and about what I saw in the stores my curiosity took me to. "What you saw in those stores, Professor, was what we call 'soup meat,' not regular meats." Before I could respond, he added, "And you were only in Moscow and Leningrad. In the provinces there's nothing!" I didn't challenge that, not having toured those regions myself, but I asked them to speculate on why the leadership would tolerate such shortages. "Because," piped up Roman, "as long as the *nomenklatura* has meat to eat, they don't care about what the people have or don't have to eat."

Roman Litvak was an alert, talkative young math major with a wrestler's build, from Chernovtsy in Ukraine. He was a member, with two Muscovites, Val and Mischa Podokshik, of what I called my *émigré*-student *troika* who always collared me after class for additional corrections and alternative explanations for points I made in my lectures. And also that I wasn't vigilant enough about the Soviet global threat. I had a lot to learn. "Not bad, Roman;" I said in response to his citation of the *nomenklatura,* "that's a neo-Trotskyist analysis," I teased. Trotsky had written about the privileges commandeered by "the bureaucracy" in the sphere of consumption. When once I told Roman that his comments on capitalism and imperialism sounded like Lenin, he responded, "Well, Lenin was a smart guy." That anti-Soviet Soviet pride again.

I described these and other encounters for an article in *The New York Times Magazine,* which won me a few minutes of fame. "The New Wave from Russia" drew many letters, some critical of my clear sympathy for the USSR, and was much appreciated by the Polytechnic community, the administration especially. The subtitle was: "In Brooklyn's Polytechnic Institute, Russian *émigré* students 'correct' assumptions about the country they left." The article also caught the eye of John Rimberg, a sociologist of many interests who had published a book on the film industry in the USSR, and was on the faculty of Pembroke State University in North Carolina at the time. Pembroke State's origins were connected to the need for higher education among Native Americans; the region there was populated by a state-recognized tribe, the Lumbees, after the local Lumber River. Rimberg was teaching a course on cross-cultural understanding and thought it might be a rewarding experience for his students to visit New York and meet the Polytechnic Russians described in my article. Sure, I said when he wrote me about the idea.

We arranged the date and time, I reserved a lounge and refreshments, I asked my Russians to attend, and the "cross-cultural" encounterers hit it off after my welcoming remarks. We didn't have much time. Rimberg scheduled a whirlwind trip to Manhattan as part of the one-day visit, but before they left Brooklyn they extended an invitation to me and my students to come down to Pembroke during their annual Lumbee Homecoming festivities. We accepted, enthusiastically, and for no extra academic credits – only the promise of what was likely to be a fascinating experience – I sought students and funds from them to cover the costs of the trip. Roman was of terrific assistance in organizing his comrades. "Make sure you get money up front from them, Professor, you know how Russians are," he advised. About a dozen signed on and we rented two vans. The traveling party included my daughter, Claudia, and the Monets, our old close friends from Paris who were visiting us at the time, and who were of course intrigued by the idea of heading down to Lumbee country. Jack and Rubye Monet were joined by their son, Paul; Juliette, their daughter, joined us in Pembroke after a bus-ride down. The core dozen asked a few of their friends and girlfriends to join the caravan, so the delegation came to be impressive enough. We planned for an all-night drive to Robeson County, North Carolina, and we let Roman, who boasted he could handle a vehicle better than any American, do the driving of our van while we slept.

In Pembroke we were greeted warmly by Rimberg and several Lumbee families, many of them named Locklear and Lowry. They invited us to their homes where we enjoyed their immense hospitality that July 4th weekend, 1987. On departure, we showed our appreciation by presenting them with a big, handsome *samovar* bought in Brighton Beach, and demonstrated how to prepare tea with it. The weekend was a swirl of celebratory events and pageants, among them—a dancehall party (where beer would be served, one of our hosts, a Lowry, informed me with a wink), a Miss Lumbee contest, and a performance of Randolph Umberger's *Strike at the Wind*, an action drama about the folk hero, Henry Berry

Lowry, a 19th-century outlaw who came to be known as the "Indian Robin Hood" for his exploits. My daughter Claudia especially remembers how proud she was when, as a visiting dignitary, I was personally introduced to Miss Lumbee, 1987, Kimberly Clark, a charmer with long, billowing auburn tresses. The Russians loved it all. And not just the novelty of meeting a Native American tribe up close. A surprising affinity developed between them and the Lumbees. They were in many senses both marginal peoples, often victims, in their respective societies; these Russian Jews and Native Americans told each other of discrimination and humiliations each could identify with. *Pogroms* meet the "Trail of Tears". "I can't believe," Mrs. Locklear, in whose home Claudia and I stayed, told me, "how much our people have in common with your students." My students had left their struggles behind in their birth land by fleeing from it; our hosts were still in a struggle to have the Federal Government recognize them as a legitimate Native American tribe in their birth land.

On the way back home, I congratulated my students on having experienced a colorful and educational slice of Americana. I also complimented them for making the trip, reminding them that Russians, paraphrasing the great historian Kliuchevsky on their history, were a people always in motion. Vadim, not one of my students, but a member of our party, distinguished by his bare-chested open shirt look, was determined at every turn to test my knowledge of Russian history. "You know Kliuchevsky, Professor?" Of course, and I explained how. "Who was Stolypin, Professor?" I told him. "What was *Bloody Sunday*, Professor?" I cited date, year, and circumstances. He threw other historical questions at me, but he stopped them after he asked me to name the author of *What Is To Be Done?* – a trick question since we associate that title with a famous Lenin polemic. "Chernyshevsky," I replied, and I described the novel. I don't think Vadim was showing off to me. Rather it was that strange surprise I have encountered among Russians that Americans might speak their language or know their history. Never mind that Vadim had been told by the friends who invited him to make the trip that I was a *Professor* of *Russian* History. I had to prove it, and it still surprised him that I seemed to know so much about his Russia and its history.

I've kept the "Lumbee Homecoming/ Pembroke N.C." T-shirt, with its profile of a brave in feathered head dress in brilliant red, white and blue colors. A souvenir of an unlikely trek from Brooklyn, New York to Pembroke, North Carolina one July 4th weekend.

My *Times* article, "The New Wave from Russia" was reprinted in a volume, *Jews of Brooklyn*, edited by Ilana Abramovitch and Sean Galvin, and the editors asked for an update on the original article. In "Fifteen Years Later: The Newer Wave" I looked back at that lovable cohort, and described the new Mischas and Irinas that followed. Here's the lightly edited update, which also hinted at my evolved positions on the USSR and Soviet socialism:

> After Leaving Polytechnic, those Mischas and Irinas disappeared from my view, and I often wondered how they fared these last fifteen years. I wonder as well: Do they ever think of me, and our exchanges? Except for a couple of contacts, they have not been in touch. I once ran into Roman, the most colorful of the "troika," when he came by to pick up some documents at Polytechnic. He promised to call, but he didn't. He looked chipper and prosperous, and his two-color calling card showed he was in business, which didn't surprise me. Making it in America wasn't through the doctoral degree in mathematics he once pursued. [Later I learned from Val, another *troika* member who *did* get in touch with me after he found me on Facebook, that Roman was teaching high school math in New Jersey. Val and his wife run a medical clinic in Philadelphia. Soon enough after Val reached me, Roman did, too.] Just after the collapse of the USSR in 1991, I was delighted to get a phone call from Nadia, then a medical student in Florida. She remembered my telling her class once that if ever monuments of Lenin came down, as they already were before the end, it would signal the finale of the Soviet Union. "How right you were!" she told me breathlessly. I wondered: Did she ever get her medical degree? And what did all the others think, how did they all react when the erstwhile motherland they hated and loved disappeared into the history books?
>
> There are new, successor Mischas and Irinas. If the older

group was part of the "Third Wave" of emigration, the cohort that followed was part of a New Tidal Wave. The Third Wave ebbed during the chilly Reagan years, when Moscow blocked emigration. But Gorbachev's *perestroika* and better relations with Washington opened the sluice gates again, and they remained wider than ever in the post-Soviet Yeltsin years. Formerly, the Soviet Russians were a minority enriching my classes; the post-Soviet Russians filled them wall to wall. Of the thirty-two students registered for a course I taught on "Stalin and Stalinism," all but five were from the former USSR. If it weren't for those five, the class could have been conducted in Russian. Another novelty: They came from all parts of the vast motherland, not just from Moscow and Leningrad. Identifying the birthplaces of the newcomers offered a lesson in Russian geography and history: Kursk, site of the greatest tank battle of World War II; Ulyanovsk, on the Volga, where Lenin was born, bearing his real family name; Irkutsk, deep in Siberia. And from the non-Russian former Soviet republics, they came not just from the capitals – from Kherson, not just Kiev (Ukraine); Tiraspol, not just Kishenev (Moldova); Gomel, not just Minsk (Belarus).

They got around, those Soviet Jewish families.

The new students were overwhelmingly Jewish, but like their secularized predecessors, not particularly observant. And they still came largely from respectable social and professional backgrounds, children of engineers and school administrators and laboratory heads. Another constant: they settled mostly in Brooklyn. Brighton Beach and Bensonhurst replaced Samara and Tula in their lives. Soviet anti-Semitism and the lure of a better material life brought their predecessors to our shores. That applied to the new arrivals as well, but from changed circumstances. If post-Soviet Russia has seen the revival of Jewish culture and religious expression, it has also witnessed the flourishing of a rabid Russian nationalism with ugly anti-Jewish components. The new students told me they weren't especially bothered by anti-Semitism, but their parents were worried for them, and for what a possibly uglier future might bring. In the old days, the malfunctioning Soviet economy meant long lines and chronic shortages. The post-Soviet economy eliminated the long lines and shortages, but wages and pensions are low, among other fiscal shortcomings. Old and new, the result is little faith in the future—no "perspective," as the Russians say—so why not emigrate?

The new arrivals were just as voluble, frisky, and engaging as their predecessors; they too had a presence. But since there were so many more of them, they were also much more disruptive in class. In lounges and hallways, Russian remained the preferred tongue. They were born into late Soviet culture, and raised in the dramatically changed environment of the Gorbachev years and after. So while they remembered Pioneers and Lenin Portraits and Red Holidays, they had none of that subliminal Soviet patriotism I detected in my old students. They were still well prepared for studies at Polytechnic – earlier, electrical engineering was the popular major, then it became computer science – and I could still spot all the many Russian names on the Dean's List, but their preparation in Marxism and "History of the Communist Party of the Soviet Union" didn't match their predecessors' facility in those subjects. Generally, they were politically indifferent. We didn't have those animated, sometimes heated political encounters of old. But I had changed too. I no longer hastened to defend the USSR and Soviet socialism as I once did, so what was there to argue about?

Roman, Val, and Mischa would have been pleased to know that.

☆ P★O★L★I★T★I★C★S & F★I★L★M ☆

☆From TSARS to YELTSIN☆

A History of Russia Through Film

PROFESSOR LOUIS MENASHE

SS 161 ★ SPRING MINI-SEMESTER COURSE

May be repeated for credit

Advanced Concentration Course in History

MAY 17 - MAY 31, 1995 --- EACH WEEKDAY, 9 AM - 1 PM

REGISTRATION: MAY 15 and 16, in REGISTRAR'S OFFICE

FILMS TO BE SHOWN:

ANDREI RUBLEV
ALEXANDER NEVSKY
IVAN THE TERRIBLE
PETER THE GREAT
OBLOMOV
A SLAVE OF LOVE
CHAPAYEV
COME AND SEE
SHADOWS OF FORGOTTEN ANCESTORS
RASPUTIN

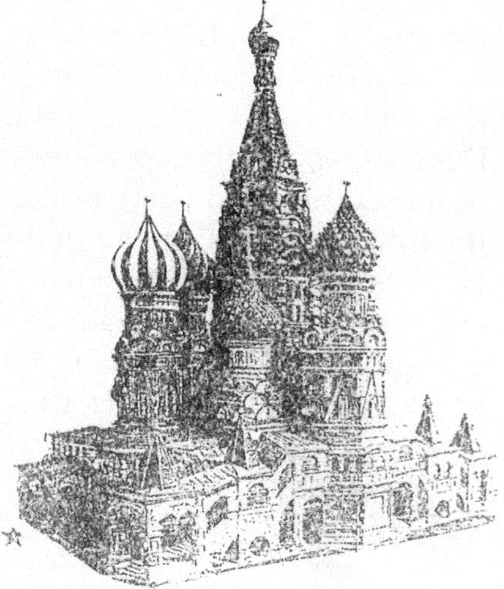

★★★★★★★★★★★★★★★★★★★★★★★

A flyer advertising the "mini-session," From Tsars to Yelstsin, at Brooklyn Poly, 1995.

XIII

ONE THING LED TO ANOTHER: History Delivered in Frames

Before the Russians came, we introduced films as learning adjuncts to the course required of all students at Polytechnic, "Main Themes in Contemporary World History". By "Contemporary," we meant the 20th century, a large chunk of time to cover, not to mention taking in the entire globe for study. We narrowed things down by highlighting certain "Main Themes" – War, Revolution, Capitalism, Communism, Imperialism, the Cold War, the Third World – instead of undertaking the obviously impossible task of delving into detailed historical surveys. It was my idea to start using some films which might be relevant to the themes we studied. Students of course loved the idea (we did, too), but we made it clear that the movies we watched were but one "source," alongside texts, documents, lectures, and the exchange of opinions for exploring a historical subject.

Films were a natural for me; films for teaching, then for formal study and reviewing moved smoothly into my professional Russianist life. My earliest cinema memories ran back to watching, as a boy, old silents of Chaplin and Keaton in my Aunt Mary and Uncle Marc's attic in Mount Vernon, New York. (I loved their home, so different from our tenement apartment in Brooklyn.) Later, my mother, a film *aficionada* herself, especially if the subjects were romance, released me many evenings from Junior High School homework to accompany her to the Commodore or Republic, two of the many local Williamsburg theaters, for the latest Greer Garson or Bette Davis opus. My father, busy in the restaurant and night-club trades, wasn't available evenings, so I was my mother's companion for those movie dates. I remember an amusing detail about one of those films, a misunderstanding that came from my mother's Ladino-inflected English. She told me we were going to see what I heard as "Tweechie Zone". What, I thought, some South Seas romance with Jon Hall and Maria Montez? No, it was a weepy romantic melodrama starring Olivia de Havilland and John Lund -- *To Each His Own*.

I had experimented with the use of film, in a limited way, by showing Eisenstein's *Ten Days That Shook the World* (Russian title: *October*) for the Bolshevik Revolution section of my course on the "History of the Soviet Union." Later, films would become major content for a range of my courses on different Russian/Soviet topics. When the Russian *émigrés* arrived, the *interface* (to use a Polytechnic term) between them and the Russian films I screened gave me a big second wind for my teaching, and for keeping me toiling in the broad fields of Russian studies.

That "World History" course developed three superlative films as mainstays, not only because they had a place in classical world cinema, but since they so well meshed with the themes we sought to illuminate: *Viva Zapata!, The Grand Illusion,* and *Dr. Strangelove.* The film, *Zapata!*, for multiple themes – a traditional society in Latin America convulsed by revolution; revolutionary leadership and the masses; liberal and other ideologies confronting authoritarian rule; the corrupting effects of political power; and more. *The Grand Illusion,* for what it told us of Europeans in the First World War, their class differences, their attitudes about the war, their divided loyalties to each other and to their flags. *Dr. Strangelove (or How I Learned to Stop Worrying and Love the Bomb)*, for its black-humored imagining of thermonuclear war between the superpowers during the Cold War. These masterpieces by Elia Kazan, Jean Renoir, and Stanley Kubrick could not be held up to close historiographic scrutiny without finding major and minor factual errors in their treatment of historical subjects. The point wasn't factual accuracy – that was my job and the function of the texts students were reading or papers they were researching. The idea was to *introduce* the subjects in an appealing way, and to identify the director's point of view as a legitimate (or illegitimate) interpretation of particular historical issues. We were also, incidentally, acquainting Polytechnic students, not normally very culturally sophisticated, with some of the finest examples of film production, and with film as art. We hoped to look at films not just for what appeared on screen, but for what was behind them, the full context – when they were made, the animating issues of the time, the controversies they reflected and confronted. T.S. Eliot put it well when he described a work of historical fiction as "much more a document on its own time than on the time portrayed." The same might be said of historical films. In the words of the critic, Manny Farber, "Every movie transmits the DNA of its time." The selected films could, in the language of historians, serve as both *primary* and *secondary* sources. *Zapata!*, for example, had to be understood as a "document" of its time if we understood how the political views of director Kazan and screenplay writer John Steinbeck affected the personalities and the story lines of the film. Hence the work as a *primary* source for politics and ideology in the U.S. in the 1950s. As for the facts of the Mexican Revolution of 1910 as presented in the film, well, that's up for analysis and discussion. Hence the work as a *secondary* source for the Mexican Revolution and its aftermath.

The films were so successful that we used them repeatedly for the "Main Themes" course, offered every semester. It got so that several of us in the Department who taught the course could reenact scenes and mouth dialogue from the films, from *Dr. Strangelove*, especially. *Well, he went a little funny in the head....and he did a silly thing, he attacked your country....Don't say that you're sorrier than I am, Dimitry!* There was something else about those three films, though I hadn't chosen them for that reason: Each had some connection to several currents in Russian/Soviet history. The overt themes of *Zapata!* were easy to spot in this regard – revolution and civil war, the revolutionaries in power, the roles of leaders and their mass followers, peasants in revolution. As Mexican themes, they all had their Russian parallels. Less visible, and certainly not to students, who tended to understand the film as a tribute to the Mexican Revolution and one of its martyred heroes—it helped that Marlon Brando played Zapata, supported by a terrific performance by Anthony Quinn as his brother—were several of the film's subtexts. Kazan and Steinbeck intended the film as a celluloid polemic against Communists and Communist-led revolutions. Don't follow leaders, they are corruptible, the filmmakers have Zapata instruct his followers. And in the role of an opportunistic intellectual attracted to political power, played by Joseph Wiseman with blood lust and the same dark intensity he later brought to *Dr. No*, Kazan and Steinbeck were caricaturing the Communist Party commissar or bureaucrat. "This is so disorganized….," he complains after a first meeting with Zapata.

A kind of portrait in miniature of the Russian Revolution appears in passing in Renoir's *Grand Illusion*. The multi-national group of officers from the *Entente* side who are interned in the German prisoner-of-war camp during WW I are permitted parcels from home. The French officer, Rosenthal, gets and shares elaborate foodstuffs sent from his wealthy family. When word comes that a big crate has arrived for the Russian officers, everyone expects vodka and caviar, especially since the crate is marked with a big letter "A" – sent by the Tsaritsa Alexandra herself. The Russians merrily lift the lid off the crate with a crow-bar only to reveal an odd assortment of …. *knigi* ("books," they mutter). Just what they needed. The Russians are so enraged by the thoughtless gift that they set fire to the crate and its contents. What Renoir had done here, by design or by inspired accident, is to distill the Russian Revolution down to some of its main ingredients – a disconnect between mass aspirations and Tsarist rule results in a firestorm of rebellion that brings down the Romanov monarchy. Renoir's essentially pacifist film of 1937—banned in Nazi Germany—was released when war clouds hung over Europe and an aggressive Germany might have to be confronted again. Or appeased, as did happen. Would another anti-German alliance include Imperial Russia's successor state, the Soviet Union? See what lines of historical probing Renoir's masterpiece could lead our class discussions?

Kubrick's masterpiece, *Dr. Strangelove,* was no less a stimulant. Obsessive anti-Communism and loathing and fear of the USSR fueled political and military policies in Cold War America. Those policies might be skewered satirically if they were personified in the form of a deranged officer, "Jack D. Ripper," who exercises his self-appointed authority to launch a thermonuclear first strike at the Soviet Union. The attempt to stop him results in Kubrick's filmic mayhem that has Americans and Russians out-dueling each other for stereotypical personalities and behavior. The American and Russian caricatures are conveyed even by their names, which are both hilariously absurdist and loaded with double-entendres. On the American side we are treated to Generals Ripper and Buck Turgidson, President Merkin Muffley, his national security specialist, Dr. Strangelove himself, and the pilot determined to unload his H-bombs, Major (King?) Kong. The Russians are Premier (Dimitry) Kissoff and Ambassador DeSadesky. Leaving aside the Americans featured in the antics, I called my students' attention to the way the (Soviet) Russians are presented. Kissoff is drunk and a bit woolly headed, while his ambassador is elegantly dressed, has refined culinary tastes and a preference for Havana cigars. He also exercises the Soviet habit of espionage, taking pictures of the War Room's "Big Board" with his hidden camera. In one episode the Russians are likened to "a bunch of peons" who couldn't possibly understand the pride of U.S. aeronautical-military technology, the B-52 strategic bomber. The DeSadesky character is not a bad rendering of qualities associated with a member of the Soviet elite. As for the other clichés—the Russian penchant for alcohol and spying, and their technological inferiority to the U.S. – they are not so far-fetched. The point, however, is that they are matched by not so far-fetched clichés on the American side. An equivalence also applies to having both sides doing their best to avert a nuclear catastrophe, which is the main lesson I drew from the film for our students in the age of MAD, Mutually Assured Destruction. They may not have fully made sense of all the sly references, even triple entendres, in the Kubrick-Terry Southern script, as in such passages as General Ripper not allowing "the international communist conspiracy to sap and impurify all of our precious bodily fluids," though the message that we may be Cold War antagonists, but we're all in this together when it comes to averting Armageddon, I hoped came across.

Not surprisingly, students enjoyed all the films – sometimes too much. Martha Livingston, the Department Secretary, used to sit in on my classes and enjoyed the films, too. I told her after class once that I thought I smelled weed coming from the students during the screening. "Oh sure," she told me, "they always light up for your films."

One thing led to another. Presenting those films Russo-centrically, and looking at them from contemporary political angles segued easily into the idea for a new ensemble of history courses for my students—on understanding Imperial Russia and the Soviet Union through film. Initiative for the special format of those courses came from historian Helmut Gruber, like me a film buff who was also interested in cinema as a teaching aid. He figured, rightly, that there should be sufficient time for a screening, which might run to two hours or more, and for introductions before, and discussion after, the film. For that, the "Mini-Course" was the solution. A four-hour daily session that met mornings over a two week period satisfied time requirements for a three-credit course, and accommodated screenings and talking about them. In the early days of the course much time was spent on unloading 16mm films from their cans, running them on Department projectors, rewinding them and returning them to their cans. Later, the advent of videocassettes, and later still, DVDs, made the screening operations a lot easier. (I know, I know, visually, nothing can match *film*.)

It was a really pleasurable and very rewarding exercise for me and my students. The courses generated buzz. The "coolest course at Polytechnic," a young graduating senior wrote me. And when the *émigrés* arrived the courses got additional vigor. I made it a habit to bring refreshments and beverages, vodka included, at the end of the mini-session. Some of the Russians got the idea and brought assorted *zakusky*. Dean Eli Pearce attended one of those sessions. He appreciated the film and our discussion, but left the classroom, shaking his head, the moment I introduced the vodka. He was right to walk out. It signaled to me that I was committing a thoughtless misstep, born of celebratory intentions that also featured a staple of *Russian culture*. Hey, it was part of the course curriculum, I could have offered in defense of the vodka. "Professor Brings Alcohol to Class for Students!" – so might the headline have read in the *Polytechnic Reporter* or in a New York tabloid. Scandalous! After Dean Pearce's walkout, I continued last-session refreshments, but washed down with soft drinks, not vodka. The Russians were disappointed. There was always someone among them who was eager to imbibe and demonstrate – "This is how it's done, Professor!" as he gulped down a shot in one swallow.

The title for the first mini-course I ran in the years-long series was *Russia in Revolution and Civil War*. Introductions always included my reminder that, *yes, we'll be seeing lots of films, but this isn't a "film course"*. Always remember, *this is a course in Soviet history*. Attention to camera work, acting, sound tracks, narrative qualities, etc., is unavoidable, I allowed. I even conducted an "academy awards" session at the end of each course. The class voted *Oscars* or the Russian equivalents, *Nikas,* for "best picture," "best actor," and so on. Usually, my picks differed from theirs. Why, an *émigré* wanted to know, did I like Elem Klimov's *Farewell* of 1982, based on Valentin Rasputin's novella, *Farewell to Matyora,* about the effects of flooding a Siberian island-village to prepare for a hydroelectric dam: the customary Soviet pattern of bulldozing anything in the way of industrial modernization. I told Elena, a computer science major who was positively indignant about my choice and preference for the film, that it was in keeping with the themes of the course titled, "The Last Years of Soviet Russia". Without citing some of the cinematic brilliance of Klimov's work, I pointed out how it showed part of the reason for the Soviet collapse, the unbridgeable distance between the Party-State apparatus and the people it purported to represent. She may have accepted that, but like others in the Russian-student cohort who uniformly disliked the film, the reaction was stubbornly negative. Was it the indefinite and dark ending that turned them off? Soviet film bosses held up releasing the film because of its "gloom". My students' "Soviet" attitudes showing again? We don't know what was happening in that fog enshrouded night of the evacuation deadline. Was the island flooded as Darya and other villagers huddled there, virtual suicides, clinging to their beloved Matyora? My preference, like Klimov's, was let the viewer decide.

That same semester the whole class agreed about Rolan Bykov's *Chuchelo* (*Scarecrow*); they awarded all film honors to the imaginatively recounted story by a schoolgirl of her unjust victimization by cruel classmates, a mean girl leading the charge. *Scarecrow* offers many insights into Soviet life in provincial Russia, even as it hints of a somber time when innocents were victimized by a merciless terror apparatus. For the Russian students, the schoolroom setting was familiar territory, adding to the film's appeal.

Another of my favorites, not theirs, was Georgi Danelia's *Autumn Marathon,* a "sad comedy"—a common Russian film trope, echoing the Chekhovian "laughter through tears"—about a Leningrad academic whose inability to say no ties him and others in his life into knots. After the film, Sofiya, a charming Leningrader, agreed on my invitation to tell the class about her beautiful city and its often painful history. She held the rapt attention of all the young men in the class, not necessarily for what she was describing, you understand. As she walked out at the end of the class, I said, "Thank you, Sofiya." Several young men followed and turned to me, "Thank YOU, Professor Menashe."

Those courses generated good, relaxed feelings. They were ideal, if slightly unorthodox pathways to teaching and understanding Russian and Soviet history. After I warned students that these were *history* not *film* courses, I always emphasized that the films were only one set, for us an important set, of "documents," but that others had a place as well, including readings in conventional history. I also justified smuggling in some classics of Russian literature along similar lines. There were, I argued, different "languages" for grasping historical events and textures of past life. For one course on "Imperial Russia Before the Revolution" we read Turgenev's *Fathers and Sons,* for another it was Chekhov's *Lady with a Dog*. The latter enriched by Iosif Kheifitz's pitch-perfect film adaptation. For conventional history? – Michael Karpovich's *Imperial Russia, 1801-1917*. For the course, "The Soviet Experience," Andrei Konchalovsky's epic *Siberiade* covered the territory, as did in very different way Solzhenitsyn's *Cancer Ward*. His *One Day in the Life of Ivan Denisovich* I reserved for the course on "Stalin and Stalinism," which also featured *HBO's Stalin,* Robert Duvall in the title role. He did a commendable job translating the Georgian tyrant for the screen. Others in the film, as in some other Western, non-Russian productions, led the *émigrés* to complain that the actors "didn't look Russian." But when the film is high caliber and its actors are stars – David Lean's *Dr. Zhivago,* for the course on "Russia in Revolution and Civil War," for example – who cares? In such cases the *émigrés* had the good taste not to complain. No one minded that Julie Christie's accent was more Cockney than Russian. And maybe her Lara could even get a pass as a good-looking Russian woman.

For that "Stalin and Stalinism" course we also watched Tengiz Abuladze's Soviet box-office smash, *Repentance,* which served a couple of purposes. The film's artfully allusive indictment of tyranny, all tyranny – its main villainous character amalgamates several figures, Lavrenty Beria, Stalin's repulsive boss of the secret police (NKVD) plus Stalin, Hitler and Mussolini – is filled with references to Soviet political and other practices. The work was also the flagship for the new freedoms in cinema and the arts in general associated with Gorbachev's *glasnost* and *perestroika,* important topics for discussion by the late 1980s. Many films made before then were brought off the shelves where Soviet film commissars had placed them out of public view. They became available on VHS, were marketed in the U.S. and made their way into my courses. I and my students welcomed Alexander Askoldov's *Commissar* and Klimov's *Rasputin* and they became regulars of "Russia in Revolution and Civil War." Another box-office hit of the period, and popular with my students as well—it captured several of their "Oscars"—was Vassily Pichul's *Malenkaya Vera* (*Little Vera*), set in the director's home city, Mariupol, a southern Ukrainian port formerly known by its Soviet tag, Zhdanov, and now threatened by Putin-backed breakaway Russians. It wasn't just the graphic sex -- a novelty for Soviet cinema -- that attracted audiences and rocketed the film to fame. And sex in film was no novelty for my students, the Americanized *émigrés* included. Rather, the work was a brutally frank description of the cultural poverty and moral degradation that filled ordinary working-class lives in late Soviet Russia. In 1989 I once asked a young Communist official in Yaroslavl, several hundred miles east of Moscow, if he thought *Little Vera*'s portrait was accurate. "One-hundred and ten percent!" he replied. The times were certainly changing. No communist's fudging, hypocrisy or defensiveness; he didn't snap back, as his forebears might have, What about unemployment in the U.S., or civil rights for Blacks?

Soviet war films were always a hit in those classes. I called them "peace films" because their messages were always implicitly anti-war. World War II – "The Great Patriotic War of the Soviet Union" – held a special place in the Soviet film canon. With a ghastly close to thirty-million dead, the war continued to resonate powerfully long after its end, and Soviet directors continuously made features out of a sense of patriotic and moral duty. Their works account for some of the most successful entries in the Soviet film catalogue. During the war directors brought out memorable films like *Zoya* (by Leo Arnshtam) and *The Rainbow* (by Mark Donskoy); after the war there was Mikhail Kalatozov's *The Cranes are Flying* and Grigori Chukhrai's *Ballad of a Soldier*, the latter two were important byproducts of the post-Stalin cultural "Thaw," and very popular with audiences in the USSR and abroad. With fine acting and accessible story lines, they were certainly popular with my students as well. Not so was their reaction to Tarkovsky's masterpiece, *Andrei Rublev,* which I included in the war-films ensemble for showing the unsettled conditions in 15th-Century Russia and for its searing picture of Tatar violence. Not even the synopsis I distributed in advance could help students find their way in Tarkovsky's narrative labyrinth. Some of my friends and colleagues have had the same trouble with the film. The hands-down winner for battle films in the several "Russia at War" courses I offered was Elem Klimov's *Come and See,* which also stands at the top of global, not just Russian, cinema for depicting the ferocity of war and the Nazi way of waging it.

All of those "film and history" courses on diverse subjects drew large enrollments, especially of seniors who needed credits in the Humanities and Social Sciences for graduation. That meant classes were filled by mature students, and they made for mature discussions. Many may have registered for the courses out of necessity but after the two weeks of film and other fare I think they appreciated the experience. I always did. The Russians in those classes were full of advice and commentary – why didn't I show such-and-such, or why did I show such-and such, they wanted to know. Our friend Roman had an interesting comment after watching *Nicholas and Alexandra,* Franklin Schaffner's epic production that conveyed sympathy for the last Romanov and his family. "This film was made by the capitalists," said Roman with a wink, "know what I mean, Professor?" Several students recommended a film I hadn't known for the *Russia in Revolution and Civil War* course, Vladimir Motyl's *White Sun of the Desert* (1969). I was very grateful for that -- *White Sun* is a sophisticated work that folds comedy into the Civil War adventure genre, a kind of light-hearted Soviet Western. It was also a welcome and revealing contrast to the older, and old fashioned comedy-adventure set during the Civil War, the Vasiliev Brothers' *Chapayev* (1934), a favorite of the public in the Stalin years, and of the Boss himself, a film *aficionado* who had final cut on all Soviet film productions.

I usually posted announcements about courses that were coming for the mini-sessions. For advertising the *Russia at War* course I once designed a flyer featuring the famous WW II Soviet poster which has the exhortation, "The Motherland Calls!," and pictures a serious, square-jawed woman looking at you, one arm raised, the other holding "The Soldier's Oath". Mother Russia herself. Across one of those flyers for a Spring mini-course, someone – was it one of my Russians? Hard to say; it was anonymous – couldn't resist responding to Mother Russia's call by scrawling a favorite imprecation of theirs, *Yob tvoyu mat'*, i.e., "Fuck Your Mother!" Ah, those Russians. Was it just an inviting target of opportunity that prompted a spontaneous, irresistible graffito impulse? Or was it some kind of political statement expressive of the scrawler's opinion of the motherland? I spotted that flyer after the course was over. Too bad; it might have been interesting to bring it to class for show and tell. What would the Russians and the natives, but especially the Russians, have to say about that vandalized poster?

All those courses with their film screenings had important side-effects on me. They certainly kept me in the Russia business when, by the '80s, I was continuing to have twinges of buyer's remorse about my decision to go into professional Russian studies. Why not carve out a new niche and *write* about those Russian films? I couldn't write as a film *critic*, I didn't have the training or inclination for that, but I could buffer discussions of a movie with political context or historical background. Soviet filmmakers operated in treacherous territory, subject to the changing political winds of the day. The subjects they chose, and how they handled them had to be carefully vetted by the cinema commissars. What subjects directors didn't or couldn't choose, or what they left out of their films were as important to understand as what finally appeared in Soviet theaters. The intelligentsia and even blue-collar movie buffs among Soviet viewing audiences understood such things. I could help U.S. audiences seeing Soviet films find their way around these between-the-lines matters. My first ventures in film writing appeared on the pages of *In These Times*. I did short reviews of Nikita Mikhalkov's *Oblomov* and Vladimir Menshov's *Moscow Doesn't Believe in Tears*, praising the former (nostalgia for the pre-Soviet past), and panning the latter (Soviet working-class life lacquered with some with rose-color). I was impressed by Andrei Konchalovsky's grand historical saga, *Siberiade,* and heard he was in town to promote the film and to seek Hollywood's interest in some of his ideas for films. I interviewed him—charming, friendly fellow, with the easy manners of one from the Soviet cultural elite—and wrote up the discussion for *In These Times*.

Someone, I think it was Pat Lacefield, with whom I was working on an updated edition of our El Salvador book, recommended I knock at the door of *Cineaste,* for placing film writings. I did, with my review of Abuladze's *Repentance*. It was accepted, and started a long and fruitful relationship with the publication heralding itself, justifiably, as "America's Leading Magazine on the Art and Politics of the Cinema." *Cineaste* is a remarkably long-lived "small magazine," founded in 1967 by a remarkably hard-working and perceptive writer on film, Gary Crowdus. With his editorial team then and now, Dan Georgakas, Richard Porton, Cynthia Lucia among them – all volunteering their labor – Gary has managed to keep the magazine afloat and in high regard on a modest budget with limited newsstand sales and subscriptions. Its non-dogmatic left-wing flavor suited me fine, as did its commitment to examining the social and political fabrics of film production. No film-crit, jargonized esthetic pretensions either. *Cineaste* also enabled me to hook up again with Leonard Quart, my comrade from *Marxist Perspectives* and *Socialist Review*. Len was a regular contributor to the magazine, and a member of its Editorial Board – N.B., *Board,* not *Collective*. No pretensions at *Cineaste,* certainly not under the editorial direction of the no-nonsense and unpretentious Gary Crowdus.

Students with me (2nd row, left). Note the "Stoli" bottles held aloft. At the end of a Russian-film "mini-session," 1985.

XIV

THE FILM CIRCUIT

I began contributing regularly to *Cineaste*—reviews, interviews, short takes and longer articles, and sat in at Editorial Board meetings, eventually getting listed in the mast as an "Associate." I was the resident Soviet-film guru. I had a broad field to cover, from the silents of the '20s to the present. Film people everywhere were always interested in Soviet cinema, one of the pioneers of the new 20th-century art form, and many of the films brought out by Soviet studios over many decades earned a place in the ensemble of recognized global classics. Add to the profile of *Cineaste* readers a probably left-wing disposition which was friendly to the Soviet Union, if not necessarily to its politics, but to its *idea*, and to its side in the Cold War. That was my profile, too. The '80s, when I started writing on film, capped a rich period in Soviet movie production, even though some of the more significant works had to wait until Gorbachev's *perestroika* to get them off the shelf. With certain exceptions post-Soviet films showed little of the quality that marked the work of their predecessors.

That decline plus the depressed mood that afflicted post-Soviet society explained the (ironic) title of the book I brought out after retirement from Polytechnic, a collection of my unpublished and published writing on film, including much of what had appeared in *Cineaste*—*Moscow Believes in Tears: Russians and Their Movies* (awarded "Outstanding Academic Title" by *Choice*, the journal of the American Library Association). The book was published by New Academia, based in Washington, founded and directed by Anna Lawton, herself a superb scholar of Soviet cinema. The book came out at the end of 2010, after two and a half decades of my activity as a Film Person, even as I held my Polytechnic positions as Full Professor of History, was for a time Head of the Social Sciences Department (four years, like the U.S. Presidency), and named Charles S. Baylis Chair in History. I continued to publish articles on Soviet-related themes—not on Guchkov and the Russian bourgeoisie—that were in that mid-range between scholarship and advocacy. But it was cinema that kept me in Russian precincts, despite the fading Russophilia and increasing disenchantment with the Soviet Union.

Academia had its pleasures, but they couldn't match what I experienced as a "Film Person." There was enormous satisfaction to getting a scholarly article or book published, not only for what that meant in the eyes of colleagues, or in the race for tenure and promotions, but for the sense of contributing to the vast body of research and information that brings us knowledge and understanding about ourselves and the world we experience, past and present. There were other endearments to academic life, the travel to conferences in different places here and abroad, meeting colleagues there to discuss shop and catch up on personal affairs, or looking for romance at them, enjoying discussions and debates over pre-Seminar cocktails or post-Seminar dinners at well-appointed university centers, all on the Department tab, the thrill of awakening young minds in the classroom. Yes, academic life offered a broad and rewarding comfort zone. I shared many of its benefits, and took good care of my responsibilities, but I always felt I inhabited its margins. Helmut Gruber was on the mark when he commented that "Louis, you have found your métier," after my doing a turn in documentary film production.

The film world pulled me in, willingly. Thanks to *Cineaste,* attending press screenings in advance of film releases made me an "insider". *Was that Stanley Kauffmann in the seat behind me?* The press kits from film producers distributed at those screenings gave me information the public didn't have, and came in handy when writing reviews. Those kits provide professional film critics with material that enters their reviews, too often without acknowledgement. But one of the biggest perks coming to the "Film Person" is travel to film festivals all over the world. My festival going was limited to Europe. Scholars get to travel too, for international conferences and seminars, but film festivals are something else. Where else would I get to meet Catherine Deneuve and Gerard Depardieu (Istanbul, for the Turkish fest), or Faye Dunaway (Thessaloniki, for the Greek fest)? There was a Portuguese fest in Lisbon, and a kind of erudite festival, the Flaherty Seminar in Riga, Latvia—at the time the Latvian SSR, part of the soon to disappear Soviet Union.

Festival organizers provided air fare and hotel lodging, plus special guided tours to visit the local sites. I sailed on the Sea of Marmora, courtesy the Turkish Film Festival, the closest I ever got to the Black Sea. Of course there was something expected of you from the organizers, an article or a review describing the festival and its films. I attended with *Cineaste* press credentials, which meant the editors there also expected that article or review from me. I always sought out Russian films, but unfortunately they numbered very few in the years I attended the festivals after the end of the USSR. So I had to fulfill obligations by watching dozens of films from everywhere, four or five daily, nodding off occasionally at screenings. But there was always the work of the productive Alexander Sokurov, a virtuoso of post-Soviet cinema. His films made in the Soviet period had been shelved until the Gorbachev reforms. At the Greek Film Festival in Thessaloniki I watched his brilliant recreation of scenes from Russian history (*Russian Ark,* 2002), and interviewed Tilman Büttner, the German cinematographer (*Run Lola Run*) who shot the film at the Hermitage in an astonishingly long, single take. Earlier, I was a regular at the "Message to Man" festivals in St. Petersburg, yearly events originally spotlighting documentary film, but more on that and the experience of *making* a film below.

My most memorable festival experience was the "Transit Zero" film conference, a singular event organized jointly by Swedish and Latvian filmmakers. The theme promoted by conference organizers was "Border crossings," geopolitical and temporal – transitioning, literally, from Sweden to Latvia; and figuratively, from the 20th to the 21st centuries; the conference took place the summer of 2000. Many of the films shown, plus the roundtable discussions that followed, had that transitioning theme in them. Latvian filmmakers, for example, trying to reconstruct their film production in the aftermath of the Soviet collapse now that a free but needy nation had shed its status as a "Soviet Socialist Republic," were very interested in "crossing borders" for funds through co-productions with European and American directors and companies. In the Swedish section of the conference we were housed and fed superbly on beautiful Oland Island, where I walked its rugged barren, "the Alvar," one chilly night. The trip to Latvia provided another kind of transitioning experience. The Swedish Air Force flew us into Liepaja on the Latvian coast in a Lockheed C-130 cargo plane. I gave the pilot the universal thumbs-up before I boarded; he was amused. Our lodging was at a former Soviet naval base on the coast, in Karosta, a Liepaja suburb. Lodging? Barracks, actually. They went back to Imperial Russian times, and were left in shambles by their former Soviet occupants. Some conference participants took one look at them and opted for a local hotel. I stayed. I slept on a primitive cot that might have been used long ago by a sailor in the Tsar's navy. Dinner featured tasteless boiled chicken, rice and tea. At a table I shared one evening with the celebrated Latvian documentary filmmaker, Hertz Franks, he put the wry question to me, grinning broadly, "So how do your American comrades like 'the Soviet Union'?" My American comrades, mostly young, did what young film-festival participants do everywhere, they party after the film screenings and seminar discussions. In a darkened strobe-lit basement in Karosta I did what they did, and I attended and danced at a *rave*, something this New Yorker had never experienced.

I made many trips to post-Soviet Russia, but those "border crossings" in 2000 were my last visit to that part of what once was my chosen world.

The 1980s were a time when film and the politics of trying to foster friendship with the Soviet Union—Reagan's "Evil Empire"—came together in my public life. In family matters, Claudia was finishing college and blossoming intellectually at Guilford, a fine Quaker school in Greensboro, North Carolina, where that famous Woolworths sit-in had taken place. Davey was a Little League baseball player, an award-winning southpaw pitcher for the "Bonnies," a venerable Brooklyn organization. Earlier, I had coached his "Red Jets" softball team, under the banner of Saint Saviour church across the street from our "cooperative" brownstone. Forgive me for mentioning again that memorable Red Jet highlight: Davey executing a rarity, especially for a 9-year old, an unassisted triple-play on a Prospect Park diamond.

Most of the Bonnies by then were made up of young players from the Black and Latino neighborhoods of Brooklyn. In his last year as a Bonnies southpaw pitcher who baffled hitters, Davey was the sole "White Boy" of the team. Once, behind the batter's box where parents congregated for a game, a father asked his wife, *Quien es este*?, looking toward me. *El padre del blanquito*, she replied. ("Who's he ?"…. "The father of the little white kid.") Baseball was good for Davey, a sport in which he showed some distinction. Of course it was awful for our nervous systems when we watched him on the mound or at the plate. He had the energy for tennis, which I encouraged, but not the patience and concentration. That was reserved for Sara, downstairs, who also shared her father's competitive intensity. Mark was a terrific tennis player and a very patient, if demanding, instructor of his children. Sara made her mark in tennis from her earliest years, and later made it to the women's team at Yale. Her brother, Eric, made it to Yale as well, but in baseball, not tennis. Davey made it to the baseball team at Guilford, where Claudia had gone, but he stayed there only two years – as noted earlier, it was, he said, a place for "tree-huggers," not for him. He finished up college at SUNY-Oneonta.

While the "Red Jets" youngsters were developing their playing skills in Prospect Park, I kept an eye on what looked like an interesting political turn in the USSR. A youngish—young by comparison with his geriatric predecessors; and healthy, also in contrast to his doddering predecessors—Mikhail Gorbachev had taken over as General Secretary of the Party after Chernenko's death in 1985. His death was preceded by Andropov's in 1984, and Brezhnev's in 1982. (A Soviet joke of the time: A guard demands a funeral admission ticket from someone. "I have a season pass," comes the reply.) Soon *glasnost* and *perestroika* became buzz words appearing in media everywhere, and needed no translation after a while. I had been so disappointed in my hopes for a Soviet Union I didn't have to keep apologizing for, that this new figure and what he seemed to represent – real, substantive reforms at last! – excited me, you bet. I would have lots of opportunities in the years to come for seeing for myself at firsthand what was going on over there.

Sheila in those days was pioneering an important benefit for the municipal workers who came to "MELS" for legal assistance, and for emotional support from the Social Services unit that Sheila headed. She noted that more and more clients who came to settle matrimonial issues were speaking, usually in whispers and in embarrassment, of domestic abuse. This wasn't an issue covered by the original benefits offered by the MELS program in 1972 and in years thereafter. Thanks in great part to Sheila's efforts and those of members of the legal and social services teams, domestic violence finally became acceptable grounds for benefits that covered its victims. Sheila, as the Union newspaper had it in a photo caption, "Opened MELS to Battered Women."

In certain circles interested in using cinema as a medium for promoting good relations with the USSR, especially when the country seemed to be heading into clearly liberalizing terrain under Gorbachev's leadership, the idea of a "Glasnost Film Festival" was born. One the most active people on behalf of the idea was the late Anne Borin, a New York film editor and a longtime peace activist fighting against rigid Cold-War attitudes. Those attitudes, on both sides, were eroding; even Ronald Reagan was warming up to better relations with the USSR, and to Gorbachev personally. Reagan's directive to him in Berlin – "Mr. Gorbachev, tear down this wall!" – was as politically prophetic as it was simple and forceful. Many of us on the Left had to admit that the arch-conservative President had touched a tender nerve. What kind of socialist society builds a barrier, a crude and ugly one at that, to keep its citizens from leaving? Not too long after Reagan's appeal, liberating developments raced ahead at breathtaking speed. Sheila and I had the pleasure of visiting the defunct Wall of the defunct German Democratic Republic and banging off a concrete chip that now sits on one of our bookshelves. The chip is atop another memento, one we brought back from Paris just after *les événements*, the May Days of 1968, a *pavé*, a cobblestone I picked up on a street in front of the Sorbonne. Such objects were used as weaponry during the protests; they were soon paved over by municipal authorities to disarm the protesters. Of course, we had dug up rationalizations for the Berlin Wall just as we had defended the barbed wire that so rudely confronted us crossing into Czechoslovakia on our first trip to the "socialist" East. By the mid-'80s I was surely running out of rationalizations. And Mr. Gorbachev was helping me shed them.

XV

PERESTROIKA, UP CLOSE AND PERSONAL

Moscow in the age of *glasnost* and *perestroika* became a powerful magnet for journalists, broadcasters, pundits, students, political tourists, and scholars who wanted to witness a major political novelty that had global, not just Soviet, significance. I joined the traffic there, thanks to Ted Koppel's "Nightline" show at ABC-Television. My old comrade David Gelber, now working in television, put me in touch with his girlfriend at the time, Betsy West, a producer for "Nightline," which planned a special on conditions at Soviet television in the changing political environment. David suggested to Betsy that she speak to me as a "Soviet expert" before making the Moscow trip. She called and kept me on the phone for three hours. One of her first questions to me was "What's that word they use for what's going on in Soviet media?" "Glasnost," I told her. Clearly, she knew zero about the USSR, past and present. What I discovered from that conversation, and from working with Betsy and other television producers in the field later, was that they may start out from scratch on the subject they're working on, but that they are amazingly quick learners. They're smart, they know where to look and whom to ask, and they toil very hard at what they do.

Soon after the phone consultation, over my hesitations, she invited me to accompany her as a "consultant" and translator. One hesitation came from insecurity about my *interpreting* skills during interviews. I needed practice. But I couldn't pass up this opportunity to find out what was going on over there, all expenses paid. I met Betsy for the first time at Heathrow in London where we came in on separate flights. Aboard our connecting flight to Moscow she kicked off her shoes and took notes from what I had to tell her about Soviet history and politics, and where Gorbachev and his reforms fit in. She hit the ground running, but I kept up with her when we arrived at Sheremetyevo in Moscow, and afterwards, too. I was 51 years old at the time, half a generation older than Betsy. I was a university professor of several decades, but I wasn't exactly a stodgy old academic. I could run with her and her crew in that hectic Moscow week.

Lodging was at one of Moscow's elite hotels, the National, where Lenin had once slept, just off Red Square. Elite, maybe, but the drapes didn't function in my room, and Betsy's phone stopped working one day in hers. The mischievous KGB, I thought. She ordered me to "do something!" That's what consultants, translators, aka Associate Producers are for. I spoke to a woman at the front desk, half pleading, half insisting that service be restored. It was, later that evening. We spent a lot of time at Gosteleradio, the Soviet center for radio and television production, checking out some of the new, livelier programming, and its producers who were sort of Betsy's opposite numbers. We couldn't determine exactly who made decisions about content for the important evening news program *Vremya* ("Time"), something evidently done behind closed doors, no doubt with input and dictates by the local Party Secretary. Or were the guidelines for picking and placing stories so well internalized by correspondents and producers, that no external word from above was necessary? A combination of both was probably the usual way it worked. A correspondent surprised us with his choice for one of the lead stories after reviewing what we thought were the more interesting ones. He chose something like industrial production in Bulgaria. It shouldn't have surprised us: It was Soviet boilerplate.

The Soviet practice of assigning a minder, part KGB informer, part helpful facilitator, to all foreign investigators was still in force. Our Elena was associated with Gosteleradio; she supervised our scheduling and arranged appointments for interviews or just meetings. My most memorable encounter was with the celebrated pop diva, Alla Pugacheva, in her upscale apartment on Gorky Street—"Brodvay," as Soviet hipsters used to call it. Her place was powerfully scented from the bouquets of roses, lots of red roses, and other flowers on every surface, including the white grand piano.

Her voice was smoker's husky and her eyes were half closed as she spoke to us in short bursts, unsmilingly. We decided she probably just got out of bed after a long performing night only because Elena told her some important visitors from American television wanted to meet her. We left quickly, discretion trumped news gathering.

Among my helpful virtues, according to Gelber when he touted me to Betsy, were my "Moscow contacts." In truth, I didn't have many of them. There were some scholars from my Guchkov-Dissertation days plus a few chance acquaintances from prior trips. No one terribly strategic for Betsy's purposes as we understood them. But there were a couple of my "contacts" we could at least have a drink with and share some conversation. For one, there was my tennis pal, Oleg Smirnoff—as in the vodka, he liked to say—who would soon be a Moscow executive for Pepsi Cola distribution in the USSR. Another "contact" was provided by Jack Monet, our good old Paris friend, who suggested I look up Meg Bortin, Reuters' Moscow correspondent, with whom he had worked at *The Paris Metro,* a short-lived English-language newspaper in the French capital. I called her and arranged for dinner with me and Betsy at the National. Meg Bortin? Of Reuters? – I expected some dowdy English woman in sensible walking shoes weary of Moscow right out of some Graham Greene novel. Wrong. She bounced through the National entrance, young and comely, an extroverted American journalist from Wisconsin. Meg filled us in on the perils of doing news reporting in the USSR, where every foreign, especially American, journalist was suspected of anti-Soviet espionage. Not long before Betsy and I arrived in Moscow, Nick Daniloff, a correspondent for *U.S. News and World Reports,* was arrested and jailed for two weeks after a KGB entrapment. "We arrest your spies, you arrest ours," one of the Party functionaries had told Betsy and me as he flashed a big grin when we mentioned the Daniloff case. *Har-Har.* Very funny. That Gorbachev was in the Kremlin probably had something to do with Daniloff's early release, as did intervention from the Reagan White House.

Then there was "my double," Steve Cohen, who always seemed to cross my path, be it in Moscow or New York. He walked into a lounge at the National where Betsy and I were having coffee, coming in to pick up something to eat for Katrina who was indisposed in their room. I introduced him to Betsy as a consultant for a competing channel, and she later met him privately. Steve was already in his well-honed role as a leading American champion of Gorbachev and his reforms.

I had an amusing encounter – amusing in retrospect—with the film director, Nikita Mikhalkov, at one of the few prime Moscow restaurants in those days, the Georgian *Aragvi*. I told him how much I liked his work, especially his *Oblomov,* and asked him what he was currently working on. *Ochi Chornye* ("Dark Eyes"), he replied quickly, with little expression and no elaboration. I took offense. I assumed he was putting me on, as if I were some dumb American who associated Russia only with vodka and that well-known Gypsy song. Ah, I said, gave him my card and wished him luck. It embarrassed me when I later learned that he really was working on *Ochi Chornye,* his version of Chekhov's *Lady with a Dog* (starring Marcello Mastroianni), and I regretted my (*really* dumb American) reaction.

Betsy and I didn't get a sense of momentous change from the many media people we interviewed and filmed. Television, however, had clearly entered the everyday lives of the Soviet population. At "stand-ups" we did in Gorky Park men told us they especially appreciated TV for *futbol* (soccer) coverage. And from I think it was Oleg Smirnoff we learned that a large number of Moscow apartment fires were caused by exploding television sets. Oleg was then and later a convinced skeptic about the possibility of meaningful change in the Soviet Union, and cynical about the reception to change among the Russian masses. Our *glasnost* and freedom of the press? Sure, mocked Oleg, it's the freedom of those in prison to publish their own newspaper. Maybe we didn't have the time to dig deeper, or didn't dig enough in the time we had, or didn't recognize some novel telltales, but I felt I was pretty much in the Moscow I had known from previous trips. It took another trip the following year to discover the signs of change that led me to believe that, look here, there's something really percolating in the USSR.

I remember being disappointed by the bland Ted Koppel special on "new Soviet television," that was the product of our trip, but it was an accurate reflection of our reluctance to make any dramatic declarations about the post-Chernobyl USSR under Gorbachev's leadership.

Nevertheless, I was very grateful for my experience with Betsy and her crew, especially because it gave me a taste of what I could expect when Marty Smith invited me to join him and Hedrick Smith (no relation) for a big PBS production on Gorbachev's USSR a couple of years later. Betsy and I got along well, and she showed her appreciation for my "expert" efforts with a wonderful gift that kept me warm in Russian as in American winters, a rabbit-fur *shapka* that also added several inches to my height. From 1986 on I was in the Soviet Union so often and at length that it gave Sheila a running line which she always delivered with a bit of an edge when she tried recollecting something that was said or that happened – "Oh, you must have been in Moscow then, Louis…." .

That line, frequently voiced, naturally added to my guilt feelings about being away from home while Sheila managed her very demanding job on top of managing the very demanding Davey, who was experiencing some learning problems in middle school. Guilty or not, still disquieted or not by impatience with the pace of change in the Soviet Union, and uncomfortable or not with my professional Russianist life, I kept turning up in Moscow, and not just Moscow, in the years after the Nightline stint with Betsy. Jimmy Weinstein, ever sympathetic to the USSR and then, like so many of us, excited by the seemingly real changes wrought by Gorbachev's leadership, took time off from his editorial duties at *In These Times* to organize a "fact-finding" mission to Moscow made up of varying shades of Lefties – Joanne Landy, a veteran socialist militant; the writer and Editor of *Mother Jones*, Adam Hochschild, among them—and he invited me to join the group. The trip belonged to the tradition of Left tourism in the land of the Soviets that began in 1917, and in 1987 Moscow – were things really changing there?—it produced a delicious *frisson* for our crowd.

Jimmy had done his homework, and prepared a list of people in Moscow who could be counted as a kind of Soviet New Left active within the still confining boundaries of the one-party state. I was still skeptical, but agreed to tag along as translator and facilitator. True, Gorby had freed the great physicist and dissident, Andrei Sakharov from his internal exile on the Volga in Gorky, but access to the city was still restricted. In the arts, often a source of subtle opposition and barometers of changing political weather, there were some striking developments like the public screening of Abuladze's anti-Stalinist *Repentance*, but only after a debate among the hierarchs about releasing it. But what was happening on the ground that would match some of these breakthroughs? I found out soon enough when I made my first effort to contact someone on Jimmy's list. Clinging to my old, secure ways for reaching people in the "old" Soviet Union away from KGB ears (my Russian students would have laughed at my thinking to evade the KGB), I made sure to use a public phone located out of the usual tourist hotel zones, and prepared to speak in the sort of coded voice belonging to some amateur agent. Sasha answered, but I made sure not to mention his name or mine. I said Hello, quietly In English, remembering Dina's warning not to be a "*spasibo* big-shot" drawing suspicion by showing off my Russian. "Yes," Sasha answered in English, "this is Sasha. Who's this?" I thought for a second to reply with a pseudonym. Nah, if he's open about his name I'll do the same: "Louis," I told him. We arranged to meet. No hiding where or when or why. Later, when I told Sasha, a young journalist with ties to other reformers inside and outside of the Party, of my fears about open phone conversation, he laughed and said mockingly and a bit proudly, "I'm not afraid, why are you?" I made other phone calls, arranged other meetings, and we were satisfied that maybe just maybe *glasnost* and *perestroika* weren't just vapid, PR slogans, and things were really changing.

The big institutional developments would come soon after our Weinstein trip, but given the open reform-minded, even radical political activity we witnessed, especially among the young, we felt considerable optimism about the Soviet future. That telephone exchange with Sasha, a small thing in the wide complex of novelties marking change in the USSR, was an important personal signal for me. At last! – freedom from fear, on both sides, between foreigners and Soviet citizens they contacted. There were contacts and contacts. The Weinstein group didn't have ABC's resources, and we were quartered in the notorious Intourist hotel, on Gorky Street around the corner from the National, but miles away from it in cost, character and reputation. Those in the oldest profession surely always practiced their craft pre-*perestroika*, but maybe more openly now? I couldn't decide if it was another sign of changing times when through our unlocked door of the room I shared with a Weinstein associate walked a young woman who sat down on one of our beds, and waited for a response from us. I promptly escorted her out. Another thought: A possible KGB provocation?

In the Soviet cinema world, documentary filmmakers were leading the effort to bring once forbidden themes before the general public, in theaters and on television. There were film studies of crime, disaffected youth, ecological damage, biographies of formerly un-personed political and military figures, and many other head-turning topics. Back in New York after the Weinstein trip I continued my work with a group of people who were active in a venture that combined interest in film with the quest for normal, tension free relations with the USSR, especially a USSR undergoing positive change. The idea had been born for a "Glasnost Film Festival" that would bring new documentary works from the Soviet Union that challenged old political and stylistic dogmas to the American public across the U.S. I fit quickly and easily into the project. It became a joint venture, as cooperation from Soviet filmmakers and their bosses was essential for getting hold of the films and arranging for their makers – directors, cinematographers, script writers – to travel with their films to New York and to wherever they would be shown. There were many hopeful starts and disappointing bumps along the way, on both sides. At our end, the usual personality and creative differences were a problem. Anne Borin, who was an important figure in getting the idea off the ground, was dropped from the project, by mutual agreement, if I remember correctly. Debates over what films belonged in the Festival, some very heated, divided our selection committee at times. Then, of course, there was financing for the whole thing—publicity, translators, travel and hotel accommodations for the Soviet visitors were the expenses we anticipated. To the rescue came Michael Brainerd, Executive Director of the Citizens Exchange Council, long a respected, well-endowed organization promoting peaceful American-Soviet interaction with individuals and organizations from both sides. A curious sidelight: Michael had been a doctoral student at Columbia about the same time I was at NYU, and his dissertation subject resembled mine, but he didn't choose an academic career. The "Glasnost Festival" brought us together again.

On the Soviet side, those filmmakers chosen for travel to the U.S. had to survive some of the Byzantine power dynamics common to all Soviet institutions, even if this was now the USSR of *perestroika* and *glasnost*. Good standing in Party organizations? Prior trips abroad? Personal connections? Unspoken nationality quotas? The late Leonid Gurevich, a celebrated documentary screenwriter who was one of the energetic Moscow figures on behalf of the Festival, told me that the number of Jews in any delegation had to be carefully measured. Leonid, himself Jewish, survived the intramural Soviet film politics and unofficially headed the documentarians who traveled to the U.S. for the Festival. While I was with the Weinstein group, I took some time out to visit Leonid at his apartment near Mosfilm Studios to discuss prospects for the Festival. Over a bottle of Bordeaux I brought for our meeting, Leonid sounded pessimistic about realizing the Festival. "Louis, *budyet festival'?*," he asked me mournfully, looking into my eyes. I looked directly into his, and answered, *budyet, budyet,* Lyonya. He gave me a reassured smile.

Fortunately, it wasn't an empty promise. The Glasnost Film Festival was a huge success, "without precedent," as a Soviet critic put it, "in the history of cinema ties between our countries." Twenty-two new and revealing documentaries accompanied by eleven of their directors and an official Soviet delegation toured the U.S. at the end of March through early May, 1989, with a premiere at the Smithsonian Institution in Washington, D.C. and a concluding reception at the Academy of Motion Pictures Arts and Sciences in Los Angeles. Soviet documentary filmmakers were "recovering long-throttled voices," in the age of *glasnost* and *perestroika,* as I wrote in the Festival Program, and American audiences could "get an unprecedented glimpse of unadorned Soviet actuality." The films themselves and U.S.-Soviet "cinema ties" were the keynotes of the Festival, but just as significant, perhaps more so, were the chances Americans and Soviets got to meet each other on college campuses and other venues to exchange information and impressions. The Festival, we felt, was doing its bit to advance mutual understanding between the two great Cold Warriors. There was misunderstanding, too. The Soviet side was at times taken aback by what they heard from some Americans, inevitably of Lefty persuasion. During one after-screening discussion of the film, *Tomorrow is a Holiday*, a portrait of a Ukrainian poultry farm whose overcrowded, dismal dormitories house workers and their families, a young woman asked for a "comment on the benefits of communal living." A Soviet filmmaker's answer for her, hand covering the microphone, was "Is she crazy?" Michele Berdy, who traveled with the Soviet filmmakers as Festival translator and interpreter, and witnessed that scene, commented, "On that night, at least, East and West did not meet." Elsewhere in her report, she describes how charmed the Soviets were by American urban architecture, the "tidy homes and yards" of small towns, and nature's glories from New England to the Pacific coast. American documentary filmmakers would have their own turn experiencing the USSR when the Citizen Exchange Council organized a reciprocal Festival the following year, also successful.

Thanks to the Festival, I developed a warm and rewarding relationship with Leonid Gurevich, and with his wife, Sima, and their daughter, Nadya, in Moscow and also in New York when the family emigrated. He – "Lyonya"—died suddenly in 2001 during one of his frequent trips to New York to visit the family. He had valued film work from his homeland base as too important to emigrate with them.

The cinema realm I was now active in gave new life to one of my original motives for getting involved in Soviet studies, that quest for reducing toxic relations between us and them, and for an atmosphere of Mutually Assured Devotion to peace. The Gorbachev wave gave me a needed Second Wind. Would his wave and my wind last? Ah, it seemed that way at the time. My work with the Festival ended on an ironic note: I wasn't around as it flourished across the U.S. I was flourishing in another film project, this time across the USSR.

Street-vendors art proliferated during *perestroika*. I bought this three-dimensional portrait of Gorbachev asking, "Have you restructured yourself?" in Moscow, 1989.

XVI

PERESTROIKA, UP CLOSER

Martin Smith, an experienced and alert television-documentary producer, headed his own company, and was looking to film the exciting new developments unfolding in the USSR. He had shot an interesting film there, an examination of the state of Soviet science, with Loren Graham, a distinguished historian of that subject, as his consultant and on-camera correspondent. Marty knew the ropes about filming in the USSR and working with Gosteleradio. I got to know him not through the Soviet circuit, but through little league baseball – his son, Zachary was our shortstop for the Red Jets, the team I helped manage. Marty, of Lefty and anti-Cold War disposition, was impressed by the El Salvador book I co-edited, and especially by the article I did on my interactions with Soviet *émigré* students for the *New York Times Magazine*.

I was busy with preparations for the Glasnost Film Festival in the Fall of 1988 when Marty called with a proposal. He was about to embark with Hedrick Smith on a major PBS production examining what was happening in Gorbachev's USSR. Rick Smith would be making his first visit to the USSR since he won a Pulitzer Prize for his reporting as Moscow bureau chief for the *New York Times* in the 1970s, and he and Marty were putting together a team for this big venture. Marty invited me to lunch at Fanelli's, one of his favorite SoHo pubs, and he laid out their plans for a four-part series, one hour each on different aspects of the dramatic reforms taking place under Gorbachev's leadership. I no longer had any doubts about those reforms at this point. The transformations in the economy, the arts, and politics were real, the skepticism from some U.S. pundits notwithstanding. These were not just cosmetic alterations with Moscow's PR hyping them. Moreover, from what we heard, and from what we were to discover ourselves, there was a palpably different *atmosphere* in public across the USSR, looser, more open. Dare we say *freer* overall? Over hamburgers, Marty described for me some of his ideas for film coverage of this new Soviet life in the Gorby era. Then he asked, would you come aboard as an Associate Producer? *Gulp*! I sipped my beer, and furrowed my brow as if giving it some thought, but it didn't take long for me to consider the offer and tell him, *Sure*! Mentally, I quickly figured I could do the job – a year's work – as part of the sabbatical I had coming to me. Almost *pro forma* I asked Marty what sort of compensation did his budget itemize for me? He shuffled some papers – also *pro forma*, I think – and gave me a figure that I mentally added to my projected sabbatical half salary. Very satisfactory. As we shook hands on the agreement, he told me that before my "appointment" was official I had to meet Rick Smith and get his clearance. I had other clearances to negotiate.

"Moscow? Again?," said Sheila, only slightly uncooperative, when I told her of Marty's proposal and my acceptance. But she understood the significance and prestige of the project, and how important it was for me as a stimulus for my waning commitment to Soviet studies. "And I thought you were giving up on the Soviet Union and Russian history," she said. All Sheila asked was a guarantee that my time over there would be punctuated by plenty of visits back home. Granted. In fact, much of the work on the documentaries was conducted "at home," in Marty's offices on Lafayette Street, in a building I knew from my visits to the Russian Library there founded by Rose Rubin and her wealthy pro-Soviet comrades long ago. Claudia, in her last year at Guilford, asked for another guarantee. "I hope," she said, in a voice that allowed no disappointment, "that your duties won't prevent you from attending my commencement." You bet I'll be there, I assured her. And will there be time to begin surveying and visiting some boarding schools we should be considering for Davey's educational needs? Actually, that would come later. At Polytechnic, I had to get approval from the Department and Provost for the sabbatical. As with all sabbaticals, there had to be an acceptable academic reason for granting mine. I didn't have to argue much that although my sabbatical wouldn't be for the usual scholarly research purposes, my project was valid enough as it pertained to advancing our understanding of the contemporary Soviet Union. My sabbatical was green-lighted, even enthusiastically by Poly adminstrators. *Did Steve Cohen face similar domestic and academic issues, I wondered.*

I got in touch with Rick and he suggested we meet at the celebrated Algonquin, where he was staying in New York. For some reason—I think it might have been how journalist Jack Monet described him when I asked him what he knew about Hedrick Smith – I anticipated someone "courtly." "*Courtly*?!—are you kidding?," Marty laughed, when I told him what Jack told me. If he smoked, Marty said, Rick would have ashes scattered down his shirt and tie. I understood what Marty meant, even if he exaggerated the sloppy bit. Rick, despite a distinguished career in journalism and as a well-known author of best-selling books – I used his *The Russians* in my Soviet History classes—was a regular guy, and we hit it off immediately at my "interview" in the Algonquin lobby. Among some general exchanges, we chatted about our respective qualifications for the forthcoming on-the-ground coverage of developments and novelties in Gorbachev's USSR. His spoken Russian was rusty, he said; mine was fairly fluent, I told him. Russians, I boasted, often thought I had a Baltic or Caucasian accent, not an American one. How about vodka? he asked – you can't avoid drinking over there if you want to fit in and do as the Russians do. No problem, I answered. Many years later I heard an echo of Rick's reminder from Diana Taurasi, the world's greatest woman basketball star who played for a Russian team: "And you can't not drink," she said. "You must drink. It's just part of the world [there]. Any Russian team: You win, you drink. You lose, you drink."

The next time I saw Rick it was that winter of 1988, in Moscow. Before long we headed down south to check out Stavropol, Gorbachev's home turf. Rick and Marty complemented each other well and were superb partners to work with. They were both six-footers. Marty, the taller and thinner of the two, had handsome chiseled facial features that recalled David Bowie. Rick, as befits his Scottish origins, had a soft, ruddy face topped with straight, lightly colored sandy hair. Both laughed easily, were very sharp (not just about Russia), and worked very hard. Rick took notes on pages he stripped off 4"x 6" notepads he carried with him at all times and wrote on everywhere. Once, from my urinal next to his, out of the corner of my eye I noticed he paused from emptying his bladder to jot down something on one of his pads. He used the massive collection of notes for ideas and data pertaining to the documentary, of course, but they were also his field notes for fleshing out the splendid chronicle he published after filming was done, *The New Russians*. (Like all great journalists, he was a superfast writer.)

Rick outdid Marty in one notable regard: handling his vodka. Marty's cheeks would flush a bright red with just one snort. When people remarked on this, he would smile defensively, "It's the English schoolboy complexion in me." I recall only one point of strong disagreement between the two Smiths. Rick proposed having his wife, Susan, join us in the USSR. "I need her with me," Rick said. Marty thought it was a bad idea: "You don't bring your spouse to the office," he would say. Rick held his ground, and Susan joined us. She was personable, easy to get along with, and often displayed an amusing curiosity and amazement about what she was seeing and experiencing. "Red Square, wow!" just like any American tourist, not the wife of a well-known, prize-winning journalist, one of whose specialties was the USSR. She was fun to be with, and shared some of my adventures—with Soviet security—in one incident.

In the old days, pre-Gorby, there were stories about foreigners, Americans in particular, having anxiety attacks and general emotional discomfort as visitors to, or living in, the USSR. Even with Gorby. Betsy told me someone at the ABC Moscow bureau suffered a nervous collapse and had to leave the country. An Intourist guide once explained to me that it was American visitors who were most prone to anxiety attacks and even breakdowns. Dark tales about Soviet totalitarianism had something to do with it. That Big Brother was always watching you led to a kind of persistent low-level unease, even paranoia for some. The absence of simple amenities added to the disquiet. There wasn't a corner drugstore open all night where you could pick up some dental floss, or a nearby café or diner to grab a quick bite after hours. Language was a barrier. And meeting locals was a big problem. Much of this changed with *perestroika*. One major difference was a dramatic relaxation in U.S.-Soviet relations, and with it the feeling, a hope, even a certainty, that the USSR was now a friend, not a foe; that transformations wrought by *perestroika* would also make the land more amenably "Western," more "European". I got an astonishing answer from a floor lady at the Hotel National to the question I posed everywhere and to everyone: What's the most important change you've noticed since 1985? She replied at once, inverting the usual formula: Americans were not so frightened here anymore. She illustrated by making a gesture of someone looking suspiciously over his shoulder. No more of that, she said. Someone else, an office worker in Yaroslavl, told me, "Just being able to meet you and talk to you, a foreigner, is the biggest change."

Above, I used dental floss as emblematic of the eternal Soviet condition of consumer shortages (the *defitsit* problem), the things that, as Russians mourned, were available everywhere else in the world, in "normal" societies. The banana is another emblem that reflects Soviet shortages and consumer yearning. Back in the old days I remember strongly missing bananas, my usual daily source of potassium at morning breakfast. Once, doing as Russians do, I got on it when I saw a line somewhere in Moscow. I had with me, also as Russians always had, a small bag, an *avoska,* "just in case". *Bananas*! They were small and greenish, from Cuba, I think, and I bought half a kilo. They were a big disappointment, inedible, hard as rocks. Maybe passable fried, but I didn't have time to turn them over to Russian friends. Anya von Bremzen reminds us, in her superb memoir, *Mastering the Art of Soviet Cooking,* that "a story about Soviet food is a chronicle of longing, of unrequited desire …. a simple banana – a once-a-year treat back in the USSR – still holds an almost talismanic sway over my psyche." In his amusing memoir, *Little Failure,* another *émigré,* Gary Shteyngart, reports his father's amazement at coming upon bananas in Vienna on their way to the U.S., a "miracle," he said, "a banana. Who has ever heard of bananas in winter?"

I can't resist citing more evidence and testimony about the power bananas exerted in the Soviet experience – in their absence, when they turned up, and for other reasons. Maria Baibakova, daughter of an oligarch and herself prominent in the art world, remembers tasting her first banana at 5: "It took me half an hour to eat it because I would bite it off in really, really small bites to get the taste out of it." Serafima Leyfman, an emigrant living in Brooklyn, describes treating a banana as a delicacy: "We might spend a week eating it." On the ugly side, bananas serve as symbols certifying Russian racist credentials. In soccer matches Russians habitually throw bananas at Black players. Irina Rodnina, an Olympic Gold-Medal ice-skating champion, once posted a photo on Twitter doctored to show President and Michelle Obama gazing at a banana offered by a white hand. In the Perm region recently, a banner in public display pictured a greedy looking Obama staring at a banana marked "Ukraine".

Bananas in other roles: here are two incidents they figure in, from different angles. In St. Petersburg, after the Soviet collapse, I spotted some peels on the *Nevsky Prospekt* sidewalk, and kicked them away off the curb into the street, for obvious pedestrian safety reasons. "Remarkable," commented the Russian scholar I strolled with, "I understand why you did that," she said, "but a Russian never would have done it." (That statement belongs to another category describing Soviet life, carelessness about collective concern in the society purportedly committed to collectivist values.) At St. Petersburg's *Dom Kino,* the city's central film establishment, sometime in the Yeltsin 1990s, I teased a cinema journalist about her skepticism in regard to the new post-Soviet freedoms and transformations. "Look," I said, "you now have bananas!" "Yes," she shot back, "that's about all, unfortunately!"

In Moscow our PBS team was assigned – the old system still prevailed—our Gosteleradio minder, once again Elena, our Elena of the ABC documentary a year earlier, remember her? I got to know her well enough that she introduced me to her young son, who remembered me as *Dyadya Looey* ("Uncle" is commonly used in friendly respect). Elena ran into a couple of problems with our new team. The other Associate Producer working with us, Natasha Lance, complained about Elena's body odor, and kept her at a distance. Natasha had a point, but Rick and I didn't mind. I once told Bernie Koten after my early visits to the USSR that I was aware of a distinct scent in crowded metro cars. Bernie, who used to run the old Russian Library on Lafayette Street, was a seasoned Moscow visitor and he insisted the scent emanated from collective body odors of the unwashed public. Did Elena belong in that cohort?

Elena may have noticed Natasha's aversion, but said nothing. She did complain, however, when we told her once to get lost before a scheduled interview. We felt we were breathing the freer air of *glasnost* and *perestroika*, and could take liberties with archaic institutions like assigned (KGB) minders. A dissident we were interviewing would surely feel inhibited by Elena's presence, knowing for certain she was a KGB asset whose job it was to report on the interview. "I never heard of such a thing," Elena protested, "no one has ever treated me like this before." We spoke Russian and did our own translating, we told her, so what was the point of her presence, as if we didn't know.

Elena, we figured, reported this breach of customary Soviet practice. But there were no after effects from our sidelining her, no cancellation of visas, not even an official reprimand. The absence of such measures meant things were really changing. The four of us, Rick, Natasha, Elena, and I made it amicably to and around Stavropol that winter. Of course we were met there by the local Gosteleradio representative, a jolly Zhenya who promised us a hearty reception in Gorbachev's native village when we returned for filming. Stavropol was a handsome provincial town with an impressive scenic overlook, and untouched by overbearing modern Soviet architecture. Rick jogged on a frosty morning while we walked the un-cleared icy streets. Zhenya's hospitality extended to having a local sauna opened especially for us one evening. It was a first for me. After enduring the invigorating heat, I declined to plunge into the waters of the adjoining pool; Natasha did, with an ear-piercing scream when she hit the water. No vodka that evening, but plenty of it flowed after our filming in the region the following spring.

At a Stavropol movie theater we noticed Pichul's *Little Vera* was playing, the film we had heard so much about, that, like Abuladze's *Repentance*, was drawing global attention and big box-office activity in the USSR for daring to take on once-forbidden subjects. We didn't have time to see it at the Stavropol theater, but I asked the middle-aged woman selling tickets if she had seen the film, and what did she think of it. She had; she shrugged and said unsmilingly, "*protivny*" (disgusting; repulsive). That reaction contrasted with the response of a young Communist official mentioned above who thought its depiction of sordid working-class life in Mariupol was

"110 per cent" accurate. On another occasion, later in Leningrad, a cabbie agreed about the accuracy, but complained, Who wants to see that stuff in a movie? "We have enough of it in real life!"

That spring we filmed in Privolnoye, the village where Gorbachev was born and raised. The local Party organization treated us to a sumptuous banquet with, we assumed, local and regional officials. The feast took place around "Victory Day," May 9, the date of the German surrender and the end of the Great Patriotic War. Rick quite properly thought to offer a solemn toast honoring the great Soviet sacrifice, and the victory over Nazi barbarism. I too raised my vodka, seconding Rick's remarks and expressing gratitude for the gracious and generous reception we were accorded. Those at the table numbered about a dozen men apart from the American filmmaking group, and I was surprised by their impassive faces and their failure to reciprocate or offer friendly comments of the sort that thanked us for remembering, or that complimented us on our Russian, or how much we welcome U.S. visitors. A couple of years later I watched another documentary on Gorbachev, not ours, that had a scene of a banquet in the same place where ours was held, and around the table sat, I would swear, the same impassive figures. Clearly, this, like ours and probably many others, was a well-rehearsed event of feigned hospitality staged for visiting filmmakers for political purposes. A kind of *Potemkin Village* scene, you might call it, or an example of *Pokozukha*, as the Russians call the phenomenon, "for show". Just a guess, but those stolid guys were probably bored from having to attend these numerous events, or perhaps they included local *KGBistas* annoyed to be called out for tame work not in their line.

While we were in the region, the North Caucusus, we decided to film in Kislovodsk, one of the many sites in the area famous for spas and their curative waters. Party big-wigs from Moscow came down there for R &R, and it was the local Party chief for the Stavropol *krai* (region), who was responsible for greeting them and arranging everything for their comfort. That's how Gorbachev, then Stavropol boss, caught Andropov's attention when the General Secretary came down for a visit. In one of the grand hallways at one of the majestic spa buildings, our cameraman, Jean de Segonzac, wanted to film the big space in a tracking shot, and asked me to get him a carriage of some kind to carry him and his Beta-Max videocam the length of the hall. I asked one of the workmen there for a *kolyaska*, and he promptly brought out a large dolly. Jean had his tracking shot. I cite this incident as an example of one of the very many and very diverse tasks in the Associate Producer "job description." I translated; I ordered food and drinks; I suggested stories and planned for the interviews and filming to bring them to life (the mandate of the documentary filmmaker: "tell a story"); I booked hotels for us; I made zillions of phone calls to people connected to prospective stories; I did pre-interviewing in preparation for the on-camera interview; I attended big Moscow rallies of the democratic opposition and interviewed a young activist, Boris Kagarlitsky, on camera at one of them, and asked for an interview with Boris Yeltsin at another. (He turned me down, saying he already gave one to American television – but this is for American *public* television, I pleaded, to no avail); at an important open meeting between officials and residents of Moscow's Brateyevo district, Marty asked me to direct the shoot with a Soviet crew while he and our crew were busy elsewhere. Soviet television journalists and crews envied our Beta-Max; the Brateyevo meeting was shot with their camera, and you can spot the decline in quality of that sequence in Part I of *Inside (A Taste of Democracy)*; and because Marty and sound engineers thought I had a good voice, I supplied the English that dubbed the Russian of several speakers in the documentary; when Sergei Stankevich, a liberal-minded Deputy to the new Congress who was featured in Part I of our film, came to the U.S., Marty asked me to be his personal guide. Our travels took us to Los Angeles for a media convention, where part of our documentary was previewed, and to Washington, where we had an informal lunch at the office of Senator Bill Bradley, who was fascinated by the democratic directions the USSR seemed to be heading in.

That's a pretty good list of some of the many tasks expected of the Associate Producer. I worked hard; we all did. But I learned the prevailing motto was "Work Hard, and Play Hard!" Nothing debauched, of course. Rick and I had our tennis racquets with us, but we never found the time to get on some courts. We heard that Yeltsin was a tennis aficionado, and invited him to hit with us (and be filmed), but he declined. I jogged a lot, as did Rick. Dining and the vodka that fueled conversation and high spirits after a day's work were a must. After the Privolnoye, then Kislovodsk shoots, we repaired to a big and crowded restaurant in the latter. After some *zakusky* and a round of our own drinks, a man, clearly local, approached our table. Swarthy, smiling, he asked for confirmation that we were an American television crew, identified himself as a *Karachai,* and ordered vodka and *konyak* for the table. He suggested we come and film in his native *Karachai-Cherkess Autonomous Oblast,* so that the West might learn of conditions there and (we inferred) support a movement for greater independence from Moscow. We thanked him and said we might try to visit someday. The disputed territory of Nagorno-Karabach in nearby Armenia figured in Part IV of the documentary, *Coming Apart,* on political turbulence in the non-Russian republics.

Soviet citizens with a cause who approached us hoping for publicity was a common occurrence in the new *glasnost* environment. I remember several women cornering me at the entrance to Gosteleradio headquarters, pleading for camera time for some religious issue. They recognized me from our work on the controversial hunger strike conducted on the steps of the "Red Church" in Ivanovo.

Rick described his delighted surprise when he and Marty were doing some experimental filming not far from the Kremlin in Moscow, on the Great Stone Bridge in preparation for later work on the documentary. He remembered the days in the 1970s when people shunned reporters and their questions, and wondered if the strollers on the bridge would react the same way. Marty's camera would surely scare them away, he feared. But no; they and the camera were magnets for the strollers who soon gathered around them and, after some courteous remarks about Reagan's visit, began pouring out their complaints on shortages, housing, and health care. Rick's Moscow visit after 14 years, heralded, he understood, a voyage of discovery in the decidedly novel Soviet environment.

After our merry dinner in Kislovodsk we piled into our van, handled by our designated driver, and headed back to Stavropol, singing all the way. Zhenya provided the Russian ballads, we contributed American pop and folk songs. *Work hard; play hard.*

Sheila frowned when I told her we would be returning to Stavropol in the Spring of 1989 for filming. She and Claudia both suffered from bouts of anxiety whenever I spent time in the USSR, even if it were Gorbachev's USSR. Davey wasn't subject to that malady. Once, in the 1970s Sheila called the Astoria Hotel in Leningrad where I was staying, and was told no one with the name Menashe was registered there. *Panic*! She got in touch with our friends, Jonathan and Jane Harris, scholars and old Soviet hands, and asked for help in locating me. They tried to reassure her that it was probably a case of a typical Soviet screw-up, but they went so far as enlisting the U.S. Consulate in Leningrad in the hunt for Louis Menashe. But then Jane called the Astoria again for Sheila, and this time they placed me there. We even talked, and she calmed down. We were in Stavropol on December 7, 1988 when an earthquake of "devastating" intensity struck nearby Armenia. Claudia, in Greensboro, North Carolina for her final year at Guilford College talked by phone to Sheila in New York, with maps of the USSR in front of them, wondering if I was anywhere in earthquake proximity. *Uh-oh*. Claudia told Sheila that Stavropol is "not far" from Spitak, the earthquake epicenter. She exaggerated; Stavropol's "not far" actually was over 300 miles north. They followed news reports closely, but Stavropol was never mentioned in accounts of the earthquake. They relaxed. Especially after I called from Moscow when we flew back.

A word on vodka consumption described frequently in these pages. As Rick pointed out when we first met, and as I knew, imbibing was unavoidable. It was the alcohol of choice – 100 grams, please – at restaurants, at homes for dinner invitations, at snacks after a hard day's night of filming and interviewing, at celebrations and banquets of every kind, from birthdays to film openings. I could handle the stuff, but I couldn't match some Russians. I gasped as a guy at a nearby table in a Hotel National restaurant chug-a-lugged a full half-liter bottle, a common size, without a pause to catch his breath. "Bravo, Sasha!," his table companions shouted, alarmingly in my mind. That could have killed him, I shouted in turn. They didn't hear me, and I didn't press the issue. I enjoyed vodka, and almost never drank it in excess. Once in Leningrad, though, I literally miscalculated a date in the foggy aftermath of an evening's multiple toasting, and turned up hours late for a dinner appointment. Greg Guroff, a Russian historian of my generation who had worked at the U.S. embassy, and was a consultant for WGBH, the Boston PBS affiliate, on our project, often arranged meetings with his contacts for interviewing and filming. I noticed that Greg always declined invitations to down some vodka when it was offered at some of those sessions. I asked him why. "It would kill me," he replied, explaining that if he accepted all those invitations proffered often and almost daily in his work, it would do very serious damage to his liver.

For me, vodka and its buzz had the added benefit of calming the Essential Tremor that frequently shadowed me. There was a hitch, however. Russians, at home especially, usually serve the beverage in small, delicate glasses, *riumki*. In receiving or picking up one of those filled with vodka my hand would visibly shake, causing some embarrassment for me, and some concern from the hosts. At bars and restaurants I would request a sturdy, tall glass for my drink. No shakes then. At a dinner with Marty and Rick for the filmmaker Vasily Pichul (*Little Vera*) and his wife, Maria Khmelik (who scripted the film), we rose for a toast to their success, *riumki* in hand. My hand shook as I clinked the others' glasses. "Steady there," Rick said, kindly. It ruined the pleasant evening for me; it's something I haven't forgotten, you notice. I guess I could have followed Greg's abstinence model, and always requested mineral water in place of the "little water" (*vodka*, literally). Well, that would have killed half the fun and chummy warmth of the whole enterprise.

The Moscow atmosphere when we returned from Stavropol was electric, as it was throughout the Soviet Union. Elections had been held nationally for delegates to a Congress of Peoples' Deputies. The elections were historic, the first really free, competitive balloting since delegates were elected to the short-lived Constituent Assembly of 1917, closed down by the new Bolshevik government after a few sessions. The Communist Party, heirs of the Bolsheviks, had a strong showing, especially in the provinces, where some ballot stuffing probably took place, but the elected deputies numbered scores of figures who voiced dissent and opposition, from inside and outside of the Party, from Yeltsin to Sakharov. People were glued to their TVs, watching in disbelief as speakers offered politically charged criticisms and raised controversial subjects openly and fearlessly at the Congress *in the Kremlin*. I used to do morning runs along the Kremlin walls, an exciting enough exercise (the walls of the *Kremlin*!), but it was even more exhilarating to freely enter those walls with my Ministry of Foreign Affairs Press Center credentials, issued as a representative of *Pee-Bee-Ess*, to witness the historic goings on at the very historic Congress. For a Kremlin interview with some deputy minister or other, I even got to sit at one of those green-baize covered tables described by many a journalist and memoirist.

The televised Congress, the Congress itself, the publication of non-conformist periodicals like *Ogonyok* and *Moscow News*, the appearance of formerly taboo films and literature, the broadcast and popularity of pioneering television shows like *Fifth Wheel*, the visible cracking of the once "monolithic" Party, and – most of all, really, the *free atmosphere* enveloping all of this, restored my faith in the inevitability of positive, long-lasting change that would move this place to real socialism. And might move me back into serious Soviet Studies. And the newly untarnished socialism of the USSR might even give a leg up to socialist movements in the U.S. This Gorbachev phenomenon promised so much more than the Khrushchev thaw and reforms, puny by comparison, and short-lived, in any event, crushed by the Brezhnev reaction and the "stagnation" (*zastoi*) that ensued.

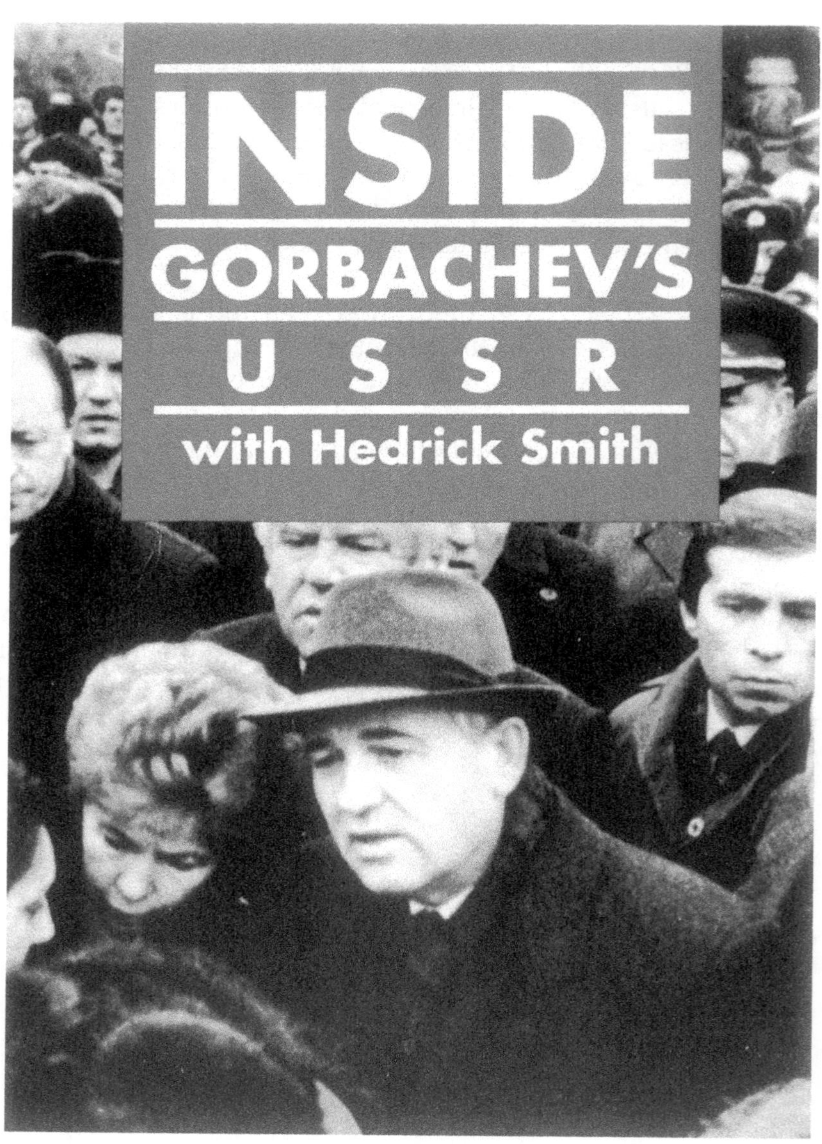

Publicity card for *Inside Gorbachev's USSR with Hedrick Smith,* 1990.

XVII

FROM THE BOTTOM UP

One of my first, very pleasant, surprises, of the *Inside* trip came when I walked out of our Intourist Hotel on Gorky Street late one morning, and was greeted by what we called back home a *demo*, of some size, young people mainly. What's that about?, I asked a *militsioner* (policeman). *"Mitting,"* he replied, using the word for demonstration; he said it with a shrug and a kind of *what else?* smile that told me this is what goes on these days. *Amazing*! A big demonstration, a Soviet citizens' demonstration, not an officially organized one for official purposes, an officially *tolerated* one on an important boulevard a stone's throw from the Kremlin. It was one of the many I've got to pinch myself moments that followed. Too bad Rick and Marty and the camera crew were elsewhere. Rick would have termed this, as he was to do often during filming, a clear result of an energetic Gorbachev rousing a historically dormant population. We had lots of discussions about this. He emphasized the passivity of the Russian people; I disagreed with that kind of generalization, and kept citing instances when the opposite was true.

As for this big demo, it certainly couldn't have taken place at any other time in Soviet history after Lenin and before Gorbachev. But it wasn't grateful to the promoter of *perestroika* either. One guy held up a sign reading, in English, "Gorbachev is A Talking Machine." Why do you think that? I asked him. "He's just a chatterbox, that's why," he answered. More rhetoric than real reform. There may have been traces of condescension and mockery in that assessment as well. As we learned soon enough, undercutting the image we had back home of Gorbachev as an eloquent statesman-leader beloved by the Soviet masses, he was often ridiculed for his

Southern hillbilly accent, and for his tendency to run on and on. My Russian-*émigré* friend Artyom Englin put it this way: When Gorbachev speaks about something, he goes around it, beside it, under it, through it, on top of it, but never directly to the point of it. As for the Soviet masses, it didn't help their regard for him when early on Gorbachev instituted strong anti-alcohol measures. Production cutbacks, limiting sales hours, etc. The oft-told joke I heard there and from *émigrés*: A guy can't stand waiting any longer on an endless line for vodka, and announces he's going to shoot Gorbachev. He returns soon after, abjectly: The line was longer there.

That demo on Gorky Street calling for widening political reforms before elections to the Congress of Peoples' Deputies was one of many instances, great and small, of *perestroika* from below, the really astonishing phenomenon of the Gorbachev years that we witnessed and filmed. One materialized in the Moscow "microdistrict" of Brateyevo; another on the steps of a church in Ivanovo.

As I've mentioned, much of the work for the documentary was done at the headquarters of Martin Smith Productions on Lafayette Street in the building that once housed the Russian Library. I spent many an hour there in my Monitor Record days researching Moldavian or Tadzhik culture for the liner notes I wrote that backed the LPs of the music from those Soviet Republics brought out by Monitor. I hadn't worked in an office and kept office hours since full-time graduate work closed my career at Monitor. As faculty, my university office, where I prepared lectures, graded papers, and met students, had a certain relaxed *academic* flavor; a "real-world" office working on pre-production for a documentary was different. The setting meant business, but it also involved creativity. Marty had an easy style as a boss overseeing a staff made up of aspiring young filmmakers who also knew how to send out a telex to Moscow. A film editor was part of the team, and, I discovered, a more important component of the project than I had known. At her console working on the tapes fed to her after we returned from over there, she was every bit a creative and decision-making part of the filmmaking team as Marty the director, Rick the correspondent, or the film crew out in the field, and me, the Associate Producer. Sharon Sachs was a quiet, very capable editor and an impressively dilligent worker. I still picture her eating her lunch at the console table. The *auteur* theory of filmmaking has its merits; clearly, Marty put his own, distinguishing stamps on that end product, *Inside Gorbachev's USSR*, for which he was Executive Producer over all four parts, and Producer of Part I, but I came away from the whole experience with the conviction that filmmaking, both documentaries and features, was very much a collaborative effort, with input from different sources.

I loved showing up at Marty's offices every weekday morning, and working into early evening. That schedule mirrored Sheila's at MELS; there wasn't the flexibility and luxury of my academic calendar, but with help from Davey's sitter, Rose Duggins, we managed the household regime. On one of those mornings at Lafayette Street, the Worm of that Kremlin night long ago made another of its frequent, gnawing appearances. Maybe this is what I should have been doing, working in film instead of toiling in the Russian precincts of academe? Well, in a way I was doing both with this present project since it had the USSR as its focus; I was a Russianist-cum-Sovietologist, remember. As such, my professional background assisted Marty and Rick (and Sherry Jones: see below), while I in turn benefitted from a wealth of experiences in Gorbachev's USSR on the ground different from what I might have gathered as a scholar researching in libraries and archives. Actually, researching a story for the documentary was not all that different from investigating a subject for an article or for a lecture in my teaching, but ah, it was so much more exciting to be filming. Get thee behind me, Worm, or else I might flee academia; the present arrangement suited me just fine. What's more, there was a nice, hopeful political twist to it all. Soviet socialism, Russian studies, working to change America was the mash-up that set me on my professional-political path. Disillusion with Soviet socialism contributed to some of my disaffection for Soviet studies, and took some starch out of political work – not only was Guchkov irrelevant, but over time Lenin joined him in irrelevance. But now, thanks to the General Secretary from a village in Stavropol *krai*, and the reforms he fronted and symbolized, Soviet socialism was acquiring a human face. It seemed finally to be on the right road, comrades; it might become the model we thought it was long ago. Such considerations – boy, was that wishful thinking, as it turned out—energized me anew as a political activist with Soviet specialist credentials. Should I try to revive the Park Slope chapter of the New American Movement? Did the New American Movement still exist? How were small-m movement gurus like Eugene Genovese and Jim Weinstein handling the new look in Moscow? Gene would wind up in the arms of the Catholic Church, while Jim, up to his dying day, never lost his faith in socialism, and his empathy and hopes for Russia, Soviet and post-Soviet.

Anyway.... Gorby was the standard bearer at the top for *perestroika,* but amazing developments gave it meaning from below. As Sergei Druganov told us, "What's going on is a radical restructuring of people's way of thinking, a radical *perestroika* of a person's relationship to society." At Marty's office I pored over newspaper and periodical articles reporting on what was going on over there. I kept looking for leads to possible good stories for Part I, "The Taste of Democracy". Something caught my attention, a conflict between residents, numbering some 60,000, in Moscow's Brateyevo "microdistrict," and local authorities. The district, already choking on fumes from the factory complex in its midst, faced plans for additional industrial construction. They had enough; they formed a "Self-Governing Committee," proposed an alternate "Green" plan for development, and ran a referendum on the issues. We decided this was a perfect story for the documentary, spent much time filming and interviewing in Brateyevo, and captured in microcosmic form the way *perestroika* was stirring things up in a democratic direction – as well as the roadblocks it faced.

Sergei Druganov was a lawyer and one of the leaders of Brateyevo's "Self-Governing Committee". I attended a meeting of the Committee one evening —if you look hard enough in the film you can see me sitting in the rear among dozens of Brateyevo residents, with Eddie Baranov, our current minder, beside me. There was free and lively discussion under Druganov's chair, measures were proposed, and voting supported them. I watched in wonder. How did Soviet citizens, throttled for decades by Party and State from any form of independent civil activity, learn this stuff? How did they know how to run street demo's, design posters, conduct meetings, organize referendums, mobilize the angry citizenry? The partial paradoxical answer: they were well tutored by Party and State in these things, according to the tight norms of Party and State, only now they were turning them back on Party and State and untrammeled by those norms.

We filmed a meeting of the District Soviet (Council) about industrial plans for Brateyevo, stacked, unfortunately, against its residents. Marty tapped me to direct a Soviet crew for the filming. No special guidance from him, only this amusing detail – make sure, Marty instructed me, that when "authorities" speak, they should be shot from below. I passed that on to the Soviet crew, and they understood why immediately. In contrast, we filmed disgruntled Brateyevo residents as they filed out of the meeting – "This blah, blah, blah can go on ....," said one, "With one-party rule, nothing will change." She hit on an important point. According to the Soviet constitution, the Party in effect held a monopoly over political power in its "leading role". Later, the end of one-party rule was one major signal of the coming collapse of the old Soviet order.

In Ivanovo, the birthplace of the first Soviet of Workers' Deputies during the 1905 Revolution, we witnessed another clash between citizenry and Party-State authorities. We hadn't planned on this story. We were in the Russian heartland; Ivanovo was an industrial center known for the conservatism of its ruling establishment, and we wanted to explore attitudes there about the coming elections to the Congress of Peoples' Deputies. I think we also scheduled some visits into the countryside to find out what collective farmers in the region had on their minds. The evening before heading out I chatted with a local journalist who mentioned, casually, that there was a public hunger strike in town. *A what? Where? By whom*? Maybe his casualness was a studied casualness, just a cover for a media-savvy tip that would whet the appetite of an American film crew hungry for a good *perestroika* story. I rushed back to tell Marty and Rick what I just heard. Four women, a round-the-clock hunger strike on the steps of a church; it holds archives now and they were asking for its re-opening as a center of worship.

Marty said never mind; we should follow through on the pre-elections story. Rick disagreed, as I did. It sounded too dramatic to pass up. We went out to reconnoiter. Yes, there they were, lying under blankets, bundled up against the chilly evening air. A supportive crowd gathered at the fence around what we learned was called the "Red Church," from the color of the bricks of its walls, and to distinguish it from another in town. I couldn't keep my eyes off the face of one of the women, broad and Slavic with high cheekbones in silent martyrdom. A cascade of thoughts and associations as I stared: *Holy Russia/Dostoevsky/Andre Rublev/Avakuum/ Old Believers/Platon Karataev/Petrushka/Mother Russia/Eternal Russia/ Moscow, the Third Rome….* Thinking about my reaction now, I chalk it up to some of the romantic, faux mystical feelings that got me into Russian studies in the first place. Besides, when I saw her again at a dinner sometime after the hunger strike, the luster of Russian suffering had worn off.

Despite Rick's fears that local security wouldn't let us film the women at the Red Church, and Eddie Baranov's insisting we couldn't because we weren't sticking to our agreed schedule, we filmed and did the story. I had my own personal encounter with Ivanovo security when we returned for additional filming. With us was Borya, a young Muscovite we hired to help with lugging and loading equipment, and with other odd jobs. He seemed to have been targeted for harassment by local police and security services. A stern looking plainclothes man stopped Borya as I walked with him, and asked for his ID, the internal passport carried by all Soviet citizens. He left it in Moscow, he answered. It was odd and dumb of him to neglect having on him one of the most important official *dokumenty* governing Soviet lives. Or was it not odd or dumb, but deliberate on his part? We later speculated that Borya was possibly a plant himself cooperating with local security. Come with me, the agent barked at Borya, and you too, he gestured to me. Susan was with us, and looked worried; Rick, experienced old Moscow correspondent, passed me the telephone number of the American Embassy. We were escorted to a non-descript office where I was asked to show my passport and press credentials, which I did. Borya got a be-careful-next-time lecture. Then they let us go. I think they were just having a bit of fun with us, and also trying to make our work a bit more difficult, just to let us know who was boss in those parts. Here was the other side of my Holy Russia musings – Russia of the secret police, of suspicion of foreigners, of harassing foreign media, of arbitrary arrests and detentions. I got a double baptism in Ivanovo. One at the Red Church; the other at a police station. *That worm again.*

Galina, one of the "Three Sisters of Minsk," Singapore, 2014.

Alla and Natasha, two of the "Three Sisters of Minsk," London, 1997.

XVIII

"THE THREE SISTERS" OF MINSK

For a segment on how the truth about the Soviet past of terror and "liquidations" was being recovered from under the lies or silences of official history, we went to the Byelorussian SSR and its capital, Minsk. Byelorussia (now Belarus) was badly affected by fallout from the Chernobyl disaster. Newsstands sold maps of the region around Minsk that marked hot zones to avoid. Several people we met asked if we could bring them Dosimeters next time we travelled to Minsk, which we did on one of our return trips. Many complained of illnesses brought on by the toxic fallout. When seven years after my Minsk experiences I developed a detached retina – of unknown origin according to my ophthalmologists – I immediately suspected time spent in the Byelorussian countryside as the source. One of those hot zones? As a Russian radiation specialist at Chernobyl boasted sarcastically, "Soviet radiation is the best radiation in the world."

Working closely with each other in the field every intensely active day on the film, I felt I had made friends for life of my fellow crew members, that our relationships would last long after the documentary was made and broadcast. It didn't work out that way. The collegial friendships were ephemeral. Paraphrasing Bob Dylan, *colleagues will arrive, colleagues disappear*. Jean de Segonzac and Foster Wiley, our skilled operators of the Beta Max cameras, and Maryse Alberti, another fine cinematographer, and her boyfriend, the jolly sound-man, Scott Breindel – they remained only in my distant, fond memories. I did keep in touch with Marty long after filming, and later at a distance, watching his many outstanding investigative reports for PBS's "Frontline" series. For which, incidentally, he not only produced, but was his own handsome on-camera correspondent, and a relentlessly effective interviewer. I was perhaps closest to Rick during the many months of researching, interviewing, comparing notes, sharing often differing opinions, bending elbows, and filming. In one unforgettable night we found ourselves locked into our Moscow-to-Riga train compartment, hoping our bladders would hold out until we could pry open the seriously locked door. Rick mentioned that he had already prepared an improvised urinal. Prying didn't help; it was only when we unscrewed the whole fitting with my Swiss Army Knife that we were liberated. I later sent Rick an industrial-strength screwdriver as a holiday gift. Earlier that evening on the train, we met and chatted with a West German journalist working on *perestroika* stories, and exchanged impressions. Rick excused himself to head for the bathroom down the corridor, in his stocking feet. He came back muttering about the wet bathroom floor. Our German colleague couldn't refrain from commenting that "anyone who walked that way into a public Water Closet in Russia doesn't know Russia." I, in turn, couldn't refrain from informing him that he was speaking of *Hedrick Smith*. His suddenly wide eyes and red face were equivalents of an apology; he then addressed Rick deferentially. He also offered some story leads after Rick assured him he wasn't filing.

Incidents like that made for bonding, and I've had several friendly contacts with Rick and Susan over the years since then. Rick, productive as ever, turned out many books and television documentaries on diverse, non-Russian themes since *Inside Gorbachev's USSR*. Oddly – or maybe not so oddly given that ordinary Russians and Byelorussians were prone to personal warmth and depth of feeling for you not long after meeting you – it was several Byelorussians I met during work on the documentary that I maintained friendships with even after work was completed, and long since.

Filming the mass grave site at Kuropaty forest outside of Minsk, one of Stalin's killing grounds where hundreds of thousands were shot during the Great Terror, yielded one of the most powerful sequences in the second part of the documentary, *Comfortable Lies, Bitter Truths*. (From a comment Rick often heard from Russian friends: "It's easier to live with comfortable lies than face the bitter truth.") In the Byelorussian SSR, where old Soviet habits were still deeply ingrained in a rigid Party-State establishment, we were of course assigned a facilitator from local state television. I'm glad it was Galina Laskova. A filmmaker herself, she understood completely our documentary's intentions and identified with our pro-Gorby, pro-*perestroika,* pro-liberalizing sympathies. She put us in touch with Zenon Poznyak, who led us to Kuropaty and framed the grim story for us. She also introduced us to a fellow Byelorussian documentary filmmaker, Arkady Ruderman, whose courageous films on taboo subjects angered officialdom – on the Soviet invasion of Czechoslovakia, or police suppression of a street demonstration in Minsk, for example. His works were denied public screenings and he turned to touring and showing them at film clubs and other venues as a kind of cinema-troubadour.

More than their personal contributions to the making of our documentary, Arkady, to some extent, and Galina, very much so, became my personal friends. I worked with Arkady again on Sherry Jones's award winning film for PBS described in the next Chapter, *In the Shadow of Sakharov*. He was an extremely smart and engaging guy, with a fine sense of humor about the troubled times he was documenting. He was, alas, cut down at the height of his career in an automobile accident on a film job covering civil strife in the former Soviet republic of Tadjikistan; he was 42 years old. The handsome Galina was a bright and thoughtful young woman with an easy smile, and whose open face with delicate features reminded me of my favorite aunt Lily. In one of those unforgettable Russian – correction, Byelorussian here – moments laced with melancholy, she broke down in tears when we parted in Minsk after our work was done there. I hope to see you again, in New York, maybe, I tried to cheer her up. No, no, she said drying her eyes; I'll never be able to leave this place, I'm not Jewish, and I have no relatives abroad. Flash forward almost two years later: A telephone call from Galina Laskova, responsible for foreign relations on behalf of the Byelorussian Committee for The Children of Chernobyl. She was in New York with three girls who were suffering from Chernobyl-related ailments on a fund-raising tour that called international attention to cases like theirs'. Come on by, I told her, and Sheila and I hosted Galina and her three wards, Alexandra, Elena, and Margarita, of an afternoon in Park Slope. The girls loved bananas (of course!) and chocolate ice cream sandwiches. Galina burst into laughter the moment she greeted us – you were right, she said to me, I *would* see you again in New York! But she was very skeptical about the prospects for *perestroika*.

Galina's travels abroad did not end with her trip to New York. On a related mission in Europe, she met and later married a New Zealand healer and motivational speaker and writer, Clif Sanderson. Together they journeyed far and wide for many years helping others in medical and spiritual endeavors. Galina left Belarus permanently behind her, settled in New Zealand, continued to travel, carrying on Clif's work after his death. We spoke recently by phone after she sent me an e-mail with photo attachments from Singapore.

Galina's crying about not being able to leave the (then) USSR reminded me again of that old Soviet joke: *How many Jews want to leave the Soviet Union? Answer: 250,000,000*! Galina was one of the three non-Jewish *Minchankas*, whose lives after I met them were transformed thanks to the collapse of the USSR. The right to travel freely or emigrate was a basic human right denied to Soviet citizens by the State. The exceptions were accorded to those with relatives abroad, fictitiously or not, among Armenians, ethnic Germans, and Jews, hence the joke citing the last group. The outstanding historian, Sheila Fitzpatrick, sums up well the sense of confinement experienced by Soviet citizens. She spent much time in the USSR, and enjoyed close friendships with many Russians, but "I would not for a moment," she writes, "have contemplated living in the Soviet Union, because if you lived there, you were trapped: the moment you lost the ability to leave at will (which I possessed, but not [her friends] Igor and Irina or any other Soviet citizen), it became a prison. We all knew that, and that's why there was always a collective sigh of relief when the plane lifted off from Moscow." (From her revealing memoir, *A Spy in the Archives*.) In my experience, no sighs at take-off, but always exuberant cheers when we touched down at New York's Kennedy. Once, at a group Russian-conversation session, our mentor Artyom, who was a journalist before emigrating, declared hotly that living in the USSR meant swallowing two *poods* of shit every day. (A *pood* was an old Russian measurement equal to 36 pounds.) A favorite story from the West in his circle was James

Thurber's *The Secret Life of Walter Mitty*, he told us. We all had secret lives, alternative lives filled with unrealized hopes, he explained.

At their modest Minsk apartment for tea and sweets I met Galina's good friends, the sisters Natasha and Alla Drozd. I called them collectively, "The Three Sisters," yearners, as in Chekhov's play, only it wasn't Moscow they sought, but the wider world beyond Soviet borders. Alla was a virtuoso of the violin who earned her living working at Byelorussian film studios, while her younger sister Natasha was still studying psychology locally at the graduate level. No tears when we parted, but we agreed to stay in touch.

In touch we stayed over the many years after the Soviet end. A decade and a half after our meeting in Minsk I saw Alla in London where she worked as an *au pair* for an English family – one way of making her way out of Belarus for the West, and earning some money. She now boasted an English-accented English and hung out with some Bulgarian *émigrés* on their way to Australia. They were kind enough to offer me a bed for a couple of nights. As a Bulgarian-Byelorussian-American threesome we played tennis, and over beers at local pubs, we reminisced about the old *Soyuz* and its satellites, and tried to envisage their future lives. I never learned what happened to the Bulgarians. I think Alla lost touch with them, but she is now Alla Takemura, living in Tokyo with her husband Noburo, a poet. I assisted Natasha in getting a visa for a "professional" visit to the U.S. I wrote that she would be a welcome lecturer in our Department at Poly on some topic of her specialty. If not for the "Welcome, Natasha!" sign in Russian I held up in the arrivals area, I don't think either of us would have recognized each other. It had been over a decade that we met in her Minsk apartment. She was a quiet girl in her teens then; she was a mature young woman now, affable and willing to try out her English. She stayed with us in Park Slope as she got to know Sheila and David, and explored the city. At Poly she delivered a poised and informative talk on Psychology in Belarus, in Russian, with my old friend Oleg Smirnoff hired as a capable simultaneous translator. We stayed in touch like good friends after she left, and several years later she too surprised us: Natasha was now Natalia Drozd Skar, and happily re-settled in Norway with her husband Jostein. A birth announcement followed not long after we received that news; welcome, Per Nikolai!

I mentioned earlier that Oleg lives in New York with his wife, the mid-Westerner Julia Sloan. I sponsored Oleg's Green Card application, not without some hesitation, because of my personal financial liability, but I was confident about his business skills and general trustworthiness. He was very grateful. At his wedding party I presented him with a bottle of his favorite beverage; no, not that – he loves Cranberry Juice. As a quite successful International Development Consultant Oleg shuttles frequently between New York and European points east of the Elbe.

Galina. Alla. Natasha. Oleg. Below we'll meet Julia. They got around, those erstwhile Soviet citizens. To cite Kliuchevsky again – he wrote of Russia as a land of people in motion. He had in mind the internal colonization of the vast Eurasian plain during the centuries of Eastern Slavic history, but his description could have been updated to include the migrations of people seeking better lives than what the Soviet and post-Soviet republics offered.

How many Jews…?

Publicity card for *In the Shadow of Sakharov*, 1991.

XIX

SHERRY AND SAKHAROV

Sherry Jones, a feisty Oklahoma blonde (Texas born), ran her own production company in Washington, and had some experience filming in the USSR. Marty tapped her to direct the second part of the documentary, the section covering developments under the general theme of *glasnost* (and its enemies), titled *Comfortable Lies, Bitter Truths*. The two other parts, *Looking for Perestroika* (on reforming the economy) and *Coming Apart* (the non-Russian republics seek independence), were directed by Marion Marzinsky and David Royle, respectively, under Marty's overall supervision. I had little to do with either of those sections, but I do remember telling Marty I thought Marzinsky was anti-Soviet, unlike me, at the time, and might be unsympathetic to Gorbachev and *perestroika.* He was, but no matter; he did a good job chronicling the difficulties reform ideas and innovators faced in moving the massive and massively inert Soviet economic bureaucracy forward.

Sherry at middle age—I helped her celebrate her 40th birthday at a Georgian restaurant in Minsk—was a sharp and dynamic woman with strong organizational and leadership skills who enjoyed a valuable association with the superb cinematographer, Foster Wiley. She was less enthusiastic about Rick, whom she knew from their common interest in Washington politics. They were both "Washington junkies," she told me. I was taken aback by her confiding to me her low opinion of his political viewpoints, but no hostility between them showed in the course of making the documentary. She was a professional, I don't think Rick harbored any ill feelings about her, and they worked smoothly together. She shared with us and the Russians a notable talent for handling alcohol, beer especially. I had some complaints about Sherry, certainly not about her drinking; I considered that a plus in our work. She ran a much tighter ship than Marty, and often treated me, I thought, with some disrespect; she let me know in many ways not to forget that I was for her an *Associate Producer*, after all, not a *Polytechnic Professor*. I translated for her, and filled her in on details of Russian history, but as an AP, it also meant, say, my making sure the crew had satisfying snacks and meals promptly. Out of her earshot while we rode somewhere outside of Minsk, Foster said to me amiably, "Hey Lou, we're taking bets on how long it will take for you to punch Sherry out." Comforting to hear him say that, when I was beginning to be bothered by "What am I doing here?" feelings; a different kind of worm, this one, not unrelated to the other, big, one. Why am I in Russia, still rooting for the Soviets? Why am I now among other things a *gofer* for a film crew? Aw, shucks, I said to Foster, I can take it; I know she's under a lot of competitive and deadline pressure to produce and she's a little edgy for it.

In the end, Sherry and I got along fine; I respected her skills and creative instincts, even as she came to appreciate my Russian-area expertise. She also had a love for Russia and Russians with a passion that went beyond her obligations as a Producer for *Inside Gorbachev's USSR*. She took lessons in Russian. "Yellow blue bus," she told me was her instructor's cute way of easing her into saying "I love you" in Russian (I.E., *Ya liubliu vas*). She kept thinking ahead about possible subjects for new, Russian-themed documentaries that would bring her back for filming. "You really like this place, don't you?" I said to her once when I picked her up at Moscow's Sheremetyevo airport. She didn't disagree. Unsaid by me, but understood: *You sure like it more than I do.*

I was especially glad to take part in a couple of episodes on Sherry's watch. Greg Guroff, a consultant on the project, pointed out to her that bells and bell ringing occupied an important place in Russian history, in both secular and religious realms, and maybe something should be keyed to that in *Comfortable Lies, Bitter Truths* – you know, as in: Gorbachev was *ringing* in new times. We decided to head up to Rostov, one of the towns with ancient roots comprising the "Golden Ring" northeast of Moscow. There I experienced both the highs and a lows of traditional Russian culture in metaphoric and literal senses. We arranged for some of the expert bell ringers of Rostov (*zvonary*) to demonstrate the extraordinary art of Orthodox bell ringing for us. We climbed the tower of the Assumption Cathedral where they met us at the top; around their hands and legs were ropes attached to the clappers of the massive bells. Up close to them, it was really, *really* loud when they went into action, but I didn't hold my ears as we took in the wondrously complex polyphony of the tolling bells. Sherry got her opening for her *Comfortable Lies* – a terrific collage of sonorities and pictures of the bells as Rick announced, "A friend told me, this is the sound of *glasnost*."

That was traditional Russian culture's sacred "high". The profane "low"? After climbing down from the bell tower I looked for a rest room. I was directed across a courtyard to what I asked for. I could have found it from the odor—a wide and deep open trough invited me to do my business there. All in the life of an associate producer filming in Holy Russia, I said to myself as I walked away. Back in Brooklyn, reporting my experience to Artyom at one of our Russian conversational sessions, I expressed my amazement that a major religious center and popular site for tourists didn't have more amenable facilities. Ah yes, he said, no surprise; I often hear from Americans how impressed they are with the Kremlin and the Hermitage and the Metro, but Oh!, they say, Oh!, the toilets….

We met and filmed many fascinating figures in those fascinating times of *perestroika*. Most applauded Gorbachev and his reforms, and we naturally sought them out, not only because our sympathies were with them, but because it was the point of the documentary—to spotlight the individuals active in this historic endeavor. At the path-breaking show, "The Fifth Wheel," specializing in the new Soviet television journalism of exposure, we met its courageous director, Bella Kurkova, and one of her thoughtful producers, Alexander Krivonos. We accompanied them on a shoot intended to reveal some of the estates of the Leningrad *nomenklatura,* walled in away from public scrutiny. Police stopped us on the way, and made it clear we weren't welcome and could go no further. "How stupid!," shouted a frustrated and embarrassed Bella, "and in front of the Americans….". A good lesson on the limits to *glasnost* and *perestroika* that confronted its champions and beneficiaries.

A staunch opponent of the Gorbachev program is someone I remember very vividly, Nina Andreyeva, the Leningrad chemistry teacher parachuted into controversy by the old guard of the inner circles in the Party and Government. Her essay, "I Cannot Forsake Principles," surely authored by others, appeared in the conservative newspaper, *Sovietskaya Rossiya,* in March, 1988, and generated much public jousting between reformers and defenders of the old guard. Should we offer Andreyeva camera time to air her "Principles"? We had to, in the interests of documenting the full *perestroika* picture, including its opponents as well as its champions. Would she agree to be interviewed and filmed? You bet she would; she was eager to state her case before us, even knowing that, like most in the American media, we didn't favor her critique of the Gorbachev reforms and didn't share her discomfort with the pronounced liberalizing atmosphere evident everywhere.

We expected an ideology-hardened, unfriendly battle-axe who wouldn't hide her latter day Stalinism and polemical skills for an American film crew. That image did not entirely accord with her appearance and hospitality. In their very small, very neat apartment, she and her husband, Vladimir Klushin, a Marxist-Leninist pedagogue, hosted a lunch of sandwiches, salads, soft drinks, and sweets for us. (On the Party tab, we guessed.) Andreyeva, stoutly built, wore her dark hair short, and smiled at us as if we were all old friends. I swear she blushed deeply when she shook my hand. Sure, she spoke to American journalists. Several times she mentioned "*Dahveed,*" warmly and sort of boastfully. I gathered she meant David Remnick, then the *Washington Post's* Moscow correspondent. She and the equally voluble Klushin seemed delighted with the attention her article brought them. Later for the camera she asked rhetorically, what is *glasnost*? "If...everyone can blather anything he wants, then psychiatric hospitals are the clearest examples of *glasnost.*" And what's the worst thing? – "Disorder, disorder!" she said animatedly. Klushin chimed in and summed it all up as "the ugly face of freedom."

We were hearing voices that augured the coup attempt of August, 1991, the failed *putsch* that sought an end to the Gorbachev reforms, and even placed him in house arrest for a short while. A new commanding figure emerged from those events, the "populist maverick," as he was usually dubbed in the American media, Boris Yeltsin.

I mentioned earlier getting Yeltsin's ear while he stood on a podium waiting to speak at a Moscow rally, in 1989, asking him for an interview. "I already gave one to you Americans, to ABC," he said. "But this would be for American *public* television," I pleaded. He shook his head and went back to his notes. We had heard that Yeltsin was a serious tennis player, and since Rick and I had our racquets with us, we wrote to his office, challenging him to a match. A nice subject for Foster's camera, lots of action; a sit down interview would come after we all toweled off. We got no reply to that ploy. Someone in our crew commented that Yeltsin could be one of those figures who seemed important then, but of no consequence later, so why bother. We did get a bit of Yeltsin commentary in the final cut, but didn't highlight his or its significance for future political developments. We couldn't predict Yeltsin's future importance, how could we? It's a hazard of trying to record contemporary history, in print or in film; you're likely to confuse, in the swirl of events and personalities, what's really momentous and enduring, and what's only transient. Journalism, including documentary-film journalism, may be the "first draft of history," but like any draft, it may need correcting. If we had the documentary to do all over again, it might have been corrected to something like *Yeltsin's Challenge to Gorbachev's USSR*.

But these are all reflections in retrospect. Looking back, I came to understand that ours was an overly *Gorbocentric* documentary, making it appear that the essential political dynamic operating in the USSR was simply one that pitted an inspirational Gorbachev trying to arouse an apathetic nation. A Gorbachev focus was natural, given all the attention he got in the West. But it was much more complicated than that bi-polar dynamic, with fissures everywhere in the political sphere, both right and left, in the upper reaches and down below, and with, especially, centrifugal ambitions in the national borderlands that only independence would satisfy. Still, we could boast of producing a lively and an in-depth rendition of the historical events taking place in the USSR, 1989-1990, and the documentary was recognized as such. It won the prestigious Alfred I. DuPont Columbia University Award for "Excellence in Broadcast

Journalism," and Long Island University's George Polk Award for "Documentary Television Reporting". I was proud of being a part of the production. And also impressed by television's reach. An article I could publish for some periodical on the Left or in some scholarly journal about the Gorbachev reforms might be seen, perhaps even read, by at best several thousand readers. The *Inside* documentary for PBS drew some ten million viewers.

Then it was back to the gray world of the Polytechnic Department of Social Sciences, where I was named Head, a position I was to hold for four years. No fireworks there, no faculty carping and back-biting, just devoted teachers of future engineers and scientists; my colleagues and I shared the sense of a common mission, and that made my job easy. Nothing new there. But my classrooms in the 1990-1991 academic year were now animated by my recovered enthusiasm for the USSR, and for the socialism that I associated with it. I screened the documentary for my classes, and tried to convey the exhilaration filling the air from Leningrad to Stavropol in those days. "Bliss was it in that dawn to be alive," wrote Wordsworth as a witness of the French Revolution in its early pre-Terror period, "But to be young was very Heaven!". I wasn't as young as the witness Wordsworth was in 1790 – I was already fifty-five exactly two hundred years later – but I could identify with Wordsworth's feelings. Well, maybe it wasn't bliss precisely, but certainly elation, high optimism, and a sense that I was very lucky to be a part of all those historic moments. Michael McFaul, later U.S, ambassador to Putin's Russia, was there at the same time, as a graduate student working ostensibly on his dissertation in a Moscow that David Remnick describes as "a pageant, irresistible to anyone with a trace of democratic idealism and fellow feeling for the Russians. The sense of historical drama was unmistakable." For McFaul, it was "Like being in a movie," he recalled. An apt metaphor, and, *ahem,* we were making a movie about that movie. In more sober, civic minded tones, the Russian novelist, Mikhail Shishkin, remembers "that marvelous feeling when the Soviet era was ending, and, for the first time, I could consider myself a citizen of my country, responsible for its future….The totalitarian system was molting before my eyes. It was an astonishing feeling: we had been raised to be obedient slaves, and then, all of a sudden, you were taking responsibility for all that was around you."

Oh, the power of television. A woman in Minsk nearly swooned, cross-eyed, when I told her I was with "American television." (She was organizing a beauty contest, and we were looking for possible stories for Sherry's *Comfortable Lies.*) At home, not as a Russia specialist, but as an Associate Producer for the PBS series on the USSR, I was in demand at numerous campuses in the New York metropolitan area to report on Gorbachev and *perestroika*. Embedded in lots of anecdotes was my main theme, the awakening of Soviet civil society, and how the academic and governmental experts had failed to anticipate Gorbachev and that awakening. Later, that failure of anticipation was even more acute when the Soviet Union vanished. I was reporting on *perestroika* for university audiences, and emphasizing the birth and possible development of a Soviet democratic socialism, music to the ears of Lefties in those audiences.

Supplemental income from speaking engagements was very welcome. Claudia had finished up at Guilford and was out on her own in the Washington, D.C. vicinity. Guilford had given her a taste for the South, and Washington had that southern flavor, within easy proximity to New York to boot. Later she completed, with distinction, a joint Master's Degree in Public Health and Social Work at Boston University. Davey, who made it clear he did not favor entering "the family business," attended the local Park Slope private school, Berkeley-Carroll, for a couple of years before transferring to Gow, a boarding High School near Buffalo specializing in education for students with different learning issues. Davey experienced Attention Deficit Disorder from an early age, battled his way through Berkeley-Carroll, and excelled at Gow. He later spent two years at Guilford, following, we hoped, in his sister's footsteps, but he left abruptly, the summer before his junior year. As I mentioned earlier, a school for "tree huggers," he said, was not for him. Sheila continued her efforts at DC 37's MELS on behalf of Union members, most of whom really constituted the working poor. Often she had to fight off the opposition of some of her colleagues, for either their bureaucratic nit-picking or for their ultra-Left political postures, both of which interfered with delivering concrete benefits to the Union constituency. I always thought that at MELS Sheila was doing more productive, meaningful *political* work, i.e., making life better for people, than I ever achieved in my writing for radical publications or participating in this or that ephemeral organizing group or grouplet. More and more I felt I was engaged hopelessly in the narrow Left margins of American political life. My "socialism of the heart" remained, but by the '90s I was no longer actively engaged in Left culture or community. Sometime in the delirious '60s I wagered against a skeptical Helmut Gruber that a mass socialist movement would develop in the U.S. "in our lifetimes". (He's won that bet, though the "Democratic Socialist" Bernie Sanders succeeded in mobilizing millions of mostly young supporters behind his run for the Democratic Party's Presidential nomination in 2016. That meant something: Might there be some kind of American "socialism" in the future, after all?) The collapse of the USSR, and with it the dreams of a humane socialism there that might animate socialist politics in the West, had something to do with my disengagement at the time. About that, later, but first, enter Sherry and Sakharov.

After successfully tackling Gorbachev, *glasnost* and *perestroika*, under Marty's direction with Rick as correspondent, Sherry began considering various figures and topics that would bring her back to the USSR for another Soviet-themed documentary, this time with complete control of her own production. Scanning books on the Soviet past, a fascinating episode of cultural rebellion in the post-Stalin '50s caught her attention: the *stilyagi*, youthful emulators of Western "style" who thumbed their noses at establishment norms. It would have been a great subject for a good historical film, but she put the idea on a back burner. (In 2008, the Russian director, Valery Todorovsky, made a splashy musical, *Stilyagi*, "Hipsters," in the English translation.) Instead, Sherry decided on a biographical portrait of a towering Soviet figure, the great physicist and courageous dissident, Andrei Sakharov, and she asked me to come on as an Associate Producer.

Clearly, the initial frostiness between us had fallen away in the course of working together on *Inside*. "Fondly," she signed off in messages to me after *Inside*. I appreciated her skills as a documentarian, and she valued my historical smarts plus my ability to get along with Russians and win their confidence for the project we were working on. It crossed my mind later, reflecting on my experience with Sherry, that at each of the opposite points of my Russianist career, at the beginning and near the end, I worked for two strong, talented women, Rose Rubin and Sherry Jones. Another kind of "synchronicity."

Even though I was scheduled to take up the Headship reins of the Department at Poly that autumn of 1990, I enthusiastically accepted Sherry's invitation. Another chance to experience the unfolding of *perestroika* on the ground was something I couldn't pass up. Was Soviet Socialism with a New Face real and prospering? My requesting and receiving one more semester's leave was not a problem; someone else could lead the Department while I was away. Here was another example of the amenities at Poly for which I was ever grateful, never mind the comparatively, by academic standards, inferior salary scales for us.

Sherry knew the ropes of working in Moscow, and how to benefit from the new environment. She was aware that many Muscovites, eager for dollars, and encouraged by the looser regulations on such matters, were prepared to vacate their apartments and lease them out to *valiuta*-bearing foreigners. Later, she would even *buy* a place as a secure base for future productions. Nancy Shoss, the other Associate Producer, and I were the advance scouts for finding an affordable and well located apartment. Nancy was the oldest among us, and about to retire from filmmaking, but she had enough will and energy to do her very capable part in the early stages of the Sakharov documentary. In addition to apartment hunting, Nancy and I were charged with locating people for possible filming and we began scheduling pre-filming interviews with them. We found a one-bedroom plus sofa-for-sleeping apartment at a solid old building on *Ulitsa Klimashkina* (Klimashkin Street), conveniently located in the *Krasnaya Presnya* district, not far from the Byelorussian Railroad Station, with metro stations in easy walking distance. I had the bedroom, Nancy slept on the sofa-bed in the living room; the apartment was small enough for us to hear each other snoring at night after our very active days – Sherry kept us busy from Washington, filling our time with her suggestions, requests, assignments. A stickler for pre-production details like keeping her crews well fed, she also arranged for catered meals for us; through one contact or another she located an excellent Moscow cook, Yuliya Berezinskaya, who prepared delicious roasts and soups for us periodically. I remember especially her excellent, authentic, *gefilte* fish, really *filled,* not the small loafs you find in jars back home.

In January, to have an apartment ready for Sherry's Moscow arrival, I found another place, available for the month, located in an older section of the city, near the *Arbat,* on *Skatertny Pereulok* ("Table-Cloth Lane"); that one had two bedrooms. I'll describe it below.

Before I left for Moscow in January, my friend and Park Slope neighbor, the superb figurative artist, Simon Dinnerstein, asked if I would do him a favor. Seems there were cousins from the clan still living in the old land, and the family had kept in touch by mail across many years. Could I, Simon asked, mail an envelope with a letter and some art work to his cousins in Moscow, if it's no trouble, when I'm there? Of course, I told him, but it might be better, more secure, for me to hand-deliver it; I'll be happy to do it. Simon sounded out the street address for me, carefully, ***Klee-mosh-keen*** -- do you know where that is? A long pause before I answered, after I swallowed hard – tell me the number of the building, Simon. Nine, Nine Kleemoshkeen Street, he said; they live on the fourth floor. *Whoa….* I couldn't resist responding casually: Oh sure, it's the floor below mine when I lived there last autumn, I told him with a straight face. We then both broke out in exchanges of amazement about this against-all-odds coincidence. It ranked high up there with that synchronicity at the *Bibliothèque National* decades earlier. I took this one as a good omen for our work on Sakharov ahead.

P.S. I delivered the envelope. The cousins, the elderly couple, Yefim and Irina Kobyoynsky, invited me in for tea and cookies, and couldn't believe it when I told them I was not only a messenger from Brooklyn, but their Moscow upstairs *neighbor* not long ago.

Living in our own apartments, not hotels, gave us a better taste of life in Moscow, though of course we didn't suffer the daily hardships endured by Muscovites. We had access to some of the foreign-owned, well-stocked new superettes for most of our needs, but we shopped locally for the occasional milk or bread, we took out our trash, and watched as pyramids of cabbage heads grew outside of neighbors' doors, enough amassed for pickling to last the winter. The location of the January apartment on Table-Cloth Lane could have been made to order for our documentary. I quote from my report to Sherry about the apartment and its whereabouts:

"Its location is terrific, even if the plumbing isn't so great. Who would have dreamed that we'd locate two minutes from where AS grew up? Granatny Lane, now Shchusev Street, is one long block, and one of the nicest streets in Moscow. It's named for the 'outstanding Soviet architect' Academician Alexei Viktorovich Shchusev (1873-1949), who only happened to have headed the project which produced the Lenin Mausoleum. His bust stands in front of an official looking structure across the street from the impressive ensemble of buildings housing the Union of Soviet Architects. At Number 3 is Militia Station No. 83. I take this to be the site of the bombed out Sakharov house. Across the street is a building just as described in AS's memoirs: 'Our building faced an old and stately private mansion (said to have belonged to Marshal Kutuzov), surrounded by extensive grounds; it now housed the Bureau of Weights and Measures of the All-Union Institute of Standards'.

"Around the corner is the handsome domed neo-classic church where Alexander Pushkin and Natalya Goncharova were bethrothed. The Timiryazev statue which AS mentions is at the foot of the Tverskoi Boulevard promenade (a section of the Boulevard Ring where you and I have fast-walked and jogged); it's at the intersection of the Ring and Gertsen Street, and this comprises 'Nikitskie Vorota,' the old gates to the city."

Shots of these locations in the film would serve to illustrate Sakharov's intelligentsia and religious family roots.

In our Table-Cloth Lane apartment Sherry had one bedroom, I had the other. There must have been talk about our living-together arrangement, but, no, it was all strictly business, in service to pre-production. The apartment had a temperamental toilet, but it had a working TV and a telephone; it was all we needed. Mornings, Sherry and I went over lists of people who knew, worked with or were related to Sakharov. I made the phone calls to reach them and set meeting times and places. For exercise after breakfast and phone calls, Sherry liked to fast-walk, and I preferred running, but in Moscow's January weather I chose fast-walking too. In our heavy overcoats and winter footwear we took different paths, but sometimes we crossed each other coming from opposite directions. See... you... later... Sherry! I called out between frosty puffs. Well bundled Muscovites who passed us took our exercise in stride.

Some women were particularly striking in their great coats, high boots, cloche hats, berets, or *shapkas,* resembling some latter-day wives from *boyarin* famiies.

That fall and winter, the euphoria of early *perestroika* had evaporated. The mood was darker and tense. People spoke of a coming civil war. Gorby was being attacked from Right and Left, while Muscovites were complaining about food and clothing shortages. The new McDonald's off Pushkin Square was a huge success, but in elevators, on the street, riding with cabbies, I heard the same thing: *There's nothing in the stores! You can't eat glasnost*! A *dozen eggs costs two days' wages*! As someone put it, "Soviet power still existed, but the food ran out." There were marches and demonstrations. Sherry and I even marched in a big one calling for greater democracy and a deepening of *perestroika*. Oh, the thrill of this for me, you bet; me, a veteran of scores of demo's and marches in New York and Washington, in campaigns for civil rights and against the war in Vietnam, here I was voting with my feet with Russians in the cold streets of Moscow. And one more thing: Washington had launched "Operation Desert Storm," the first Gulf War against Saddam Hussein's Iraq. The media and conversations among ordinary Muscovites were full of commentary on Scud rockets and Tomahawk missiles. It was strange being in another country, the USSR, no less, while my country was at war; without probing the issues and reasons for the war, I even felt a dose of patriotism. Anyway, we had a documentary to make.

That was the atmosphere we worked in during our research into the life and activities of Andrei Dmitrievich Sakharov, the legendary Russian physicist, "the father of the Soviet hydrogen bomb", and fearless dissident, who also became in many eyes the "moral conscience of *perestroika*" before his death in 1989. "A *miracle*!" is how Alexander Solzhenitsyn described Sakharov—Solzhenitsyn was another kind of miracle himself. From the ranks of the privileged Soviet scientific elite, rewarded by the Kremlin with perks making them a special, favored caste provided they worked loyally for the regime, there appeared this major figure who turned against the whole Soviet system and gave his every breath to fighting for the ideals of freedom and justice, denied at every turn by that system. Was it an "Oppenheimer Complex" that prompted him to take his place beside Soviet dissidents and do battle with the Kremlin and the KGB, a form of contrition and atonement for helping to put that powerful weapon in the hands of Soviet leaders? Robert Oppenheimer, a father of the U.S. atomic bomb, was said to be appalled by the fearsome results of the weaponry he helped devise, and went on to oppose the construction of the "super," the hydrogen bomb. We learned, from the many physicists he worked with, that Sakharov did not suffer from the "complex," nor did they. The general feeling among them was that during the U.S.-Soviet confrontation of the Cold War in the early '50s it would have been perilous for the U.S. to retain sole ownership of the thermonuclear bomb. That feeling had something to do with Soviet or national homeland patriotism and security, but it was also an assessment based on simple balance-of-power considerations for preserving peace. As the physicist, Efim Fradkin, told us, no matter how democratic we knew the U.S. to be, the temptation to use a weapon it monopolized would be too great. What most concerned Sakharov when he was still in the Kremlin's good graces were the awful consequences of above ground bomb testing that spewed radioactivity into the global atmosphere, and he was instrumental in persuading Nikita Khrushchev to support negotiations with the Kennedy White House that led to the Nuclear Test Ban Treaty of 1963.

That "worm" of doubt and anxiety – "What am I doing here?" – rarely bothered me while I worked on *In the Shadow of Sakharov*, as Sherry was to call our documentary. There were many moments, mainly in early autumn at the start of our round of meeting people and preparing "pre-interviews," when I wished my interpreting skills were better honed. By the end of January, however, I was interpreting, if not with totally suave, professional ease, with considerably better skill and accuracy. *How do you get to Carnegie Hall?.....*

The work I was involved in and the people I was meeting and getting to know in those days was so exciting and in every sense so full of historical significance that the doubts about my romance with Russia were temporarily smothered. Sakharov had passed away a year earlier, but I was in touch with other historic figures, men and women of Sakharov's two cohorts, the physicists and the dissidents. There were naturally some encounters with Soviet officialdom and with Soviet rulesdom. Sherry was eager to get some hot material to dramatize the story, and wrote to Minister Konovalov of the USSR Ministry of Atomic Power and Industry, for permission to film at the *Ob'yekt*, the facility where Sakharov and the bomb-makers worked in secret under KGB direction. She also requested film footage of the hydrogen bomb tests themselves. Sherry identified PBS as America's leading *non-commercial* television – such a designation perhaps might appeal to a Soviet *socialist* functionary for its good ideological connotations. In other, similar circumstances, with a similar intent, PBS was translated for us by some Russian assistants as *Narodnii Televideniye* – "Peoples Television," which had a fine, *Soviet*, ring to it.

Minister Konovalov denied the request for filming at the Sarov installation, known by its code name, Arzamas-16 (and known by Soviet wags as "Los Arzamas"). The location of the secret facility was already public knowledge at the time, but when I mentioned it to Liuba, the younger of Sakharov's two daughters, during an interview, she and her husband exchanged suddenly worried glances, and she changed the subject. Better not get into such a sensitive area with this too inquisitive *Americanets*. Otherwise she was quite agreeable in discussing relations with her father. Suspicions and caution still turned up often in our work. The efficient, affable and helpful Kostya, who headed the "International Department" at *Dom Kino*, Moscow headquarters of the Soviet Filmmakers Union, became a friend during and after filming, and we kept in touch with him after the Soviet collapse. Not only did Kostya reveal he had worked for the KGB at *Dom Kino*—all major organizations, especially those with any connections with foreigners, housed an agent—but that he was convinced I was his CIA opposite number. Sherry then began calling me "Agent Menashe." Well, I told her, if I was the CIA spook for our operation, she was my "Control".

Minister Konvalov did offer us footage of the H-Bomb tests – for a price. We knew they were very hungry for dollars. I don't remember the exact numbers, but negotiations went something like the following. They must have done some research into what television time or film rights for broadcasting cost in the U.S., and came up with some numbing figure in the tens of thousands of dollars. Impossible for our budget, Sherry told him, but we can afford $3,500. How about that? It's a deal, he said at once, and we got our dramatic, mushroom cloud footage.

The industrial city of Gorky, now returned to its original name, Nizhnii-Novgorod, where Sakharov was exiled for seven years, had been closed to foreigners. Keeping him isolated from foreign journalists and from the eyes of the world was a reason they sent him there. Ironically, the installation at Sarov was nearby. Naturally, we wanted to visit Gorky, and stake it out for filming later. We were delighted to learn the city was now "open" by the end of 1990. Except that it wasn't. We were disappointed when the Ministry of Defense told us Gorky was still off limits, and we could go there only with KGB permission. The Moscow KGB office put us off by telling us only the local Gorky KGB could green-light us. Forget what they told you, laughed Seryozha, our young hired driver; it's typical official Soviet bureaucratic nonsense. And Seryozha's reaction was a typical young Soviet response. Let's just go, he said, and off we went unimpeded for the 400 kilometer drive. The high-end hotel we wanted to check into, the handsome and handsomely situated "Rossiya," however, shut its doors to us. The director there insisted the city was still closed to foreigners, and if we wanted to protest, you can take it up with "the organs," he snapped at us. With a wink from Seryozha, we headed for the "Tsentralnaya," a very provincial hotel right out of a Chekhov short story. No problem there.

The city was renamed for its most famous son, Alexei Peshkov, whose *nom de plume* was Maxim Gorky -- Maxim "the Bitter". It stands at the confluence of the Volga and Oka Rivers, and was a center of Russian commerce and industry before the Revolution; its annual St. Makary Fair was nationally and internationally known. Fine old homes that belonged to wealthy members of the pre-Revolutionary "merchant" class, the *kupechestvo*, are some present-day remnants of that commercial past. (In my projected study of the "Russian bourgeoisie" in Tsarist Russia, Gorky – Nizhnii-Novgorod – and its economy and social strata would have been good subjects to look into. Just an idle thought, as I muse on having visited the city as an Associate Producer for a documentary on Sakharov, not as a scholar in search of the Russian bourgeoisie before the Revolution.)

In Soviet times the city and the region were known for heavy industry, particularly in the military sector. The most famous plant was the Gorky Auto Works. We noted the oddity of little auto traffic when we were there, and that the roads were notoriously bad. As a closed city eight hours away from Moscow by overnight train, Gorky was for Soviet authorities a natural internal exile spot to send Sakharov. Foreigners and especially foreign correspondents couldn't get to him, and all visitors, locals as well as those from out of town, were tightly and easily monitored. The apartment assigned to Sakharov was at the far edge of the city, about a half hour by public transportation from the center. I tried unsuccessfully to get some maps or a guide book, and ascribed their non-availability to the Soviet "closed city" mentality.

We visited the four-room plus kitchen apartment where Sakharov and Elena Bonner lived during the exile, No. 3, at 214 Prospekt Gagarina, on the bottom floor of a 12-story building, part of housing complex set in ample grounds. There were observation points around the building, and across the way was a postal station where their mail was closely screened. The apartment was later converted to a museum, but a plaque was already up at the building when we were there: *In this house, from 1980 to 1986, lived, in exile, the Nobel Laureate for Peace, Academician Andrei Dmitrievich Sakharov.* A rack for flowers was filled with evergreens, and a few feet away a pine-tree sapling had been planted in Sakharov's memory by a local charitable society. At the Oblast (Regional) Clinical Hospital where Sakharov was force fed twice during hunger strikes—and also secretly filmed on another occasion to show the world he was in good health—I met the doctor in charge, Oleg Obukhov, 60-ish, with thinning dark-red hair, thick glasses, and an affable manner who could be your friendly internist. He assured me how well Sakharov had been treated, and how under his leadership the hospital was the best and most respected in the region. "The *nomenkatura* is treated here," he reported with pride. "Even American tourists who fall ill on Volga River excursions are treated here." "A real *Dyed moroz (Santa Claus), isn't he?*" commented Nina Zvereva, a local TV journalist who accompanied me for the interview. Dr. Obukhov is used to these interviews by now, Nina said; he repeats the same responses word for word.

Sakharov was not totally isolated in the Gorky apartment. With permission from the authorities, of course, many individuals were allowed to visit him, some from Gorky and the region, others from

Moscow. We tried meeting as many of the locals as possible in the several days we were there, seeking their impressions and reminiscences of the celebrated exile in their midst. I was struck by Felix Krasavin, a literary-minded intellectual who worked as a machinist after doing time in the Gulag before the modern dissident era. He knew Elena Bonner from childhood and claimed, interestingly, if not necessarily accurately, that it was Sakharov who turned Bonner on to politics and opposition, and not the other way around, as commonly thought. Both of Sakharov's daughters shared the accepted interpretation, resenting Bonner for it, and blamed her for alienating their father from them. Krasavin's wife, Maya, was a physician who treated Sakharov and Bonner on several occasions during the exile. Maya and Felix liked to bring Sakharov jam and cabbage, and they complained that every such visit had to be approved by the local procurator. Felix had the attitudes and habits of an old political prisoner. He was dismissive of any organized activity, believed only in the individual, and did not identify with the dissident movement. When we told him we had driven to Gorky he questioned Seryozha closely about his car. I noticed Seryozha removed the car's windshield wipers and side-view mirror each night after a day's work, a common practice among private auto owners in the auto-scarce USSR. But Felix wasn't interested in the security of windshield wipers. As the three of us talked he passed me a handwritten note that advised me "not to talk about these things [political matters and meetings with locals] in your car." This may have been the USSR of Gorbachev and liberalization, but in Felix's eyes, the "organs" were still prowling. I wondered then, but didn't probe further, did Felix assume Seryozha was an agent, or was he sure that the KGB had already planted a bug in the unguarded car at night?

Among Sakharov's permitted visitors were former colleagues from Moscow as well as physicists and other scientists from Gorky and the region who helped him keep in touch with developments in his field. I met a group of the locals one evening, exchanging credentials before I reported on our work and aims for the documentary. I explained that my "real job" was teaching Russian and Soviet history to undergraduates at a predominantly engineering and science school in New York, Polytechnic University, as it was named then. Where in New York? someone asked. In a *rayon* (district; region; the closest to *borough*, I thought) called Brooklyn, I replied. *"Ah, Brookleen Pauwley*!," the questioner exclaimed. The work of Poly's excellent researchers in polymer chemistry, chemical engineering, and microwave technology, among other areas, had acquired a global reputation. I was touched and very proud. Never mind "Associate Producer," I told Sherry later; they were more impressed that I came from Brooklyn Poly! You're well known on the Volga, I announced to my colleagues at a Faculty Meeting when I returned.

That Volga left a strong impression on me. Facing some very wicked winds coming off the river one late afternoon on a Gorky street near an embankment, I experienced, really for the first time, the intensely ferocious cold of a Russian winter. It's something I've never forgotten. Moscow, Leningrad, Ivanovo, Minsk, the Baltics, the North Caucasus, and many other places I had known across the Soviet Union in my winter travels had been mild compared to those icy blasts that hit me from Mother Volga.

Inevitably, and sadly, the many dozens of relationships established in the course of research, interviewing, filming, or socializing that go into making a documentary are ruptured when the Producer announces – Sherry actually said this after the Gorbachev shoot -- "It's a wrap!" The film is in the can, we pack our bags and go home. I left the USSR at the end of January, and delivered a nine-page report, with "Suggestions and Ruminations" for Sherry's assistance when she returned with her crew for filming that Spring, and for some guidance when she and Foster edited the material and prepared a script. There were exceptions to that "rupture," as I mentioned above; I made lasting friendships that grew out of my work on *Inside Gorbachev's USSR*, and later from attending film festivals in post-Soviet Russia, but none, save for Sherry herself, as a consequence of *In The Shadow of Sakharov*. There was someone, however, who remembered me from an interview and called me at home when he visited New York. It was none other than the venerable Scientific Director at Arzamas-16, the physicist who could rightly boast to having had a central role in parenting the Soviet atomic and hydrogen bombs, Yuli Khariton. More exactly, it was his grandson, Alyosha Semyonov, who called on his behalf.

Khariton received a Ph.D. from Cambridge University in the 1920s, supervised by Ernest Rutherford at the famous Cavendish Laboratory. He had co-authored a paper in 1939 on the possibility of creating nuclear-power reactors, a first – the Soviets were well prepared in the physics of atomic energy to make productive use of information gleaned from atomic-bomb espionage. When I asked Khariton, discreetly, about the role of Klaus Fuchs in the development of the Soviet A-Bomb, he answered, discreetly, well yes, intelligence (*razvedka*) was involved. But Sherry and I didn't dwell on such matters; we were interested in his impressions of Sakharov, who worked under him at Sarov. Our session with him was not entirely productive. Khariton was well into his 80s then, short and frail, but it wasn't his age or physical condition that slowed down our exchanges to the point of tiring us (not him), it was his insistence on speaking a halting English, as if he wanted to exercise and keep in shape the language he knew from his time at Cavendish. We got some general things from him. When he learned of the U.S. Atomic Bomb, he "realized we had to work harder." (Stalin made sure they did. His enforcer at Arzamas-16 was the repulsive head of Soviet security, Lavrenty Beria) His reaction to the development of the Soviet H-Bomb – he "had a feeling of safety for the country." He had enormous respect for Sakharov as a genius of unique capabilities, but thought of him as naïve in political matters.

I forget how it came up, but Khariton was intrigued by my Sephardic background, and especially that my family came from Salonica, Greece. He came from the Petersburg Jewish intelligentsia, and there may have been Greek lineage in the family. That perhaps explains the call to me when he and his grandson were visiting New York. I was delighted and flattered to hear from them, and invited them to dinner at our place, emphasizing that Brooklyn, and Brooklyn's Park Slope, should figure in everyone's New York itinerary. I mentioned that a Russian *émigré* once told me how pleasantly surprised he was by Brooklyn, having heard it was dingy and without much greenery. (I didn't mention that another Russian *émigré*, Zhores Medvedev, who lived in England, told me he thought Brooklyn's Brighton Beach – "Little Odessa by the Sea" – was quite ugly.) I enlisted my brother-in-law Seymour's services to pick up our guests at their Manhattan hotel, and drive them to the Slope.

Sheila, on short notice, prepared meatloaf with mashed potatoes and broccoli, and I tossed a *Greek* salad according to my mother's recipe. Maybe over elated by the occasion – it's as if the Soviet equivalent of a Robert Oppenheimer or Edward Teller were in our dining room—and in its Judeo-Hellenic spirit, I drank too much *ouzo* while they had red wine, and so I remember very little of the evening. There was coffee and Sheila's excellent apple crisp for dessert. We confined dinner conversation to chit-chat – what had they been doing in New York, what were their plans, could we help, etc. Much, too, on my family background and our Ladino language. I couldn't very well broach weightier matters and pose some searching questions to Khariton, the sort of stuff Sherry and I avoided when we interviewed him for fear of alienating him. Why, for example, did he add his signature to that notorious letter from scientists denouncing Sakharov during a furious Kremlin campaign in 1973 against "the Father of the Soviet H-Bomb" for his "anti-Soviet" activity? Khariton's signing much disappointed Sakharov. Clearly, Khariton's notably long tenure as Scientific Director at Arzamas-16 —from 1946-1991; from Stalin through Gorbachev—depended on enormous circumspection in political matters. Unlike Sakharov, with whom he may have sympathized in private, for Khariton the devotion to science, even science in service of the totalitarian state, trumped any struggle for individual liberty and democratic reform. Besides, getting involved in such things could only get you into trouble. When Sakharov's critical tract, *Progress, Coexistence and Intellectual Freedom*, with its call for "convergence" of the capitalist and socialist systems to insure peace, was published abroad in 1968, Khariton's worst fears came to pass about the "unique" figure who worked for him: Sakharov was now persona non grata at the Sarov Installation, and he closed his office door there, never to return.

After Sakharov's death, an official obituary was published, signed by Gorbachev, Politburo members, and many Academicians, including five who denounced him in 1973, among them: Yuli Khariton. A Moscow driver commented to me at the time, in the familiar cabbie-sardonic style, that, of course, "they" attacked him while he was alive, but "they" praise him now that he's dead. "That's the way it always is with us," he said. The cabbie's assessment recalled the similar bitter sentiment we heard earlier from Sakharov's cousin, Irina, who cited lines from Pushkin's *Boris Godunov*.

The Khariton visit was an odd and unexpected footnote to my experience of *In the Shadow of Sakharov*. In his "shadow" I got to meet many of the important figures associated with the great physicist and heroic champion of individual freedom and human rights. Prominent fellow scientists like Mischa Levin, Vitaly Ginsburg, Vladimir Fainberg, Vitaly Goldansky, and Khariton himself; prominent fellow dissidents like Vera Lashkova, Sergei Kovalev, Tanya Velikanova, and, of course, his wife and fellow combatant, the formidable Elena Bonner. Sakharov's widow was, despite warnings, very accessible, and very cooperative when we interviewed her. Some of these and other figures appear in the documentary relating their experiences, and they also offered commentaries on Sakharov the person and Sakharov the majestic historical figure. The bard Bulat Okudzhava placed Sakharov for us in the Russian tradition of "Holy Fools" who dare speak those truths to power that others shun. We never got to him, but Dmitri Likhachev, the venerable scholar of Russian literature and culture, cast Sakharov in these terms: "He was a genuine prophet. A prophet in the ancient, primordial sense of that term, that is, a man summoning his contemporaries to moral renewal for the sake of the future."

It has been said that long after Brezhnev is forgotten, Solzhenitsyn will still be remembered. How do Gorbachev and Sakharov compare as leading actors of their epoch, and how will history evaluate them? The former political prisoner, Vassily Meilanov, was once asked if he were grateful to Gorbachev for introducing the liberties that the dissidents now enjoyed. "No," he answered, "I think he should be grateful to me. It was the positions adopted by dissidents like me that helped to bring a new generation of Soviet politicians to power." Natan Sharansky – among the most famous dissidents, and fighter for prisoners' rights in the Gulag – expanded on that view: "Without the stubborn, unrepentant dissidents and their supporters in the West, there would have been no changes." At Sakharov's funeral, Bonner told Gorbachev that he had lost his most valuable ally.

Sherry's 90-minute production is an engrossing documentary,

a dramatic account of an extraordinary life set against a historical background with a *perestroika* denouement. It was a mix of standard documentary techniques along with at the time riskier elements like re-enactments that have now become part of the documentary style. Added to the many talking heads and archival footage, was some handsome scene-setting photography by Foster Wiley, and there were several of those re-enactments – of dissidents typing *samizdat*, of members of the KGB's 5th Directorate, responsible for watching over and reining in the dissident movement, searching apartments and hauling off suspects destined for the Gulag. I was very pleased and proud to be a part of another award-winning PBS documentary, and naturally, I got several additional minutes of "Associate Producer" fame as I travelled the paid lecture circuit and sometimes screened the film. My friend, the film scholar and popular teacher of Russian language and literature, Kolya Galichenko, invited me to deliver the Lansdowne Lectures in Soviet History at Victoria University in Canada. The family pediatrician, Dr. Aaron Meislin, who continued treating Davey into his teen years and beyond, invited me to address the New York Pediatric Society and show excerpts from the film. I mention this only because I'll always remember his telling me that the Society Budget couldn't afford an honorarium, but that I would be treated to "an excellent dinner".

Sherry and I kept in touch after she and her crew finished filming in the Spring of 1991. I read and we discussed the script for *In the Shadow.* I caught some errors, made some suggestions for adding or discarding some minor things, but on the whole I thought it laid out Sakharov's life and backgrounds quiet well. I remembered Nancy Shoss's dictum that a script should be unintelligible in the reading; that coherence would come only from the film's realization of the script. I read Sherry's script before I saw the finished film, and found it quite intelligible, maybe because I could picture many of the scenes and subjects from my pre-interviews with the many dissidents and physicists. On those interviews: Sherry had given me a valuable lesson in interviewing techniques. She had picked up some Russian in our work, a few words here and there. One of them was *koneshno*, "of course," and she pointed out that if the person interviewed answered, *"koneshno,"* it meant I had asked the wrong question, i.e., included or implied the very answer in my query. The question should be open-ended and provoke an answer genuinely reflecting the interviewee's thoughts or feelings, not the interviewer's. Always remember this, I said to myself, if I do another documentary, maybe even my own; so many inviting Russian/Soviet historical and contemporary topics to explore. But I didn't pursue that idea; it sank along with my affection for Russian studies.

It was a privilege working with Sherry and her teams. I respected her and them, and I think she and they came to respect me, and what I brought to the documentary, a willingness to get this Professor's hands dirty with the prosaic details of filmmaking, as well as my, *don't forget!*, erudition about Soviet history, politics and culture. Anyway, after many miscellaneous calls and correspondence with Sherry in the summer months of 1991, I heard from her again late in August. Davey came home late on a Sunday night to tell me "Gorbachev is sick and has been replaced." Thanks, Dave, but what's that all about? I turned on WINS—"You give us 22 minutes, we'll give you the world."—and heard some very spare bulletins confirming what Davey told me: TASS had announced that Vice President Yanayev was assuming Gorbachev's duties owing to an unspecified illness. Nothing more. At 6:12 a.m. the next morning (according to my diary) the phone rang. "Sherry? Yes, I'll wake him," I heard Sheila say. "She probably can't wait to tell me that *Inside Gorbachev's USSR* won an Emmy," I whispered. (It hadn't and wouldn't.) She had other news for me: *"There are tanks in Moscow. Gorbachev's been overthrown. Turn on CNN!"*

XX

THE TRIPLE WHAMMY

Carlos Marx, nothing
Engels, nothing
Bakunin and Kropotkin, nothing
Leon Trotsky, lots of nothing
Stalin, less than nothing
—The Village Fugs
(Melody adapted from the Yiddish folk song, *Bulbes* (Potatoes): *Sunday—potatoes, Monday—potatoes, Tuesday—potatoes, etc.*)

I had a foggy reaction to news of the *putsch*, not because the awakening that morning was so sudden. A stream of thoughts in a swell of anxiety. My first thought: How does this ugly development impact Sherry's script for the Sakharov documentary? Then: How will *Inside Gorbachev's USSR* look now? Both films intended to throw a positive, hopeful light on democratic signs of political change in the USSR. So my first reactions to the disturbing news connected the events to the films I had worked on, even before I considered, professionally, the larger implications of what was happening. Where was the "awakening of Soviet civil society" we had witnessed? *Perestroika* had not "restructured" the Party, and the political establishment, or the "organs" after all. Were Soviet totalitarianism and the armed power of the state against society about to enjoy a new lease on life? Would this power grab yield another return to the old, undiminished character of authoritarian Russia? Reform never went very far in the past; the State always reasserted itself against Society. We seem to be watching an old movie, the crushing of Soviet socialism with a human face, just as the Czech Spring had been crushed two decades ago, and by Soviet tanks then, too.

This flood of thoughts were followed by others of a more personal nature. It was turning out that the rosy picture I had painted for myself of a renewal of the Soviet Socialist idea was more wish than reality. Party and State were reasserting themselves in the old mold. My picture didn't account for that when I reported on what I learned from making films about Gorbachev and Sakharov to different audiences, and in lectures to my classes on "The Contemporary USSR". I could hear my Soviet-*émigré* students mocking me for my naiveté – We told you so, Professor, they would say. Well, here and there, my assessments built in some wiggle room -- "surprises are always possible," but it was more out of rhetorical convention than conviction.

And my thoughts inevitably turned to Steve Cohen. We were both *philosoviets* at one time, in joint opposition to the *sovietophobes* of the establishment. What now of his reputation as a leading Gorbachev champion? During the brief period of the *perestroika* years I had several encounters with him, a couple of them not so pleasant. On the pleasant side: at a conference of Slavists, we beamed and winked at each other with smug satisfaction over how we were vindicated by developments in Gorbachev's USSR that knocked theories of an unchanging, and unchangeable Soviet totalitarianism into a cocked hat. In New York, on another occasion, after a screening of Alexei Gherman's *Checkpoint/Trial on the Road*, a once embargoed film that came off the shelves thanks to cultural *perestroika*, we met to exchange opinions. I appreciated Gherman's undertaking a forbidden theme – a Soviet soldier going over to the Germans – but I didn't think it ranked high as film, I told him. Cohen walked away, sneering, "You've been hanging out with too many Americans, Lou." Was it his greater Russophilia or greater enthusiasm for Gorbachev – greater than mine -- that affected our old comradeship? At a session we arranged with him and Katrina in a private room at the Hotel National in Moscow, Rick, Marty and I thought we might benefit from some of his insights into what was going on and what he thought might lay in the future after those delirious days of *perestroika*. Except for Marty, we all did our share of vodka swilling as Steve talked. I interrupted him at one point to offer my own take on something, and he didn't take it lightly. Whose opinions do you guys want, mine or Lou's?, he snapped. His view on things differed from ours, and was sadly, even ironically, mistaken. We were exploring and emphasizing democratic activity from below, while he insisted we should be looking into the reforms coming from the top, from inside the Party.

Well, we saw where the Party was going. With the assistance of the KGB, certain Party leaders organized the *putsch* in order to head off the planned new Union Treaty scheduled for August 20. But from the beginning it became clear this was no Pinochet-style application of force; no mass arrests, no executions, no silencing the media; no sealing of borders. This was a soft and very shaky *coup* attempt. The bumbling plotters even held a televised press conference that bared their quavering incompetence. Someone told Robert Conquest, "We've been ruled by morons for...years; this is the first time it's paid off." The sinister would-be *coup* turned into the comically operatic. Enter Boris Yeltsin at political stage center atop an abandoned tank in front of the "White House," the Supreme Soviet, announcing resistance to the *junta* and demanding Gorbachev's return.

The curtain came down on the *putsch* in three days. In New York, street violence was erupting at the same time. The Crown Heights neighborhood of Brooklyn, a community divided in an uneasy relationship between the Hasidic Lubavitchers and the predominantly Caribbean Blacks, exploded in antagonism over the accidental death of a Guyanese youngster hit by a swerving auto driven by a Hasid. At the time, we were in Spring Lake, New Jersey for a brief holiday we had planned earlier with Jack and Rubye Monet, in from Paris. Fortunately, there was a small TV in the modest rooming house we lodged at, and we managed to follow the events in Moscow and Crown Heights, toggling from one broadcast to the other off that set sitting on the rooming house porch, shaking our heads in silent wonder as we watched the reports from both fronts.

Whew! My panicky thoughts triggered by Sherry's news of the *putsch* turned out to be prematurely, needlessly alarmist. Gorbo was back, but in the shadow of Boris Yeltsin, the "populist maverick"; the Party was in disrepute; in Eastern Europe the satellites had broken free of Moscow; the Baltic republics were following in their path; a new, really reformed USSR was bound to emerge after having survived a scary, reactionary challenge. My old faith was being restored, sort of. It was still there, but didn't burn very brightly. I couldn't make sense of things, and of my own muddled feelings. I had no certainties. I was much amused by the conspiracy theories I heard in both Brooklyn (from my students and *émigrés*) and Moscow (from various friends). The *putsch*, they were convinced, was scripted by Gorbachev, or by Gorbachev and Yeltsin, to free their hands in order to fashion a decentralized Soviet Union with the State purged of Party control and leading the country in a democratic direction. In cruder conspiracy versions, the two politicos were simply consolidating their personal power.

As for Sherry's documentary, she had no trouble tweaking the original script to account for the new Soviet Union that seemed to be emerging. She cleverly opened with what Sakharov had completed just before his death, a draft of a proposed constitution for a freely united federation of Soviet Republics. *In the Shadow of Sakharov* went on to win several prizes for documentaries, including one in Moscow, where Kostya arranged a screening at *Dom Kino*.

At Polytechnic, where I had returned as Head of the Social Sciences Department for the Fall, 1991 semester, a strange academic melodrama played out that had some twists for me. The larger-than-life media baron, Robert Maxwell, was awarded an honorary degree in 1985 by Polytechnic University and joined the Polytechnic Board as a member the following year. His connection to Poly came from his friendship with President George Bugliarello, who coedited the quarterly journal, *Technology in Society*, published by Maxwell's Pergamon Press. With much publicity and an enthusiastic reaction at the school, Maxwell announced a $10 million gift to Poly as he assumed his Board responsibilities. Moreover – naturally, I really perked up when I heard this – he wanted Poly "to play a significant role in helping the Soviet Union rebuild" in the aftermath of the failed *putsch*. Well, well, now. I assumed he had in mind Poly's distinguished faculty of engineers and scientists as helping hands in the "rebuilding," but surely there might be a place for, um, a Soviet expert like me in that effort?

After I met Maxwell I began to feel that it wasn't such a crazy idea. The school arranged for him to greet the Polytechnic community at a special convocation. I got on the receiving line. At my turn, Bugliarello introduced me as Professor Menashe, who has "produced documentaries on Gorbachev". As he shook my hand, Maxwell, this very imposing figure with an English accent, bellowed, "Gorbachev is a good friend of mine!" I thought afterwards, is Yelstsin a "good friend" as well? Then I began planning and musing. I'll write Maxwell about his announcement to have Poly help rebuild the USSR, and how I might be able to fit into whatever Maxwell/Poly-financed programs develop. And how about establishing an endowed "Gorbachev Chair in Soviet Studies"? Or, depending on where and how the political winds were blowing, a "Yeltsin Chair"? I would gladly volunteer to be its first holder. I was the resident Polytechnic specialist on the Soviet Union, after all; no need to shop elsewhere for a candidate.

Alas, this figure who swept into the Polytechnic like a "gallant knight" to the rescue, as the *New York Times* described him, had many chinks in his armor. About a month after I met him on that receiving line, Robert Maxwell disappeared at sea off the coast of the Canary Islands, having jumped or accidentally fallen from his luxury yacht. The suicide assumption got some credence from revelations of many irregularities in his companies' books. Polytechnic's current hopes for riding out perennial deficit problems sank with him, as did my suddenly revived interest in pursuing Soviet Studies. I would continue ambling along, teaching Russian and Soviet history, publishing essays and reviews on diverse Soviet topics, and widening my reach into the cinema field. But the zeal was no longer there. The Maxwell fiasco was yet another deflating experience for me. A bigger one followed soon after. With a whimper not a bang, the Soviet Union dissolved.

Some might disparage the whole Soviet experiment as a giant historical fiasco, with dubious achievements bathed in blood and terror, not to mention its leading role in fomenting international anxieties. Vladimir Putin attached a different meaning to the dissolution of the USSR, by implication stressing the experiment's positive character when he later described the end as "the greatest geopolitical catastrophe of the twentieth century." The liberal historian, Yury Afanasyev, had this gloss on Putin's assertion: "The

Soviet Union's geopolitical catastrophe was not that it fell apart, but that, upon falling apart, it remained…an autocratic, aggressive imperial Russia."

My reactions at the time of the collapse were curiously mixed and on the whole decidedly cool, unlike those of many friends and colleagues. Denise Youngblood, a prolific historian of Soviet cinema at the University of Vermont, said she cried when she heard the news. Ron Radosh, by then, December, 1991, well into his rightwards U-Turn, had what seemed like an odd reaction for someone who was always anti-Soviet in his lefty or conservative phases. He called me to tell me he felt a "void" after hearing of the Soviet end. He was much more a political animal than I ever was, and in a sense more emotionally connected to the USSR from his earliest radical years than I was in my professional life. The USSR meant more to him existentially, even as he came to hate it. Stanley Ofsevit—who introduced me to Sheila and to Marxism-Leninism, and whose faith in the Soviet Union remained unshaken after our first visit to the USSR in 1962, the time when we muffled our disappointments about the place (I rationalized more than Sheila) – Stanley was so upset about *THE END* that he refused to talk about it when I asked him for his reaction. I thought about writing a reflective piece based on interviews with those who had some direct or indirect connection to the Soviet Union—"Scholars and Fellow Travelers React to the Fall," or something like that. At a Columbia University Seminar I spoke at, I used a rather lame line that usually got laughs in my classes, among friends and even among scholars: "Does anyone remember the Soviet Union?" John Cammett, the Gramsci scholar, once a good friend and comrade, an Editor at *Science & Society*, and, I believe, a member of the Communist Party, USA, attended the Seminar. At that line of mine, he muttered "Very funny," and walked out.

Professionally, I joked in a letter to Rick Smith that I felt like a "man without a country." For a journal article, I compared the vanishing of the USSR, and some of the reactions to it, to the trauma experienced by Akaky Akakievich when his splendid winter coat was swept off his back in Gogol's masterpiece, *The Overcoat*. I expressed some of my initial "post-Soviet" feelings in a letter to my friend Jonathan Harris, a Political Scientist specializing in the USSR at the

University of Pittsburgh. Hear my wounded tone: "I feel orphaned. A bit betrayed. Seduced and abandoned. I could still do Soviet history – there will always be a Soviet history—but the thrill is gone. Maybe it means a return to Russia, my first love. But maybe it's just regrets that I didn't do, say, Iberian studies. It's so much nicer to spend time in Barcelona than in Moscow. Besides, it would have involved my roots." The themes of my "buyer's remorse" together with a longing for other professional and personal paths had me in an obsessive grip over the next decades.

In early December, 1991, the heads of Russia (Yeltsin), Ukraine (Leonid Kravchuk) and Belarus (Stanislav Shushkevich) gathered at a hunting lodge in Belarus and announced unceremoniously that "the Union of Soviet Socialist Republics is ceasing its existence." On December 25 Gorbachev addressed the people of the Soviet remnant, defended his *perestroika* and pleaded for maintaining "the democratic achievements of the last few years." We were witnessing the operation of the pitiless law of unintended consequences. Gorbachev came to reform the Soviet system; he left to bury it. I thought of De Tocqueville's brilliant insight that the "most critical moment for bad governments" came with their "first steps toward reform." The Soviet "critical moment" was a crisis lasting seven years that Party and State could not overcome. The evening of December 25 the Soviet flag came down at the Kremlin; the Russian tricolor flew there now. Maybe it was indifference masking deep disappointment, but I don't remember where I was or what I was doing when I heard the news that the Soviet Hammer and Sickle were consigned to History. Or maybe it's because there was no exact moment of Soviet death; the system was in a months-long death rattle since the failed *putsch*. I could still tell you exactly where and how I learned of the Kennedy assassination, or give you the details of my 9/11 experience. Sheila and I were riding a bus down Fifth Avenue after a doctor's visit on November 22, 1963 when we heard the bells of St. Patrick's cathedral tolling the death of the President. Claudia called us from Washington on that day in September, 2001 to tell us planes had crashed into the twin towers of the World Trade Center. We raced to our rooftop to watch black clouds rising from lower Manhattan where the towers stood, then we called Claudia back when we heard reports that another plane was heading towards Washington. Claudia lives in Capitol Hill, and the massive dome of the Capitol could be a likely target. Get down to the basement for safety, we told her. She felt more comfortable by staying upstairs to remain on the phone line with us to follow events together. I also remember getting numerous phone calls and email messages of concern and sympathy from friends everywhere, from San Francisco to St. Petersburg.

No such messages arrived offering condolences to me on the demise of the USSR, and I wasn't bothered by their absence. It would have been interesting to compare notes and feelings with my Soviet *émigré* students during those fateful events taking place in Moscow, but classes were suspended for exams, then came intersession. Besides, these weren't the politically minded, militantly anti-Soviet kids of the emigration "Third Wave" I jousted with in the early '80s. I think the new *émigré* cohort of the '90s had no particular love or dislike for the motherland of their youth, and no particular feelings one way or the other about the Soviet collapse. I regretted not being in touch with the earlier bunch with whom I shared many moments in and out of the classroom defending the USSR (me) or attacking it (them). Oh, to hear Roman or Dina or Valery describe their reactions to the disappearance of the Union of Soviet Socialist Republics!

My Soviet Russian affair was filled with disappointments. The welcome Khrushchev reforms, highlighted by the anti-Stalin "secret speech" to the 20th Party Congress in 1956, and the "thaw," the loosening of restraints on the arts, were markers of a hopeful socialist renewal. The Brezhnev retrogression that followed laid those hopes to rest until the amazing arrival of Gorbachev and *perestroika.* Time again for renewed hopes! Well, *perestroika* failed to breathe socialist life into the system and Yeltsin, who had no sympathy for the Communist Party or the Union, made it clear there was no life at all in the old system, the legacy of Lenin and Stalin. In my eyes, that made Yeltsin in a way a bigger historical figure than Gorbachev.

Gorby, we can't praise you enough for breaking with the past – but praise you only up to a point; you still wanted to preserve the system, while Yeltsin moved to destroy it. For Yeltsin's independent Russian Federation, I nurtured new hopes. I settled for a back-up rationalization for continuing my Russian affair. OK, so

Soviet socialism didn't work, maybe a new democratic-capitalist Russia might be on the horizon, realizing the ambitions of the Russian population, their eyes cocked to the West, for what they understood to be a "normal" life. I remember talking at length to my pal and old comrade, David Gelber, and a colleague of his at CBS's important TV newsmagazine, "60 Minutes," on the Russian situation. I suggested they should do a story, maybe even a full documentary, on what surely was one of the most important developments of our time, the transformation of once Soviet socialist Russia into a capitalist "normal society." Gelber didn't bite, but other documentarians, Sherry included, did turn their cameras on Yeltsin's Russia. What they found, what we all saw, was an often intoxicated leader waging a brutal war on the Chechens and giving away the store as he enriched a new class of oligarchs in order to keep political power. True enough, he protected freedom of the press and other civil liberties, and he kept the Communist Party from staging a political comeback, even bombarding the White House when another coup attempt seemed imminent, that very building in front of which he had fearlessly defied the earlier *putschists* from atop a tank. But his skills did not extend to governing efficiently, and – what I came to understand in retrospect as his chief misstep, a big one – he named Vladimir Putin as his successor when he retired from office. Maybe an energetic Putin would set things right? But this once obscure KGB operative soon revealed restorative ambitions, not for the recreation of the USSR, but for a new Russian imperium based on a Church-State alliance tinged with xenophobia and advancing ultra nationalist, ever expansionist goals, while suppressing basic liberties and jailing political opponents on trumped up charges along the way, even having some liquidated.

What remained after all of those hopes of mine were fractured, after those personal *kronstadts*? Only the pain of having suffered a *Triple Whammy* over the decades. Khrushchev's *Thaw*? – Wham! Gorby's *Perestroika*? – Wham! Yeltsin's *Democratic Capitalism*? – Wham!

"Message to Man" Film Festival Poster, St. Petersburg, 1995.

Jury members at the "Message to Man" Film Festival. I'm at lower left; Volker Schlöndorff, center; Festival Director Mischa Litvyakov standing, right. St. Petersburg, 1998.

Julia in Paris, 1999.

"Professor Soap" sings *Let There Always Be Sunshine* at an after-Festival party, 1998. Photo by Kathryn Arnold.

XXI

L' ENVOI. I CAN'T COMPLAIN

Pust' vsegda budyet solntse,	*Let there always be sunshine,*
Pust' vsegda budyet nyebo,	*Let there always be blue skies,*
Pust' vsegda budyet mama,	*Let there always be mama,*
Pust' vsegda budu ya!	*Let there always be me!*

I got that from Pete Seeger. Knowing his politics and his love for bringing people together through song, I think Pete would have been proud to know that I performed that charming Russian ditty – in the original and in translation—from atop a table at a high-spirited party at St. Petersburg's Hotel Oktyabrskaya after the day's film-festival screenings. The party ended with a fist-fight between two very high-spirited festival participants. Both Russians; they weren't "*Arabi*" as I heard a woman sneer dismissively, when a crowd I joined watched two men butting foreheads in a restaurant in Moscow's Hotel National years earlier.

Those are among the scores of memories I still retain of my long-ago Russian affair. I can't complain. The *Triple Whammy* I experienced can't wipe away those memories, the sweet ones and the sour too, like the ones I just described. The "Message to Man" Film Festival was the occasion for so many of them, mostly, not all, sweet. The Festival was an annual St. Petersburg event that began as a strictly documentary showcase when that city was still Leningrad. I attended regularly, thanks to an original invitation arranged by Anne Borin, who worked closely with Festival organizers. She offered advice on general planning, and also programmed the American films she selected for screening, often with their makers to present them. Anne was a great enthusiast for film and for film as a medium of peaceful exchange between the U.S. and the USSR. She complemented her soulful enthusiasm with boundless energy. *Burya Anne,* "stormy Anne," the Russians called her. That had a double edge. I emphasized the compliment side when I translated it for her -- you get things done! But Anne wasn't pleased; she thought it bespoke a certain wry resentment of her driving the slothful Russians too hard. Both edges probably true.

My first trip to the Festival came the winter of 1993; it was also my first trip to post-Soviet Russia. Festival organizers later changed the annual event to the summer to boost attendance; visitors would experience warmer weather and Petersburg's glorious White Nights. I accompanied a group of U.S. filmmakers on that trip, and proposed taking an Aeroflot flight from Amsterdam when we missed our KLM connection. As encouragement, I suggested to the group this might be a convenient introduction to the Russia they were about to experience. "No way!," said Jan Oxenberg, the documentary filmmaker who brought her brilliant work, *Thank You and Good Night,* to the Festival, "I'm not taking a chance on my life by flying Aeroflot!" The rest of the party agreed; no Aeroflot introduction to Russia for them either. Such was the reputation of all things Russian, Soviet or post-Soviet. We wound up spending a couple of pleasant days in Amsterdam, courtesy KLM, waiting for an acceptable flight to St. Petersburg.

Never mind Aeroflot, the Russia they experienced when we got there did little to alter Jan's and others' anxious preconceptions about the place. As if to confirm the general Russophobia, the Sony Hi-8 Jan bought days earlier in Amsterdam to film her St. Petersburg experience, was torn from her shoulder one sunlit afternoon by a young man who ran off with it on the crowded Nevsky Prospekt.

Film theaters were showing *Batman Returns* and *Basic Instinct*. Newsstands were covered with porn magazines. A rise in street crime and burglaries were now a fact of life in the troubled, transitional Russia after the Soviet collapse. Festival organizers warned us that break-ins had taken place at our hotel, the sprawling, down at the heels Oktyabrskaya, dubbed "the Gulag" by the California filmmaker Louis Venosta. Don't leave any valuables, film and other equipment especially, in your rooms, they told us on arrival. When she heard from some Dutch filmmakers that even their food had been a target of thieves, Jan and her partner insisted on having their valuables, food included, locked up every night in a special room provided by the hotel and Festival organizers.

Yes, things were rough. The Festival itself had problems just staying alive. Director Mikhail Litvyakov told us the event was almost aborted because of insufficient funding, a constant headache over the years. As I kept telling my filmmakers group, the Russians will get through this, as they've managed to overcome all the other adversities that have invaded their history. I think it was Martin Walker who wrote that not only could Russians tighten their belts, they would eat them if necessary. I noticed a generational divide in those troubled post-Soviet circumstances. For someone I got to know then, a young Petersburg native in his mid-twenties, things were splendid. Working at a private, consumer merchandise firm, he earned more monthly than both his parents did together. For his parents, things were traumatic, not necessarily for financial reasons, he explained, but from psychological sense of general disorientation. Back in Brezhnev's time, life may not have been entirely sweet, but at least you knew that tomorrow would be like yesterday and today. The comfort of stability was gone for my friend's parents, but it was the drama of change and the hopes that came with it, that were so alluring for him. As for his grandparents and their generation? They were less discomforted by change for another reason. Their attitudes resembled what someone told me in the days of *perestroika*, "we survived Stalin, Khrushchev, and Brezhnev; we'll survive Gorbachev too!"

I told our filmmakers the Russians would survive Yeltsin too. Hearing of the hard times, our delegation opened their charitable American hearts as best they could. Help took the form of giving the Russian staff at the Festival our dried fruit, jars of peanut butter and Wash 'n' Dry's. Translators got packs of instant coffee and lots of note pads. The Gypsy woman outside the hotel entrance got lots of spare change. One of my most distressing Russian experiences took place a few years later when I was in town at the same hotel for another Festival. I made the mistake of taking a dollar bill out of my wallet and giving it to her when a Gypsy woman with a child in her arms approached me, hand extended, across the street from the Oktyabrskaya. Before I could walk away she grabbed my arm as several other women came out of nowhere, all shouting *Bumagy*! *Bumagy*!, and trying to grab at my coat when I broke into a run. "*Paper*! *Paper*!"—currency, that is, and especially U.S. currency, is what they had in mind; no loose coins for them. They ran, too, and chased me, but I beat them to the Oktyabrskaya entrance. The next day the newsstand dealer across from the hotel who had watched yesterday's chase lectured this naïve *Amerikanets* with the admonition, never, never give them dollars!

The tradition of my bearing gifts for people at the festivals grew out of survival skills I had developed when in the USSR for more than a quick visit. Don't forget to pack your bags with dried fruits and nuts, small cans of tuna fish, condensed soups, instant coffees, candy bars, trail mixes and other non-perishables from home to assist you getting through those days and nights in that Soviet land of consumer shortages and missing amenities, like 24-hour diners. After the collapse, when everything was available—hey, I saw some Snickers here at last, and bananas, of course—I continued the practice of bringing in survival fare. Often, to get away from official Festival luncheons I repaired to my hotel room for a bit of canned tuna with good Russian black bread. What I didn't consume, I distributed, but I also made sure to bring more than I could consume. People came to expect dried fruits and pistachio nuts from Professor Menashe. Festival organizers always placed young women with translating skills at the reception desk to greet foreign visitors and assist them with visa problems, street directions, film schedules, and the like. As a frequently invited guest of the Festival I got to know some of the women regularly stationed at the desk. For them not just pistachios; I hit on the idea, with Sheila's input, of gifting decorative soaps of the most precious sizes, shapes and colors. Soon, I was receiving requests for these things. From Julia I learned that in her circle I was now known as *Professor Soap*!

Julia Arkhipova spoke an excellent, pleasantly accented English and had great people skills. Her striking appearance also had something to do with getting attention. She possessed a kind of feline, willowy grace about her. Men naturally clustered around her wherever she was at the Festival. She was married at the time, but it was one of those men, Louis Venosta, who captured her heart. They continued a relationship in Europe and the U.S., eventually married and now live in New York, where I see her occasionally.

Tanya Kosovtsova was an interpreter at the Festival, specializing in helping visitors who spoke German. A single mother of middle age, with Finno-Slavic-Tatar facial features – those high cheek bones and slanted eyes—Tanya was a geographer at Leningrad University who earned some needed extra income from her work at the Festival, which also included serving tea and refreshments for guests at Mischa Litvyakov's office, which is where I met her as I was interviewing him. Later, when I bumped into her again and we talked cinema, she was delighted to learn that one of my favorite late-Soviet films was Georgy Daneliya's *Autumn Marathon* (1979), that *Sad Comedy* I mentioned earlier. Buzykin, the harried translator and Leningrad University lecturer has trouble juggling all the exhausting parts of his life – morning jogs with an insistent foreign scholar, his teaching and translating, his demanding friends and family, and keeping up with a younger woman in an extra-marital affair. Tanya knew exactly where scenes of the film were shot, and she offered to take me to the University for a walk through the hallways and classrooms and on the nearby streets that appear in the film. I accepted and enjoyed the tour; sometimes, I told her, I felt like the vexed Buzykin myself, minus a young mistress. Naturally, I asked Tanya, in line with my custom of asking whoever I met if she played tennis. Of course, she said, and arranged for me to hit with her and some of her men and women friends on a less than well-groomed local clay court. The friendly Tanya turned out to be a tiger of an opponent on the other side of the net, but I took a set from her. She asked if I wouldn't mind giving her the knee supports she noticed I wore. One of her friends asked if I could leave that new, unopened can of Wilson balls behind. Sure; the supports for her and the can for him. I kept one of their balls, old-fashioned white and so hard it hardly bounced.

Across the Neva River on the bank opposite the University is one of St. Petersburg's most attractive spaces, Palace Square with its Alexander Column as an architectural exclamation point to the expanse. *I crossed that Square on horseback one wintry afternoon*. Alla Drozd (now Takemura), the *Minchanka* I knew from my work on

Inside Gorbachev's USSR a few years earlier in Soviet times, was in St. Petersburg during the Festival with a delegation of Byelorussian filmmakers, and asked me to show her some sites in the city she had never visited. I was flattered by the request – what did I know of Peter's City except for the sections around the film center that I got to know during the Festival? But my memories of residing at the Hotel Astoria two decades earlier, and doing some exploring when I had time left over from daily morning-to-evening research at the Library, were still strong. I remember those delicious potato *piroshky* I usually had for lunch, sold off street carts. The library cafeteria and the crowded *stoloviye* were not for me. The *piroshky* looked and tasted just like the *knishes* I knew from school days in Williamsburg where they were also sold off a cart, on a street opposite P.S. 50 by a chubby guy probably born in the pre-Soviet Russian Empire. *You vant vun*?, he would ask as I approached.

I gladly agreed to be Alla's guide, and off we went during a break in the Festival program. Down we walked on the Nevsky Prospekt towards the Neva. We wandered about in the Astoria vicinity. I pointed out the adjoining hotel, the Angleterre, recently built on the site of the earlier one, the place where the poet Sergei Esenin committed suicide by hanging. Plans to demolish the original Angleterre had drawn protests and a demonstration from Leningraders anxious about preserving the city's architectural and historic treasures. They lost.

One of those treasures, the majestically domed St. Isaac's Cathedral, was in sight. Alla wanted very much to inspect the interior, but it was closed that day. Before long we found ourselves ambling about in Palace Square, and noticed an odd scene, a young woman stood at the base of the Alexander Column (another treasure) holding the bridles of two horses and stamping her feet in the open winter air. We also noticed that a film we both wanted to see was about to start at the kino center a distance away, with no time to negotiate the Square that lay between us and transportation. As we discussed next steps, the woman waved to us and with beckoning gestures let it be known the horses were available. Alla and I looked at each other: Why not? The last time I sat on a saddle had been ages ago on a trail in Prospect Park. I forgot what height horses like these big Russian nags were, but with a stool and some help from their handler I managed to get my foot into the stirrup and pulled myself up onto the saddle of my all-black mount . Alla's was a roan. She had much less difficulty getting aboard. With the horse girl walking between us, we headed out across the Square, towards another horseman, Peter the Great, sitting on his rearing charger in Falconet's dramatic statue commissioned by Catherine the Great, and memorialized by Pushkin's haunting poem, *The Bronze Horseman*. I wore my heavy, long greenish winter coat, Timberland boots, the wide purple and gray woolen scarf knitted by my mother-in-law Bea, and my tall black *shapka* – there I was, an American Hussar and his Lady in the vicinity of Senate Square, where officers and some 3,000 men had a stand-off with Tsar Nicholas I's troops in the failed "Decembrist Revolt" of 1825. "I hope you appreciate this tour," I shouted to Alla as we began to pick up some speed; the horse girl was now trotting between us. My thought: How do you exclaim *"Whoa there!"* in Russian? In a few minutes we approached traffic, the motorized kind, where the Nevsky Prospekt and Dzerzhinsky Street end at a come-together point. *Then we were in traffic*. That's enough, eh? I suggested to the horse lady. She agreed, grabbing our bridles with a smile. Oh, I was proud and confident getting off my charger, you bet. Alla couldn't stop laughing. I think I gave the horse girl a $20 bill, who accepted it, wide-eyed. We hailed a passing private car, as was commonly done (did I still pay the driver with a couple of packs of Marlboro's I long ago learned to always carry with me?), and made it back to the Festival in time for the opening credits of that film I can't remember the name of, or why it was so important to see. It was the last time I saw Alla in Russia. I saw her twice again, once when she worked as an *au pair* in a London household, and again more recently in Brooklyn, where she was staying with a Byelorussian friend. As an accomplished violinist, she had applied for and won a Juilliard School fellowship to study in New York for a short period. She's now back in Tokyo with her husband Noboru, and teaching music to youngsters. You recall that her sister, Natasha, has settled in Norway, as Mrs. Jostein Skar, with their son, Per Nikolai. Alla and Natasha – and Julia and Galina and Oleg — all exemplify what a Petersburg filmmaker described to me as the greatest freedom resulting from the Soviet collapse, the *freedom to leave*. A sad comment on the seven decades of Soviet socialism that traveled a road, someone said, leading nowhere.

The last Petersburg "Message to Man" Festival I attended had Volker Schlöndorff as its Honored Guest. He was friendly and chatty, and I noticed the celebrated director of *The Tin Drum* was a big cigar smoker. So was I then, and he enjoyed the *Maria Mancini* I gave him. Those were the days when I always had those cigars with me. On my way to the Hotel Intourist in Moscow one warm evening, a hooker – the front of, and even inside the hotel was favorite terrain for picking up foreign clients – a hooker noticed the cigars I had in the breast pocket of my shirt. "I love a man who smokes cigars," she exclaimed in a voice that could almost be heard across the other side of Gorky Street. I flashed her a smile in return as I entered the hotel.

I was Jury Chairman for Short Films at the last Festival I attended. Originally a strictly documentary film event, the Festival expanded into fiction and also increased the volume of invited films in and out of competition in different categories. Festival organizers thought they were making their event more attractive and competitive --Petersburg hosted other film festivals—by going beyond documentaries. This of course disappointed the documentary purists who looked upon the "Message to Man" as the major Russian venue for their film form. As jury chairman I had an opportunity to amplify their cause when I announced winners in the short fiction film category from the stage of the crowded main theater. Yuri, the very hip and very capable Festival interpreter, stood next to me and kept smiling in agreement as he transmitted my words after I named the winners. It was disappointing, I said, that a Festival originally committed to documentary cinema, had strayed from its mission. I was also critical of what seemed to me like an indiscriminately chosen high volume of films for Festival screenings. I spotted Mischa Litvyakov in the audience, and turned to him with the scold, loudly and in Russian, that "fewer is better"—*men'she, da luchshe, Mischa*! Immediate applause greeted my comments. People were standing, clapping and signaling to me their approval. *Prolonged, stormy applause* is the way *Pravda* would have described the reaction in Soviet times. My finest hour at the Festival! Proud, but also feeling a bit guilty and ungrateful toward the hospitable Litvyakov for my oratorical indictment. Backstage I was mobbed by film enthusiasts seeking my autograph. A reporter for a Petersburg newspaper collared me for a short interview – and completely mangled what I told him in the published article, more his invention than my observations.

When I later told Yuri of my amazement that a reporter could so brazenly distort what he heard, he shrugged and assured me that's what Russian journalism is like. There, another example of Russians down on themselves. I encountered that sentiment in so many circumstances from so many different people. As part of our necessary survival tools during filming *Inside Gorbachev's USSR* we brought along a bottle of windshield cleaner for our van. Pasha, our driver at the time, picked up the bottle and pointed to the spray attachment. You know, he said, we have this cleaning fluid but you Americans cap it with this spray device. He said it with a great touch of admiration for you Americans, and a great touch of deprecation for us Russians. In Petersburg at one of the Festivals, a young woman heard me talking in Spanish to someone. She approached me to tell me how impressive it was to hear I knew several languages. But I respect your Russian, I started to say. "Thank you," she interrupted, "but you speak *world* languages!" From the world of rock music I noticed another put-down. The Beatles and other Western bands popular in the USSR sang in "world languages," and Russian bands imitated them. The rock historian, Artemy Troitsky, wrote that the Nomads were the first Leningrad group to start singing in Russian – and "were booed off the stage and earned no respect. The Russian language was considered somehow an attribute of conformity, the symbol of some 'hostile,' non-rock system of values."

There were other Russians with disconsolate expressions of Russian inferiority at the time, but those sprang from different sources. I remember a bar maid of middle age opening up to me when I asked her how she felt about the end of the USSR. It's all gone, now, gone, she answered. Pride, she meant. Once the whole world respected us, even you Americans. She was proud of her country once, but no more. But didn't you have serious problems at home, with economic shortages, with privileges for the *nomenklatura* that were denied to the masses—I felt queasy about lecturing her this way, but I trudged on—and failures in official ideology? She gave me a *what the hell do you know* look, and walked away to some customer at the other end of the bar.

Remembering that exchange in a Petersburg lounge, I understood full well why Vladimir Putin's approval numbers were so high. His grab of Crimea, and forays into Eastern Ukraine and Syria, thumbing his nose at NATO and Washington, and getting away with it, or successfully hosting the Olympics in Sochi, helped restore a stiff dose of great-power national pride that had evaporated when the Soviet Union broke apart.

Well, to stretch a point, I too could complain about massive losses of pride. Oh, the personal enthusiasm and pride I felt in reading history about the bold seizure of power in 1917, about the victory of the Reds over the Whites in the Civil War, about the massive industrialization drive that put tractors in the fields of collective farms and tanks in the battlefields against the Wehrmacht – and about the colossal Soviet triumph over Nazi Germany itself. I was proud of the Sputnik launch, even prouder of Yuri Gagarin's flight into space. Earlier, Soviet scientists developed nuclear and thermonuclear weaponry ahead of schedules predicted by a West doubtful of Soviet capabilities. I commended Moscow for supporting the Cuban revolution, and for coming to Havana's assistance when economic ties to the U.S. were cut by Washington, or supplying Hanoi with the weaponry to fight U.S. combat troops in Vietnam. I studied all these things as a student, then professional historian and sometime political agitator. But further study, you might say, was informed by greater objectivity and lesser cheerleading which combined to convert each plus into a terrible minus. The Great October Socialist Revolution was a sham, a successful power grab in confused circumstances by a band of Bolsheviks led by Lenin, an ambitious and unscrupulous leader willing to bathe the country in blood to preserve – another sham – the Dictatorship of the Proletariat. The tremendous industrialization effort driven by Stalin -- the authentic successor to Lenin, no doubt about it -- came with tremendous costs, measured, among other gauges, in lives, especially peasant lives, lost amidst a politics of terror over the entire population, a politics one of whose greatest monuments was the Gulag.

No need to review all the other minuses I once considered pluses. My pride in Soviet accomplishments was continually deflated. Some of that pride was periodically revived, but never fully restored. Nothing could overcome my trifecta of disappointment.

That triple whammy. It was a complicated business that in my case configured ideological with emotional strands, the Soviet Motherland contending with Mother Russia. By that I mean to highlight the twin impulses that led me to Russianist studies and Sovietology, and then alienation from both. There was my faith as a Marxist in the Soviet Motherland, the first socialist state on the planet. And there was Mother Russia, symbolizing my love of Russia, or *the idea of Russia*, borne of its literature and music. Continuous disappointments and the Soviet collapse itself subverted my once strong convictions about Marxism in general, certainly in its Leninist applications, and my robust faith in the Soviet experiment. Look, I wasn't shattered by these things, the way, for example, communists throughout the world were convulsed by Stalin's pact with Hitler, or by Khrushchev's speech exposing Stalin's crimes. There were angry/sad departures from the Party, nervous breakdowns, suicides, even. You can sense the depth of feeling occasioned by true believers ridding themselves of illusions in the confessions of Alexander Yakovlev, who once served at the highest levels of Soviet politics as a close Gorbachev associate and architect of *perestroika*. The USSR was, he writes, a "military-bureaucratic dictatorship," a "hideous system of statism, bureaucratic absolutism, economic ruin, and spiritual suppression of the individual….a society based on violence and fear…." His self-reproaching lament: "How can we, who were striving upwards to the summits of material prosperity and moral perfection, end up virtually at the tail end of civilization? The hurt, shame, and bitterness leave me no peace….it is painful to know that you have been dominated for many decades by myths, not by common sense."

When ideology takes command, common sense is displaced. But for me, ideology – socialism and its identification with the Bolshevik Revolution and the USSR it created – was partnered with a Russia infatuation in a mutually reinforcing dance. When both the ideology and the romance faded, where did that leave me? The socialist model offered by the USSR was badly, woefully tarnished. At home, I lost my faith in a future American socialism, and I dropped out of left-wing political activity. I opted for the mainstream and the politics of liberalism. Sheila and I were enthusiastic canvassers for Barack Obama in both the 2008 and 2012 presidential campaigns.

As for the Russia, non-ideological connection, that moment at moonlight by the Kremlin walls long ago was an omen prefiguring my disenchantment; the break in the strong emotional tie to Mother Russia would follow. I realized then and thereafter that not only would I never fully *understand* the place, I had to admit to myself that I didn't *like* being there. Maybe, like Turgenev, I preferred to love Russia from afar. The crudities of the political system, its managers and its crimes weren't the cause. I imagine lovers of Germany wouldn't allow the Nazis to diminish their love of German history and culture, and their pleasure in being in its land and among its people. When we travelled in Franco's Spain, its authoritarian system didn't lessen our wholehearted appreciation of the place.

By contrast, I always felt an alienating chill in the air when I was in Russia. It had nothing to do with the weather, and I'm not sure I could identify what it was exactly that threw me off. *It was lots of things*, I wrote of my original endearment. *Lots of things* also compromised my affection. There was no single thing, no single *Kronstadt.* I don't think I could enumerate all the dislikes, apart from the political system, although there were always too many bureaucratic annoyances and bad manners (and an occasional demonstration of racism). Petty and not so petty stuff. Would it be the architecture? The food? The language? The countryside? The people? (Certainly, not the people, Russia's greatest treasure.) The music? The literature? *Nah*; of course not. In each of those realms I find qualities I continue to like and respect a great deal. I still run to a Russian opera. At the Met I enjoyed terrific performances of Rimsky's *The Tsar's Bride* and Shostakovich's *Lady Macbeth of Mtsensk*. I also heard a brilliant rendition of Rachmaninoff's *Vespers* by "The Voices of Ascension" at the Church of the Ascension in Greenwich Village. (Mikhalkov used a "Vesper" on the sound track for the haunting finale of his *Oblomov*.) We took grandson Benny (age 7 at the time) to "The Little Orchestra Society's" colorful performance of Prokofiev's *Peter and the Wolf*. He loved it, as did his big sister Leah, for a video version of the work we showed her when she was younger. I try to catch Stravinsky's *Rite of Spring* and/or *Petrushka* at least once a year – some dance company or orchestra always has one or the other in its annual repertory. If a Russian film appears, I'll be sure to see it—and review it for *Cineaste,* as I recently did for Andrei Zvyagintsev's searing *Leviathan*. A much less successful production was *Doctor Zhivago*, staged as a very clunky musical on Broadway that closed quickly. It could hardly match David Lean's epic cinema version of Pasternak's novel – the film is, dare I say, much better than the book.

My recent reading has included what Russian *émigrés* are turning out, much of it engrossing, with many insights on past Soviet life, if not all with high literary distinction – the dreamy fiction of Lara Vapnyar's *The Scent of Pine*, and her amusing sketches of a band of *émigrés*, *Still Here*; Boris Fishman's ingeniously plotted *A Replacement Life*; and Yelena Akhtiorskaya's fanciful *Panic in a Suitcase*; the memoirs of Gary Shteyngart's *Little Failure*; Lev Golinkin's *A Backpack, a Bear, and Eight Crates of Vodka*; and Anya von Bremzen's *Mastering the Art of Soviet Cooking*, with its sly subtitle, *A Memoir of Food and Longing*. In that *Memoir* the author describes those standing in consumer lines back in the USSR as "united by probably the only truly collective authentic Soviet emotions: yearning and discomfort." Shteyngart identifies the chief Soviet "inheritance" as "rage and humor." All of those works are subtle, specialized instruments for grasping the Soviet experience. They also capture the pleasures and the pains of leaving the motherland and coping with America. They reminded me of my encounters in class with the young *émigrés* from the USSR and post-Soviet Russia. I read *A Woman in Berlin*, authored anonymously as a diary of her agonizing experiences when Red Army soldiers arrived in the German capital, using rape partly as a weapon of revenge. I've just finished Amor Towles's brilliantly imaginative *A Gentleman in Moscow* that sets its suave house-arrested hero in the Hotel Metropol, of all places. Elif Batuman's *The Possessed* is both playful and scholarly as she describes her *Adventures with Russian Books and the People Who Read Them* (as her subtitle has it). And every few years I try to keep in touch with *Anna Karenina*. For my next reading, the 4th, perhaps I'll try the original Russian, as I've often promised myself.

When the City University's "City Cinematheque" shows a Russian film for that popular television series, I'm among the commentators its host Jerry Carlson calls upon to discuss the work. I still retain my membership in some of the professional societies of the Russian field, including the "Working Group on Cinema and

Television," a group I helped found, now a successful organization promoting film as a serious medium for scholarly study and for understanding Russia, the former Soviet Union, and Eastern Europe. We had to work hard among scholars and professional societies for getting recognition.

At home our walls and shelves display decades' accumulation of Russian *tchotchkes* – knick-knacks like dolls, cups and saucers, plaques, wood carvings -- and featuring, of course, *matryoshka* nesting dolls, including political ones, from Lenin to Yeltsin. So many of them were gifts, often from fleeting encounters with warm-hearted Russians and Byelorussians whose names I've forgotten. There are *perestroika* mementos like a mask of Stalin worn by a late '80s street mime, plus a three-dimensional framed collage featuring Gorbachev pointing his finger at you, asking "Have You Restructured Yourself?" Over our hallway steps I still display a big poster I bought in Moscow a long time ago, of a benign-looking Lenin and Krupskaya sitting on a park bench. *Dedushka I babushka,* I tell Russian visitors. "Grandpa and Grandma" I tell puzzled non-Russians. Several years ago, Maytag sent a middle-aged repairman, an *émigré* from Kiev, for our leaking dishwasher. He did his work well; learned repairs in the U.S., he told me, "never saw a dishwasher in the Soviet Union." Before descending our parlor-floor steps he stopped to gaze, unsmiling, at *dedushka* and *babushka*. "That guy," he growled, pointing at Lenin, "a Jew, turned the world upside down!" Did he have that same measure of pride and hostility I noticed whenever my old Soviet *émigré* students talked of Lenin? On one thing they certainly were in agreement: When I asked him what Lenin died of, he responded unhesitatingly, "Syphilis!" I've learned not to dismiss that diagnosis, as I once did. Moscow still denies it, but some investigations by neurologists and infectious disease specialists abroad lend credence to the Russian street-lore diagnosis.

You get the point. My Russia screen hasn't faded totally to black. And I can't complain about what "Russian Studies" have brought me in adventures, friendships, political engagement, and a few minor distinctions in my field. As for the discomforts and disappointments, no use crying over spilled vodka. After my formal retirement from full-time Polytechnic faculty, I continued to teach on an adjunct basis, mostly film and history courses, Russian themed. But the thrill was gone; I was running on empty. Or, to change metaphors, film was just a way of kicking the can down the road. I called teaching quits several years later. *Love grows old, and love grows cold, and fades away like the morning dew.*

Love can also be challenged by competing affections. A long time ago, at some activists' meeting or other, David Gelber teasingly called attention to what he identified as my *real* identity. Have you noticed, he said, that when Louis says "we," he means the Sephardim? He hit on something; it was one of my identities, of course, along with socialist, lefty, NAM member, Russianist, Sovietologist, academic, *spasibo big shot,* but an identity somehow closer to an emotional core, to my heart, than the others. Also an identity that I didn't really cultivate fully until the others faded. Through *Cineaste* I was able to take advantage of invitations to film festivals other than those in Russia. One of them was the annual Greek festival, held in Thessaloniki, or as my family knew it, *Salonique, Selanik, Salonica, La Madre de Israel, the Pearl of the East, the Jerusalem of the Balkans*—the storied home of the vibrant Sephardic community that defined the city before the Nazis sent its members, my father's family included, to the Auschwitz gas chambers. I made four trips there, happy to meet and be hosted by my cousin Pepo Matalon, who was a Holocaust survivor, thanks to a protective Athenian family. His wife, Vincenza, a superlative cook, spared no effort to lay at my table in their apartment the dishes prepared in my mother's kitchen, from the classic *fijon y arroz*—the kidney beans and rice traditionally served Friday evenings—to the crescent shaped *bourekas* filled with eggplant, cheese or walnuts. *Ouzo,* similar to the Turkish *raki,* was always the aperitif, of course.

Each trip awakened a renewed and deeper interest in the Sephardic experience, particularly the origins and fate of the Salonica Sephardim, and my own family's connection. I wrote and published on the subject, and began reaching out to others engaged in recovering a history long overshadowed by attention to the Ashkenazim, the Jews of Central and Eastern Europe and Russia. *Sheila's people.* That history came to a tragic end, leaving Salonica to harbor a ghost of its former self. Like some lost Atlantis. This Atlantis displaced the invisible city of *Kitezh* in my mental panorama of mythic utopias.

Only the pure and pious among Russians could see the lights and hear the bells of the drowned *Kitezh*....

Each trip to Salonica also deepened painfully invidious feelings: Why hadn't I chosen "Sephardic Studies" as my professional calling instead of you know what? It was too late to reinvent myself, of course, but it bothered me. Why hadn't I chosen *Atlantis-Salonica* over *Kitezh-Moscow*? My fluency in the ancestral Ladino language would have served me well, instead of taking on Russian. Learning Greek or Turkish might have presented similar challenges, but my personal incentives for mastery might have been stronger. My father and mother had a command of those tongues. They would resort to them when they wanted to keep me from getting wind of something off limits. It was said that that every bootblack in Salonica had conversational fluency in half a dozen languages. My research travels would have taken me to Salonica and Rhodes; Istanbul and Izmir; Toledo and Lisbon. I would have felt at home in all those places in ways I never experienced in Moscow or Leningrad. Along that road not taken I would have been honoring the memory of my parents, not to speak of bowing my head to those many thousands who were annihilated for being Sephardim in Greece by the exterminating Germans. There could be a socialist motif as well: Salonica was a historic center of Hellenic radicalism. Among my mother's papers I found her transcription of a song, in Ladino, she knew from Salonica. I read it with great counter-intuitive delight – my mother and my immediate and extended families were not political, though hearts were always in the right place; in the U.S., President Roosevelt was their long-time hero. *Ijos del Pueblo* ("Sons of the People"), her socialist hymn begins, and ends with the plea: *Levantate...al grito de Revolución social* ("Rise up to the call of the social Revolution"). And also, to complete the consonances, Salonica was the birthplace of Greek cinema.

Another intriguing new development: Both the Spanish and Portuguese governments have declared a willingness to award Spanish or Portuguese citizenship to those Sephardim who can prove an ancestral connection to those Iberian lands, to ancestors who were expelled in the harsh, ultra-Catholic, ultra-nationalist atmosphere of the late 15th Century. The expulsion complemented the *Reconquista*, the recovery of Luso-Hispanic lands from Muslim domination. I'm thinking of applying for that citizenship, either for the Spanish or the Portuguese one; from linguistic and other indicators, the Menashe family origins might be traced to either Spain or Portugal. Getting that citizenship would be a personal *reconquista*.

That's enough now. As a historian, I know counter-factual history when I see it. More exactly, counter-factual biography. Or melancholic what-might-have-been day-dreaming. Oh, such jejune thoughts. I became a Russian, not a Sephardic, historian for reasons of time, place, and who I was then. Stop *kvetching*. No use crying over an unopened bottle of *ouzo* (or *Rioja*). My plaints sound like so much sore-loser, sour-grapes musings from a petulant, rejected suitor: Socialism in the U.S and socialism in Soviet Russia did not live up to my projections and failed me, therefore I turned my back on them. Or, from the point of view of a personified socialism, I am a *flat-leaver* who didn't stay the course traveled by a truly committed believer. *But I can't complain......*

Paco, as I'm known to my grandchildren, Leah and Ben, with hosts from the Turkish International Film Festival; my aide, Sinan, center. Istanbul, 2006.

The Menashe family. From left, David, Sheila, the grandchildren Ben and Leah, Louis and Claudia. At Hanukkah, 2015.

AFTERWORD

When I began sketching out some ideas for a memoir some five years ago, post-Soviet Russian studies in academia were still on furlough and public and media attention to Moscow were not what they were in Soviet times. The collapse of the Soviet Union in 1991 hastened the decline of a Russia focus in government; at the State Department it was said that Russian speakers there were now learning Arabic. Much later, during the 2012 Presidential campaign, Mitt Romney's warnings that Russia was the top geopolitical threat were dismissed as misguided in light of concerns about terrorism and radical Islamist ambitions. My own disenchantment, chronicled in the foregoing pages, seemed to fit into this pattern of writing off Russia as a magnet for contemporary attention.

All that began changing when an ambitious Vladimir Putin, who harbored resentment of the Soviet fall and of Moscow's reduced global status, projected Russian power abroad – the "near abroad" recently in Ukraine, earlier in Georgia, and later, further afield in Syria. This flexing of Moscow muscle would produce alarms in Washington about the shortage of "Russia experts" who might have anticipated Moscow's new-found confidence and aggressive behavior, and who could have helped develop policies to match. Senator Richard Burr, Chairman of the Senate's Select Committee on Intelligence, lamented the "atrophy" in Washington's Russia expertise after the end of the Cold War, and called for "doubl[ing] down on re-looking at Russia." Never mind that a massive array of Russia experts inside academia and government failed to predict Soviet behavior across decades of Cold War, and failed most dramatically when, surprise! the USSR itself folded. Why the failure of the experts is a serious subject for analysis. Still, Russia specialists can offer insights, if not accurate predictions, into Kremlin behavior. They can provide at least the context for making important policy decisions based on familiarity with Russian history and political culture.

Balanced and clear-headed policy decisions are not presently the norm in Washington under the volatile Donald Trump, but they are especially called for in the radically altered environment enveloping U.S.-Russia relations. As I write, the same Senator Burr and his Committee on Intelligence are investigating Moscow's hacking activities in the 2016 Presidential elections, and possible collusion between the Kremlin and members of Trump's electoral campaign. A special counsel, appointed by the Justice Department, is similarly engaged, and looking into the very grave charge of "obstruction of justice" by the Trump team, and perhaps by the President himself. At the summer, 2017 G-20 meeting in Hamburg, all eyes were on the encounter between Donald Trump and Vladimir Putin.

Yes, Russia is back in the news, big time. Pundits and policy makers scramble to figure Putin out, trying to predict his next moves. People have started asking me, the "Russia expert," what I think. What do I make of Putin? (Once a KGB case officer, always a KGB agent, I usually reply.) Does Putin have *something* on Trump that keeps the President from criticizing him, and seems prone to flatter him? "It's an honor to be with you," Trump told Putin in Hamburg. The President declined to brand Russia "a security threat" when asked by a Finnish broadcaster. Why do Trump and the Trump cohort seem eager to lift the sanctions imposed on Moscow by the Obama administration? Would this be payback for Putin's having had a hand in the defeat of Hillary Clinton? Can Trump, who boasts superior deal-making skills, get on with Putin to the mutual benefit of both the U.S. and Russia?

The queries put to me are in a way flattering, but I can provide only vague conjectures. I strongly suggest following the work in print, on social media or on television talk shows, of several excellent analysts with good Russia credentials -- the very sharp *émigré* journalist, Masha Gessen, whose biography, *The Man Without a Face,* describes the unlikely rise of an obscure KGB agent to the summit of Kremlin power; the prolific writer and columnist for

Newsday, the Moscow-born Cathy Young; Michael McFaul, our capable Ambassador to Moscow in the Obama administration; the brilliant commentator and historian, Anne Applebaum, a frequent *Washington Post* columnist; the ever eloquent and insightful analyst of Russian affairs, David Remnick, Editor of *The New Yorker* and once the *Washington Post's* Moscow correspondent. And be careful, I add, not to fall for any soft portraits of Putin like the one gifted to him by Oliver Stone in his Showtime-TV documentary. I also recommend keeping a skeptical eye out for very politically tendentious media. I find Fox News most egregious in this regard.

And I never fail to offer the hope that cool heads will prevail in the Washington-Moscow relationship, and certainly in any ominous clash between the two nuclear-armed superpowers. The Trump-Putin amity has now been overshadowed by mutual recriminations brought on by the hardening of U.S. sanctions against Moscow, and by the Kremlin's prompt retaliation of expelling U.S. Embassy and Consulates personnel. According to Russian Premier Dimitri Medvedev, Moscow is preparing for "decades" of conflict with the U.S. As if on cue, "U.S. Army Dusts Off Cold War-Era Playbook," as a *New York Times* front-page headline had it. Right now, as I write, the greater danger of nuclear confrontation lies in Asia, where a bellicose North Korea continues to develop delivery systems for nuclear-armed missile warheads, and threatens to use them. Whatever the confrontation, and whoever the contestants, the peaceful outcome of the scary missile crisis of 1962 always provides a model worth emulating. Donald Trump is no Jack Kennedy and Vladimir Putin or Kim Jong-un is no Nikita Khrushchev, but surely they are all sensible enough to avert Armageddon.

Hey, here I am, drawn again to commentary on today's Russia. Does all this new focus on Russia and U.S.-Russia relations nudge me to dive back into serious work in Russian studies so that I can toss my two kopecks of analysis and opinions into the inevitable discussions? Given the remarkable turn of events, does it look like I may have left the field prematurely? Did I zig when I might have zagged? Any regrets? Let's just say it's too late for yet another reinvention. Or is it?

ACKNOWLEDGMENTS

I am grateful to the following: Sheila Menashe, my first reader, always, and always discerning, and for her devotion through our many years together. Anna Lawton, my publisher—also film scholar, bi-lingual novelist, and successful entrepreneur—for her continuing support. Carole Turbin, for rewarding discussions of our common problems in memoir writing and marketing, and for her gracious agreement to read an early draft of my manuscript for endorsement. I look forward to reading the story she has to tell when it's published. She was also technically skilled and immensely helpful in preparing my photos for publication. Meg Bortin, once a journalist and a Moscow hand herself, now a writer and novelist living in Paris, who offered much encouragement after reading my "Prospectus" for the Memoir. She also proposed an interesting explanation for my choice of Russian over Sephardic studies. Could it have been what she called the "displacement effect," my seeking separation from my [Sephardic] parents? Dr. Jane Tucker, a therapist, and a friend of long standing, to whom I turned for another comment on my choice of Russian studies. She mentioned "individuation," but also sensibly pointed out that choice of a profession is a complex decision (and, perhaps, I should add, maybe not as simple as the "It Was Lots of Things" grid I laid out behind my choice in Chapter I). She'll have an informed assessment when she reads the Memoir, I'm sure. My dear son David, whose love and keen appreciation of cinema makes me proud. My loving cousins, Jack Zaraya and Wendy Sabin, film aficionados both. Ilana Abramovitch, writer, teacher, editor, and always a concerned friend. The historians Allis and Ron Radosh, good friends from way back who are ever politically and personally challenging on the phone or in email correspondence, and who offered helpful advice about my Memoir proposal early on. Ron's clipping service knows no peers. Sima Szaluta for her friendship, for our film "seminars," and especially for her care-taking assistance at our home that helped me and Sheila recover from several serious ailments (Sheila's fractured femur and hip replacement, my carotid artery surgery). My darling daughter Claudia spent time away from Leah and Ben to come help us during those difficult recovery periods. She is ever lovingly reliable. Other caring friends and family members—Susan Agee, Carole and Seymour Margolin, and Diane and Michael Zacharia—kindly helped out as well. Juliette Monet for unflagging, generous assistance at our home when we most needed it, and for her technical expertise in reproducing photos for this book. The Staff at the Elmer Holmes Bobst Library of New York University for locating documents that helped me revisit my graduate years in the History Department at NYU. Barbara and Leonard Quart, perceptive writers on film and culture, for their personal warmth and compassion. Molly Nolan, who shared impressions of the past and current History Departments at NYU where she teaches. Jacques Marchand for reminiscences of *Marxist Perspectives*, the important, if ill-fated journal he helped found. Our old and very dear friend Rubye Monet for her Bronx-Parisienne wit, and for usage help, especially when it comes to Yiddish. Ellen Perry Berkeley, a fine writer and editor who was generous with encouragement and advice about getting the Memoir published. Henry Bertoni, who invited me to the "PROFs" group of retired Polytechnic professors for a reading of excerpts from my manuscript. Fred Ciporen, BP, for politics and baseball palaver, for film going, and particularly for our post-film discussions and disagreements. David Mermelstein and Marianne McLure for friendship and comradeship. Jan Rosenberg, friend of long standing, for reading and commenting on my "Prospectus". David Gelber did the same, taking time out from his important television productions on climate change and global warming, *Years of Living Dangerously.* George ("Yusse") Steinfeld and his late, dear wife Jean, for friendship of great warmth going back to our teens. Mark Naison, Fordham University Historian and my condo comrade, for publishing advice. The great rock guitarist, Danny Kalb, for past encouragement. Joel and Sharon Schreiber, for their concerned calls. My nieces, Elaine and Linda Menashe, for their tireless loving care for their father, my ailing brother Bobby. Tove Nicholson and Stanley Ofsevit for digging up some old photos. Win at 7th Ave. Copy and Office Supplies for prompt printing and scanning. Diana Klebanow for sharing her writings on political and historical themes, and for taking an interest in my work. Renée and Simon Dinnerstein for reading and offering valuable comments on a sample chapter of my MS. Marvin and Ellen Ciporen, for their kind and thoughtful concern. Peter Agree, an old friend from the '60s, now a senior editor at University of Pennsylvania Press, for kind pointers about his fellow publishing houses. The distinguished Russian historian, Barbara Engel, for long-standing friendship, and for her perceptive comments on the Proposal for the Memoir. Gary Crowdus and the Editors at *Cineaste* for opening its pages to my writing on Russian cinema, and for publishing a version of my Chapter XIII, "History Delivered in Frames," in the 50th anniversary jubilee edition of the magazine. The late Betty Ofsevit, who, despite her fatal illness, was able and kind enough to draw on her memories of that memorable summer of 1962 when I asked her. And great gratitude to Laura Ciporen for her word-processing wizardry plus her style-and-content smarts when guiding my manuscript to publication.

A special, sad note of remembrance for two dear departed friends and colleagues: the historian Helmut Gruber, who helped launch my academic career at "Brooklyn Poly," and Anne Borin, whose infectious love of Russian cinema spurred me on.

NAME INDEX

CPSIA information can be obtained
at www.ICGtesting.com
Printed in the USA
FFHW021346231218
49920768-54545FF